# THE MAHDI OF

THE STORY OF THE D
MOHAMMED AHMED

*by*

RICHARD A. BERMANN

*With an Introduction by*

THE RT. HON. WINSTON S. CHURCHILL,
P.C., C.H., M.P.

THE MACMILLAN COMPANY

NEW YORK 1932

DIE DERWISCHTROMMEL *first published in Germany 1931*
*Translated from the German by* ROBIN JOHN

Copyright, 1932,
By THE MACMILLAN COMPANY.

All rights reserved—no part of this book may be reproduced in any form without permission in writing from the publisher, except by a reviewer who wishes to quote brief passages in connection with a review written for inclusion in magazine or newspaper.

*Printed and Published, March, 1932.*

Printed in the United States of America

THE END OF MAHDISM

The figure in the foreground is the Khalifa Abdullahi

THE AUTHOR, THE TRANSLATOR, AND THE PUBLISHERS
ACKNOWLEDGE WITH SINCERE THANKS
THEIR OBLIGATION TO

GENERAL SIR REGINALD WINGATE, BT.,

G.C.B., G.C.V.O., K.C.M.G., D.S.O.,

and

BARON SIR RUDOLF KARL SLATIN PASHA,

G.C.V.O., K.C.M.G., C.B.,

who have read this work in manuscript and made
many valuable suggestions and corrections.
They themselves played great parts in the stirring
drama of the Sudan, and it is with pride
and gratitude that their names
are associated with
this book.

To avoid the possibility of causing offence to Mohammedan readers, the Publishers desire to state that the claim of the Dervish Mohammed Ahmed to the sublime title of "The Mahdi of Allah" is not recognised by the author of this book, nor by any of those associated with its English presentation.

# CONTENTS

|  | PAGE |
|---|---|
| INTRODUCTION | xi |
| FROM THE TRAVELLER'S NOTES | 1 |
| THE TOWN | 25 |
| THE YOKE | 33 |
| THE ISLAND | 48 |
| THE STORK | 60 |
| THE BOWL | 70 |
| THE HERO | 81 |
| THE FRIEND | 90 |
| THE VISION | 99 |
| THE WARNING | 109 |
| THE FLIGHT | 123 |
| THE MOUNTAIN | 131 |
| FROM THE TRAVELLER'S NOTES | 149 |
| THE MESSENGER | 161 |
| THE BATTLE | 172 |
| THE TREE | 188 |
| THE COSTUME | 206 |
| THE PILGRIM | 219 |
| THE ROOF | 233 |
| THE HEAD | 243 |
| THE VICTORY | 262 |
| THE PULPIT | 276 |
| THE ANGEL | 288 |
| FROM THE TRAVELLER'S NOTES | 303 |
| NOTE | 313 |
| CHRONOLOGICAL TABLE | 317 |

# ILLUSTRATIONS

| | |
|---|---:|
| THE END OF MAHDISM . . . . . . . *Frontispiece* | |
| | FACING PAGE |
| THE MAHDI'S TOMB, IMMEDIATELY AFTER THE CAPTURE OF OMDURMAN . . . . . . . . | 20 |
| KHARTOUM IN THE TIME OF GENERAL GORDON . . . | 28 |
| *From a contemporary drawing* | |
| A CIRCUMCISION PROCESSION . . . . . . | 38 |
| *From the painting by Leo Diet* | |
| A SUDANESE VILLAGE . . . . . . . . | 74 |
| *Drawn by W. H. Fischer from a contemporary photograph* | |
| ZUBEIR RAHAMET PASHA, THE GREAT SLAVER . . . | 84 |
| FATHER OHRWALDER . . . . . . . . | 132 |
| MAHDISTS IN PATCHED DERVISH JUBBAS . . . . | 142 |
| A WARRIOR OF THE MAHDI . . . . . . . | 172 |
| *From the painting by Leo Diet* | |
| AN ADANSONIA TREE . . . . . . . . | 190 |
| *Drawn by W. H. Fischer from a photograph* | |
| GENERAL RUDOLF SLATIN PASHA (1927) . . . . | 230 |
| *From the portrait by Philip de László* | |
| GENERAL GORDON . . . . . . . . . | 236 |
| *From the portrait by Leo Diet* | |
| STEAMER CROSSING NILE RAPIDS . . . . . . | 250 |
| *Contemporary photograph taken during Lord Wolseley's Nile Expedition* | |
| HANSAL, AUSTRIAN CONSUL IN KHARTOUM, KILLED BY THE MAHDISTI . . . . . . . . . | 266 |
| DEAD DERVISHES ON THE BATTLEFIELD WHERE THE KHALIFA WAS KILLED . . . . . . . | 298 |

## MAPS

| | PAGE |
|---|---|
| THE NILE FROM CAIRO TO KHARTOUM | 311 |
| THE NILE FROM KHARTOUM TO LAKE VICTORIA | 312 |

# INTRODUCTION

It is always interesting to know what kind of a book the devil would have written—but the theologians never gave him a chance. It is interesting for Britons to learn the Mahdi's point of view, and Richard A. Bermann has performed this in a remarkable book now translated from the German. It is presumably the first and last word on Mahdism. All who have had a hand in the Sudan must read it with real curiosity and satisfaction. The author of this book has thrown a running commentary of light on a strange and sinister figure which fell like a distant shadow across my generation in the 'eighties. The Mahdi! It is interesting to know that his operations with fire and sword through the Sudan were based on a religious enthusiasm as sincere and philanthropic as that which inspired Saint Dominic or General Booth. When he conquered nearly a fourth of the area of Africa he was at the head of a Salvation Army which literally interpreted General Booth's motto, "Blood and Fire." This book explains an incident which was always a puzzling one in the history of the relations between the Mahdi and General Gordon; how the Mahdi sent him a dervish's outfit with an appeal to renounce the pomps of a wicked civilisation. He would rather have converted than conquered him.

The life of the Mahdi is a romance in miniature and wonderful as that of Mohammed himself. The rebellion of the Sudan was the last great outburst of the blood-red flower of Islam. The Mahdi and his Caliphate might well have endured to to-day and developed as stately a power as that of the Moors in Spain, but it was built entirely on slavery and slaughter and came in contact with maxim guns. The balance between East and West depends on the advance of knowledge of arms. When arms were equal, the East as often won, as in the Crusades. Greek and Trojan were equal until the Greek invented the first tank, which is described by Homer as a wooden machine in the shape of a horse.

When the Mahdi's successor met Kitchener, he met a weapon of undreamed power, the machine-gun. It was a fierce but unequal clash between East and West when the Khalifa was crushed at Omdurman. The Mahdi was long dead. He had died in the consciousness of his divine message and power. He had conquered Gordon. Writers do not concentrate on the battle of Omdurman as the climax of Sudan history, but on the moment when the last Christian Hero met the last insurgence of Islam. Literature will not be weary of re-telling the story of General Gordon. He is treasure trove for the romancers of history like Lytton Strachey, and here we have him recalled as the unbending steel foil to the sword of the Mahdi. That very sword survives, and it is fantastic to learn from this book that it was originally the battle sword of a Teutonic Crusader, captured by Arabs, and bearing the mark of Charles the Fifth.

The black banner of the Mahdi swept the Sudan to the booming of the war trombone made of elephant tusk. The rule of the Saints was established. The Puritans of Islam enforced Prohibition. Smoking was punished as a deadly sin. The Mahdi was a mystic and a visionary. He treated those who failed to believe in himself and his regulations as a benevolent but unsparing judge treats the criminal population. The Khalifa was his executioner.

The Mahdi raised himself to dazzling heights by the virtue of poverty and the Holy War. Against him only stood out Gordon, in whom Catholic, Protestant and Moslem saw the makings of the Saint. Never again will one man offer himself to save a city single-handed. Never again will a mystic rank as an English General. Never again will the whole British people be so stricken by the fate of one man.

Thanks to Gordon's diaries, the last phase stands out with astonishing clarity. The thought of this one man scoured the

# INTRODUCTION

desert and passed up the Nile where telegraph wires and other communications had failed. The thought of one man kept Cabinet and Sovereign and people uneasy. The thought of this one man obsessed the Mahdi, who had given orders that he should be captured alive. And the thought of one man defended Khartoum month after month, until while the Mahdi prayed, his General, the Khalifa, passed into the doomed city. No one could afterwards report what had happened save Slatin Pasha, a prisoner, who saw the head of Gordon brought in as a trophy. This grim, silent meeting between Gordon and the Mahdi has exercised the imagination and the indignation of readers and writers.

One day a Gibbon will summarise England's work in Egypt and discover splendid material for a ruthless and unrestricted pen. It is too close for the final word, for the shaping of the scenes of that Drama, for the weaving of the appropriate Chorus, but the dumb-show which in Greek Tragedy was wheeled into the orchestra (as when the body of Agamemnon was displayed in the theatre of Aeschylus), that part of the Egyptian Drama is irrevocably fixed on the stairs outside the Palace of the Governor-General of Khartoum.

After the capture of Khartoum the Mahdi had dreams of world dominion and a conquered Cairo, Mecca, Jerusalem. But he died a few months after Gordon, and was buried as a Prophet under a Dome which was destined to be a target for Kitchener's artillery. And the day came when the Mahdi's head was separated even as Gordon's was. Both believed in Empires which battled for the higher good of mankind. Neither disdained the sword, and both believed in a Fatalism so trenchant that it persuaded and held the thousands under them. In the end Gordon conquered, and the negro was delivered from slavery, which was his chief object. We read now that the cotton factory has taken the place of the slave market. The Mahdi's ends were symbolised by ascetical nudity, Gordon's by the cotton shirt. But while he lasted the Mahdi founded a State which rested, as every State must rest, upon a way of thinking. It is true that it was a mixture of a religious revival

# THE MAHDI OF ALLAH

and the shambles. When he was buried his body was entombed like that of Lenin, and his simple way of thinking continued to be exercised by the Khalifa until the coming of Kitchener.

Wonderful are the ways of England! The son of the Khalifa is an A.D.C. to the Governor-General of the Sudan, while, stranger still, the posthumous son of the Mahdi is Sir Abderrahman El Mahdi, knighted for his services to King and Empire, and in a villa on Gordon Avenue in Khartoum he still cherishes the famous old sword taken from a Teutonic Crusader and inherited through the treasury of the Kings of Darfur until it became the sword of the Mahdi, the destroyer and the slayer, the ascetic and the Sufi, the Twelfth Imam that was to come, who came and conquered, and wisely went again before he was conquered himself.

WINSTON S. CHURCHILL

CHARTWELL
    WESTERHAM, KENT

14*th March*, 1931

# THE MAHDI OF ALLAH
## A DRAMA OF THE SUDAN

# FROM THE TRAVELLER'S NOTES

*KHARTOUM:* 10*th January,* 1929

The verandah of the Grand Hotel is deserted. It is very soon after lunch and still too hot out of doors. But I seek refuge here from the tourists who are gossiping in the hall. A few hours ago the Desert Express from Wadi Halfa to Khartoum arrived; twice a week, during the season, this train brings tourist humanity from the hotels of Luxor and Assouan to this hotel in Khartoum, to more whiskies-and-sodas and more jazz in the evening.

The verandah along the hotel front is raised one step above the garden and is open to it. Beneath, on a gravelled strip, are already squatting the native dealers who, later on, at tea-time, will be allowed to display their wares on the edge of the verandah itself.

As I make myself comfortable in a deck-chair, the fly-whisk in one hand, and begin to read a book—a book about the history of the Sudan—some of these curio dealers, mixed Orientals, approach me; but they desist as I impatiently sign them to leave me in peace. Perhaps they find it still too hot even to become importunate, or more probably I am by an unwritten law the property of the one dealer who happened already to be squatting directly in front of the chair in which I have sat down. This one is impervious to any signs, and nothing will divert him from his purpose. Imperturbably he unpacks his merchandise from an oilcloth parcel and spreads it out before me—all kinds of souvenirs and curios which he intends that I should buy. As I see that there is no getting rid of the fellow, who is of a greenish dark-brown colour—I should say he is a kind of Hindoo, or rather Parsee—and he will not let me read,

## THE MAHDI OF ALLAH

I decide to irritate him and choose not to understand any of the many languages in which he at once begins to address me. It is astonishing how many European languages he seems to know!

In English he wants to sell me brass cigarette-cases, cheap trash from the bazaars of Agra and Delhi; muslin shawls, such as are sent out from England to Benares and there palmed off on the tourists. As it seems that I have no English, my fellow tries me in Spanish; he must have been in Trinidad or in Panama, where so many Indians live. I happen not to understand any Spanish either, not for him, and so I don't buy the jet-black wooden elephants from Ceylon. Goa Portuguese might be so much gibberish to me, for I refuse to show any interest in ivory carvings (although as a matter of fact I rather like one little ivory doll, representing a Shilluk warrior with a spear in his hand). I am unable to grasp, as he is now talking Cape Dutch to me, that I am desired to purchase leather-work, gorgeous scarlet cushions, made out of gazelle skin and embroidered with many colours by the clever Omdurman craftsmen.

Finally, as I do not understand any language at all, the Parsee winks at me mysteriously and produces a bundle—one that can speak for itself! In this bundle there are weapons—spears, barbaric clubs and shields, daggers that instead of sheaths are stuck into small dead crocodiles, so that the hilt protrudes from the jaws; and, above all, swords of an unmistakable form. The leather sheaths end in curious rhomboid-shaped points; the hilts in the form of a cross are studded with silver; the blade, when you draw it, is straight and broad, not a Saracen scimitar, but more like a Crusader's sword.

These weapons, too, might be faked. And, indeed, they are. Weapons like these are being offered to tourists in the mysteriously beautiful bazaar lanes of Assuan as Dervish trophies from the Sudanese battlefields.

The Indian curio dealer is standing in front of me on the lawn with a great naked sword in his hand; the gold embroidery on his little cap is sparkling in the sun and he is shouting at

# FROM THE TRAVELLER'S NOTES

me words which—no matter in what strange language of the Sahibs I may happen to think—here in the Sudan I am bound to understand:

"Dervish, Sahib! El Mahdi, Sahib!"

"The sword, la espada, Sahib, Mynheer, of the Mahdi!"

*KHARTOUM:* 11th *January*, 1929.

I am on a sightseeing excursion to the Kerreri tableland, the scene of the battle on September 2nd, 1898, in which Kitchener wiped out the Mahdist army.

On the battlefield stands the marble obelisk commemorating the dead of the 21st Lancers, who on this spot performed their heroic and perhaps somewhat unwise charge. (A very plucky young subaltern, who took part in this exploit, bore the name of Winston Churchill.) Above the monument I gain the height of a bare and stony hillock, the Jebel Surgham. From here, on the day of the battle, the Sirdar, Sir Herbert Kitchener, surveyed the country and watched the Khalifa's army marching nearer with a thousand banners. Behind them he could see the outline of a distant shining cupola. This was the tomb of the Mahdi in Omdurman.

I am sitting on a rock, with maps and books spread out before me, and am trying to picture in my mind the last great romantic battle of the nineteenth century, perhaps the last epic assault of Islam against Western civilisation.

Before me is the peacefully flowing Nile. The ridge on which I am now sitting meets the river at the point where Kitchener had his camp. It is a fortified camp; on the left flank it has a *zariba* made of thorny mimosa brush and on the other sides it is surrounded by trenches. In this camp there are 22,000 soldiers, British and Egyptian. This is not one of those fancifully improvised expeditions which for seventeen years had fruitlessly and repeatedly been sent out to smash the Dervishes. In 1885 Khartoum fell to the Mahdi and General Gordon had to die, because the relief expedition happened to be mounted very picturesquely on camels and came riding like Bedouins, all too slowly, through the desert. This time Kitchener has built his railway, which is far better than the camels, an astonishing railway straight across the bare and burning sand. That river beyond the camp is full of modern gunboats. In the camp itself, the very best of up-to-date artillery. Lots of machine-guns. The British troops, chosen from the most proved regiments, are splendidly equipped and cared for and armed with new Lee-Enfield rifles. What is more, the Egyptian troops, who this time too form the bulk of the army, are no longer, thanks to Kitchener, what they once were; they are not likely now to bolt, whole companies of them together, the moment they catch sight of a Dervish spear. Not only the negro soldiers but also the yellow fellaheen are thoroughly trained and disciplined, like European troops.

Here then, in Kitchener's fortified camp, is Western civilisation, awaiting the onslaught of barbarism: Europe armed with her deadliest weapons, Europe already preparing for her own monstrous fratricidal war, the technique of the machine age already almost perfected, the Nineteenth Century brought to its completion, pompous, grandiose, and murderous....

And now Arab drums are rumbling—and Mohammed's seventh century is marching on, unchanged....

The last of the real armies of Islam (though later the nationalism of Mohammedan peoples might, indeed, have sent armies into the field), the last of the Saracens, the last wave of that great tide which the prophet of Mecca set flowing thirteen centuries ago....

Forty thousand hot-heated, dark-skinned human beings, most of them of Arab blood and all of them still just as full of fanatical faith, just as Allah-drunk as in the days of the Prophet, quite untouched by the change of times. Men with shields and spears, with two-handed swords, some of them in the old Saracenic chain-mail. They have looted modern rifles and they scarcely use them; that is something foreign in which one can put no proper trust. Yonder in Omdurman is the Khalifa's arsenal packed with excellent captured rifles, Krupp cannon, and machine-guns. But beyond firing off one or two miserably

## FROM THE TRAVELLER'S NOTES

aimed shots the Dervish artillery takes no part in the battle. These people want to hack the white man's civilisation to pieces with Crusaders' swords!

What a spectacle! (I am dreaming it on my rock, before the empty sun-baked landscape.) What an epic spectacle, like a canto out of the *Chanson de Roland*! The Arab host is coming over the heights, slowly. In the centre the Baggara, fellow-tribesmen of the Khalifa Abdullahi, who himself leads these wild men of the desert. His vast black banner, the only black one, is high in the air; the holy texts with which it is all sewn over announce the victory, the certain, infallible victory of the Faithful.

And banners, banners, hundreds of them. Every emir carries his flag; there are white ones and blue ones and green ones and yellow ones. The battlefield now looks like a flowery meadow, with big flowers rocking in a storm.

They are coming nearer. In these hearts there are no doubts. That here near Kerreri the great decisive battle against the English would have to be fought—the whole Sudan has known it for thirteen years: the Mahdi had prophesied it before he died, and ever since on this very same ground the Khalifa has annually held his great parade to celebrate in advance the certain victory.

And then—the onslaught of the Faith against Lee-Enfield rifles, against gunboats and quick-firing batteries! Never since, not even during all the bloody horrors of the European war, has anything like it been seen. On and on they come, on and on, through such a fire as would have shaken the walls of a fortress. . . .

Slaughter immeasurable, heroism without sense! This epic assault never comes near enough to the enemy to allow those swords to be used; the losses of the Anglo-Egyptian army are minute; while the Dervishes die and die. . . .

After the great attack has been crushed they are spread out in their bright garments like white flowers on a meadow where the mowing-machine has passed. It seems almost incredible that there can still be a Dervish warrior alive; and yet, as

Kitchener now gives the order for the advance, on Omdurman, on Khartoum, twice the same paradoxical drama repeats itself, twice this assault of savage Romance against the soulless machine, this battle between war songs and lyddite shells, between banners and ironclads. . . .

I open one of the books which I have brought with me—the book of a man who saw the thing with his own eyes—and I read this:

"From the army of the black flag there now came on only a few death-enamoured desperadoes, straggling forward one by one towards the rifles; pausing to shake a spear, turning aside to recognise a corpse; then, caught by a sudden jet of fury, bounding forward, checking, sinking limply to the ground. Now, under the black banner which fluttered over a ring of dead bodies, stood only three men, facing the three thousand of the Third Brigade. They folded their arms about the staff of the flag and gazed steadily forward. Two fell. The last Dervish stood up and filled his chest; he shouted the name of his god and hurled his spear. Then he stood quite still, waiting. . . ."

Eleven thousand dead Dervishes were found on the battlefield; many thousands, who had fled with their mortal wounds, were never found. Of Kitchener's soldiers barely fifty fell in the battle.

· · · · ·

My Arab guide comes up to me and does not let me sit and think any more. I am expected to look at Dervish bones. The bones of the dead keep coming out again and again upon the surface of this accursed soil.

But I cannot yet bring myself back into the present. That day three decades ago, how far is that back? I was a schoolboy then; I devoured the war news in the papers; it was better than any stories about Red Indians! A countryman of mine, Rudolf Slatin, was among the glorious heroes of this romantic battle. He had been a prisoner in the Mahdist camp for twelve years,

# FROM THE TRAVELLER'S NOTES

had been the servant, nay, the slave, of this Khalifa. Then he had escaped—oh, what an escape out of an adventure novel! Now, on the afternoon of this day of battle, a victorious colonel, Slatin Pasha, if you please, was perhaps the first to enter conquered Omdurman, in order quickly to search the town for the Khalifa. But the Khalifa had slipped away, as General Kitchener rode in through the city gate.

What a romance, what an adventure! The boy reading about it all in Vienna was never troubled by the thought of twenty thousand slaughtered Dervishes. This war somewhere in the wilds of Africa seemed as remote and unreal as the battles of the Nibelungs which we were just reading about in school only ever so much more exciting and delightful.

War? No thought of war, no idea of actual war troubled the world of a European youth in the month of September 1898. Very few weeks later a European war was within an inch of breaking out, precisely on account of these exotic Dervish affairs. Kitchener (then already Lord Kitchener of Khartoum) had moved straight on from Omdurman, five hundred miles up the Nile, to Fashoda, where a major called Marchand had hoisted the flag of France. And Kitchener had threateningly opposed the Union Jack to the Tricolor.

It did not result in a war; or perhaps, much later, it resulted in quite a different war. The boy who in 1898 was reading about the Dervishes had no suspicion of how the wheels of the world clock were working upon each other then. Since the Fashoda incident did not lead to an Anglo-French war, it led, very slowly, to the Entente Cordiale.

.   .   .   .   .

Once more I am gazing round over this battlefield of an old and already half-forgotten colonial war. History, I realise, does not know secondary episodes. Everything is important, everything is building up our future state. Here not less than in Serajevo or on the Marne or at Versailles the fate of my own generation has been decided; in this exotic fight we ourselves were concerned; the Expected Mahdi of African Islam has exercised an influence on all our lives.

*KHARTOUM: 14th January, 1929.*

Khartoum is not one of your amusing capitals.

Thirty years ago, when Kitchener had destroyed the Mahdist army, he found Khartoum a ruin; Omdurman, on the other side of the Nile, had become the African metropolis. Kitchener of Khartoum hoisted on the ruins of Gordon's palace in Khartoum the British and Egyptian flags; there and then he planned the new Khartoum: he drew the spacious plan of a city whose avenues and squares now reproduce the pattern of the Union Jack. (This, no doubt, was done partly from patriotism and partly because it is easy to plant machine-guns at the junctions of diverging boulevards, if necessary.)

Now, three decades after, Khartoum is too spacious, too empty a city; its life still needs to develop. Three miles of promenade on the shores of the Blue Nile, shaded by giant trees. Here lie the official buildings: the Governor-General's Palace (General Gordon's Palace, but renovated and enlarged), the Government House, big enough to scare you, with echoing corridors and staircases; the Military Command, Gordon College. Otherwise nothing but innumerable shaded bungalows in long straight streets which are quite dead and empty. The real life of the capital is on the other shore of the river in that reeking, teeming African place, Omdurman. In Khartoum one plays tennis and polo; one drinks tea in the Grand Hotel, talks colonial gossip, or of one's leave and promotion. Quite a beautiful town, only a bit empty; it is as though it had burst out of its skin. There is so very much room there for yet more civilisation, for yet more tennis-playing young ladies, and Civil Servants, and subalterns, and Greek merchants' wives.

I am walking along the Nile embankment, in the shade of those big trees, up to Gordon College, an enormous building in which young and swarthy Sudanese are learning English and certain other useful arts like book-keeping or surveying—every-

FROM THE TRAVELLER'S NOTES

thing that an efficient lower employee of the British administration is likely to need, and nothing more.

My visit is concerned with the small museum in the same building, which besides stuffed birds and such things contains certain antiquarian finds out of the old tombs and ruined temples of the Sudan.

I examine at leisure the glass cases in the museum. There is all the usual bric-à-brac of ancient Egypt: Ushabti statuettes, bronze and ivory gods, scarabs, pots, necklaces, rings—then the collection of stuff from the times of the Ptolemies, the Romans, the early Christians. Everything is more or less similar to what has been found in Egypt. And yet it is different. In the sepulchre of Prince Hepzela, an Egyptian Governor of Nubia of about the year 2000 B.C., have been found the bones of a hundred people who were buried with the prince: his wives and servants. Nothing like this cruel hecatomb has been discovered among the regal sepulchres of Egypt. A strain of African barbarism is evident everywhere; it is the dominating note of the whole museum. In the tombs of the independent Ethiopian kings, a dozen centuries after Prince Hepzela, were unearthed the bones of slaughtered horses. The finds from the Pyramid of Nuri and from the tombs of Napata exhibit very clearly that negroid coarsening which in the Sudan overtook the arts of the Mediterranean countries. What grotesque perversion of Egyptian models! Everything spiritual has been misunderstood, everything fine has been distorted, made sensual and bombastic. This is still more evident in the findings from Meroë (which was not so very far from Khartoum). Here, in the times of the Romans, there did flourish something like Roman, like Hellenic art, only—great heavens! —how negroid! Venus with woolly hair, Cæsar like a nigger chief....

Besides, there are relics of a Byzantine Africa; then came Islam. It, too, in the Sudan, was a negro Islam from the start, with a strain of black blood in veins only half Arab. This is the Mahdi's Islam, an African, a barbaric, an Ethiopian Islam.

## THE MAHDI OF ALLAH

*KHARTOUM: 17th January, 1929.*

With the tramcar to Omdurman, over the mighty new bridge which spans the river at the point where the White Nile, that lazy, muddy water from the equatorial lakes and the swamps, unites with the Blue Nile, the rapid mountain stream from Abyssinia. Here, on this big fork, half Africa is assembled: fantastic Omdurman, the town of peaked negro huts and cubes of baked mud, seems to be distant from Khartoum a thousand miles and a thousand years. Omdurman is practically just as it was a quarter of a century ago, when Mahdism collapsed. Every elderly man in the streets was once a Dervish warrior who fought against Kitchener, or else he came here as a slave, with his neck in the yoke. Dervishes and the sons of Dervishes, freed slaves and children of slaves are everywhere. A few Mediterranean people are sprinkled amongst them, Greeks and Armenians, Copts and Jews. And Mohammedan pilgrims from far-off West Africa sometimes tarry awhile in Omdurman on their way back from Mecca. What a multitude in that unforgettable market! A woman of the Niam Niam on the While Nile squats in front of her *durrha* basket. She knows very well what human meat tastes like! Olive and brown Bedouins are there, Hadendoa with their queer fuzzy hair, carrying big swords in scarlet sheaths, and huge naked negroes, Shilluks, who are accustomed to stand perched on one leg, like the storks in their reedy swamps on the upper Nile; and Abyssinians who have come down the Blue Nile; half Africa. In this turmoil of barbarian humanity you see here and there a limping cripple who lacks an arm or a leg: these are people whom the Khalifa has punished for some crime or other. Although in the open booths and in the huts here and there a petrol-tin can be seen, a gramophone, a sewing-machine, nothing essential has changed: this is still wellnigh the selfsame Africa, the untouched Sudan of the Mahdi and of the Khalifa.

In the labyrinth of the huts I have difficulty in finding my way to the house of the Khalifa Abdullahi, which, I have been told now also contains a kind of museum, with relics of the times of the Mahdi.

FROM THE TRAVELLER'S NOTES

In the house of the Khalifa I fall among some of the people from the Grand Hotel, all those American young women from the Desert Express, the Dutch gentleman who is to go up the White Nile in order to photograph elephants from on board the steamer, if possible. I find them tramping along behind the coal-black Cook's guide through the many brick-and-mud houses which constitute this most unpretentious of all palaces. So this is where the Khalifa Abdullahi slept. (Yes, this is that elaborate Sudanese bedstead that Slatin Pasha describes in his book. He, Slatin, used to squat by it on the mat, and the Khalifa would admonish him to be pious and humble.) He had a real bathroom, too, with a tub out of Gordon's palace!

There is nothing for me to do but to trot along with the others—and while I do it, I keep thinking that amongst the other great figures of that exciting Sudanese drama the Khalifa Abdullahi seems the least complicated. Who was he? Just a successful soldier, and later on a dictator who managed to keep himself in power quite a long time. In the years of the Mahdi he was already the strong arm of this religious revolution, the organiser of the Dervish army. Intellectually he was never a match for the Mahdi, whose greatness and depth of mind cannot be doubted. The Mahdi alone is the brain, the heart of this new militant Church which in so short a time is able to conquer one-quarter of Africa. And the Khalifa? Just the secular arm, the bailiff. He accepts—perhaps it is a heroic sacrifice—that odium of fanatical severity which in every revolution one man has to bear; he becomes the Robespierre, the Fouquier-Tinville, the Dzerzhinsky of Mahdism. The Mahdi himself remains kind and smiling.

Then the Mahdi dies, only a short time after his victory over Gordon. There he lies buried, opposite the Khalifa's palace, in a sacred tomb (just as now Lenin lies on the Kremlin wall). For close on fourteen years the Khalifa still maintains his power. The world revolution that the Mahdi prophesied does not come; many lose their faith; but this Bedouin, whom such a strange destiny has made dictator of the whole Sudan, rules on nevertheless, in the end only by brutal force. Some four million human beings are said to have perished through him in those years....

Just an ordinary African despot, although a strong one. Slatin, who for years stood on his doorstep (here, the tourists' guide is showing us the exact spot), saw him as a monster, cold, suspicious, cruel by inclination. But Slatin himself was hardly very badly treated by him, except once, when the prisoner was found out corresponding with the Khalifa's enemies; then he was not killed, but put in chains for a time. Karl Neufeld, the German trader, who during the whole period of the Khalifa's reign was so horribly illtreated, nevertheless speaks with sympathy of Abdullahi's person. To-day, if you ask any Sudanese, he will tell you: "The Mahdi was a good man, but then the Khalifa, he was a devil!" But is not that simply the handiest explanation? Noble idealists kindle with their pure hands a holy flame; and then often, when the world is burning, some loyal helpmate of the holy one is said to be the devil of this flame!

I wander further through the rooms, behind the black cicerone. Why, the Khalifa even had a printing press, a carriage....

One thing is certain, I am thinking: a cast-iron fellow! Yet, as a prophet, rather a failure; for after the Mahdi's death Mahdism loses all inspiration, the doctrine collapses. As a regent the Khalifa seems to have been a mere tyrant, who just knew how to make his own Baggara tribesmen all-powerful in the Sudan and to ruin everybody else; as an organiser he was pitiful; but great and heroically tragic as a fighter. On the terrible day of Kerreri he stood always next to his black banner. In the evening he indeed escapes from the battlefield; a leader who still hopes, has the duty to save himself. But then, when he no longer hopes? The Khalifa Abdullahi died in this manner. For fifteen months he still held out; he retired to Jebel Gadir, the same holy mountain place from which the Mahdi had formerly launched his victorious army to conquer the Sudan, and there attempted, just as the Mahdi had done before, to incite the population by religious propaganda, and rally the tribes to his

## FROM THE TRAVELLER'S NOTES

banner; he actually succeeded in collecting yet another army, and advanced once more against Khartoum; but General Wingate's troops trapped him in a forest, some sixty miles from Abba, the Mahdi's island. There the Khalifa dismounts from his horse, spreads out the sheepskin from his saddle on the earth: now, there he will stand and will die. . . .

They find him after the fight dead on that sheepskin.

. . . . .

I stop in the middle of the Khalifa's harem (in the room which used to be full of looking-glasses) in order to search in my pocket-book for a visiting-card which I have on me. I made the acquaintance yesterday, when I was in the Governor-General's palace (in General Gordon's palace, quite near the spot where he was assassinated), of a native gentleman, a smart still youngish captain in a most dashing unform. We had a polite little chat, and then he gave me his neat little card:

---

**M. A. SOLIMAN EL-KHALIFA ABDULLAHI**

A.D.C. to Governor-General

---

Soliman, son of the Khalifa Abdullahi, A.D.C. to the Governor-General! Soliman is one of several sons of the dead Khalifa who now serve the Anglo-Sudanese Government. Charming people they must certainly be, if they are all like this one.

How the wheel goes round! How all the wheels are ceaselessly going round and round!

. . . . .

An entry in the visitors' book of the Khalifa's Palace:

"24.xi.26. Rudolf Slatin Pasha."

He had walked, so they say, a distinguished, elderly gentleman, patiently behind Messrs. Thos. Cook's guide along with the other tourists through those rooms, and this pompous black fellow of a guide had pointed out to him the spot, as he had just shown it to me, where Slatin Pasha had stood for a dozen years, barefooted, in Dervish rags, as the doorkeeper and orderly of the Khalifa. (Yes, he was something in the nature of an A.D.C., before the Khalifa's son became one in his turn.)

"No," the elderly tourist had said to the Cook's guide, "here, and not there is the spot where Slatin Pasha——"

"Sir, I ought to know! I've been for years the dragoman of Messrs. Thos. Cook——"

"And my name is Slatin!"

Too good, of course, to be true. But as a matter of fact Slatin did come here again a few years ago; he came as a tourist in the Desert Express right across the identical desert over which, a quarter of a century earlier, the romantic flight of the escaping slave had led.

I have met the hero of this astonishing romance, of one of the great adventures of history. We both, fellow Austrians, belonged to the Austrian peace delegation at St. Germain in 1919; myself as a journalist, he as the delegate in charge of the negotiations for the exchange of prisoners of war. He did understand something about prisoners.

*KHARTOUM: 20th January, 1929.*

I now usually spend the hot afternoon hours in the Zoological Gardens, on a bench beneath this huge tree. While I am smoking and reading, the gazelles draw nearer from every side, full of curiosity, and the boldest one sticks its small cool muzzle straight into my pocket.

The Zoo in Khartoum is just a bit of Africa with a wall round it. From the spot where I am sitting I can look over the garden wall and across the Blue Nile. That river is really blue, not like the beautiful blue Danube, which isn't. Beyond, on the other side of the Nile, there is instantly the desert, the home of the gazelles and hyenas. In this garden all the hyenas

# FROM THE TRAVELLER'S NOTES

and lions are locked up in cages, but the gazelles are free; it is their paradise.

(A bit of Africa where there is grass and water enough and where every lion and every hyena is safely shut up in a cage, that is the gazelle's paradise.)

And big storks are strutting about all round me. Abu Markub, the "Father of the shoe," with that grotesquely funny slipper for a beak, is promenading at liberty; you would not believe him real. And on the tree scream and chatter a nation of unlikely birds. . . .

I sit here half the day, occupied with my books.

. . . . .

A thought has shot up in my mind, swiftly, as things grow nowhere but in the tropics: I want to write the life of the Dervish Mohammed Ahmed, who became the Mahdi, the conqueror of all the Sudan, the conqueror of Gordon, the successor of the Prophet, the last bright flame of Islam. . . .

While day and night I feverishly read and re-read the books of people who have known that man, who have lived through those times, I constantly think: but will anyone believe it if I tell it again?

So improbable is the truth of this story! Reality devised so many mad things for it! The outline of the Mahdi's personality, as it emerges from the records of the contemporaries, seems so strange, so incomprehensible! A smiling mask, behind which nobody can penetrate. First, as a youth, he seems human, one of us, although in a dark-brown skin. Then he becomes remote and foreign, like a barbaric deity. And then finally the outline of the smiling idol dissolves into a grotesque caricature. . . . It is horrid! How victory makes his body swell, makes him suddenly fat, until he actually is bursting from triumph and god-like glory! What a life, what an end! This African Arab followed in everything the model of Mohammed, from whom he pretended to descend. He really succeeds in living in almost everything like Mohammed. He has his Hegira, his visions, his Medina, his Mecca reconquered, his Ansar, his Khalifas; he dies like Mohammed, is buried like Mohammed—only everything somehow is different in a subtle way, there is that African strain in everything. This new Koran has plainly become negroid; the rhythm of the drums of the primeval forest pulses through the Mahdi's fervent prayers.

. . . . .

Outside on the embankment between the Zoological Gardens and the Nile stands a negro woman with a naked baby riding in some curious way on her hip; she herself is dressed only in copper rings. A pair of black boys are there too, each standing on his left leg, while he props his right foot against his left thigh. They gaze into the Zoo, full of yearning: but the entrance costs two piastres! They do not suspect, poor, nice darkies, how much they would be paid elsewhere if they would but enter a Zoo and show themselves!

Now they are staring: on the embankment four prisoners are passing them, with chains between their legs. A very black and very big policeman in khaki, with a peaked turban like a Sikh, marches behind them; they are carrying an *angareb*; each of them supports one leg of the light Sudanese bedstead; most probably the policeman lounges upon it while they have to work.

. . . . .

This clinking of chains reminds me again instantly of the Mahdi. A clinking of chains always accompanies that story. The Mahdi begins as a breaker of chains. Without doubt he was a real revolutionary, if a religious one. He rose up against tyranny, against oppression, against the rich and the powerful.

He ends, triumphantly, surrounded by the people's fanatical love—as a lord of many slaves, all surrounded by the clinking of chains, as an African despot, like any Ashanti king. . . .

Was it worth the labour and the blood, all that limitlessly poured-out human blood?

# FROM THE TRAVELLER'S NOTES

As the afternoon wears on and dusk is coming and coolness, the Khartoum bourgeoisie appears in the gardens. To-day there is to be a military concert and a Venetian gala illumination. For the exalted ones, the English people of colonial Society, the gardens are scarcely distinguished enough, so they just send their fair and smiling children in the care of their nurses. But Mr. Ezkenazi is present and Mr. Melkonian, Contomichalos along with Stamatopulo, Vanian and Babani, and Gennaoui, Simonini, Makropulo—and *mesdames*, of course, and everybody who in Khartoum and Omdurman is trading in cotton or gum, or exports ground-nuts or senna or ivory; everybody whose skin is golden or perhaps rather greenish and whose eyes are beautiful and dreamy and whose hair is curly—Greek and Armenian traders and Copts and their ladies, forsooth, who might almost be from Paris. The younger gentlemen are dressed terribly like Englishmen, only they ought not to wear a topee when the evening has come.

And, oh, all those brightly coloured children, Melkonian children and Stamatopulo children, how they all stand round the bandstand and gaze with big beautiful eyes at the scarlet soldiers who are just tuning their instruments!

Mamma is singing out in all languages at once: "Ninon, ma chérie, don't spoil your frock, non sudiciarti, piccina!"

Rum-te-tum! The music starts: *Götterdämmerung!* Suddenly, miraculously, all the gazelles of the gardens are round the bandstand, the delicate Dorcas gazelle and the Ariel, the gazelle that is like a spirit fawn—and all put their pretty muzzles straight into the brass instruments, into the mouth of the big trombone. There is always one baby Stamatopulo standing next to one gazelle.

Rum-te-tum. Richard Wagner—*Götterdämmerung*.

On the top of that big flowering tree a multi-coloured bird begins to scream, he has got to scream louder than anything, anything, for this is *his* country here, this is Africa, Africa!

A hyena laughs in a cage, frighteningly. The gazelles shrink a little together. Darkness falls suddenly. It is very hot. I hit out for a mosquito. In the branches of that tree the coloured lamps are glowing in a most Venetian fashion. Rum-te-tum! A negro waiter brings lemonade and black coffee, the best Abyssinian sort. A fat Armenian girl is flirting audibly. I close up Slatin's book.

Now, I think to myself, if someone started shouting: "The Mahdi is coming!" they would all run. These are the people he hated, these are the ones he hunted down. The memory of him is still rooted in them!

*KHARTOUM: 21st January,* 1929.

Oh yes, the Mahdi's Sudan has become quite civilised! But in the hall of the Grand Hotel, where the young ladies from the Desert Express are writing postcards and old gentlemen are telling how they are thinking of driving by car from Rejaf on the White Nile to Nairobi, on the excellent new motoring road (via Torit and Kitgum, via wilderness, swamp, and barbarity, but all that does not exist any more, one might think), in the same hotel hall, which is so civilised and well ventilated, where drinks are so cool and dances so hot, there is an immense negro servant, with parallel cuts on his black bronze face, a giant in white wraps and red babooshes, with a vivid green sash around his almost brutally powerful body. This oldish man has seen the days of the Mahdi. He has wept, gone mad, whenever the Mahdi preached in the Omdurman mosque. And he still believes in the Mahdi to-day, I know it.

This little bit of civilisation—or isn't it simply a little bit of comfort—has been superimposed on the land of the Blacks like the harness on a beast of burden. Beneath——

This old hotel servant, who has known the Mahdi, brings me a printed sheet, the *Sudan Herald and Times*—oh yes, in Khartoum they have everything—and I read between paragraphs on the polo match and on the amateur theatricals (they recently performed *When Knights Were Bold*—very funny)—I read, between advertisements (S. and S. Vanian, Ltd., supply ready-made palm beach suits, also to measure)—I read a thing like this, under yesterday's date:

"Last evening, near the Pyramid of Dengkurs, a mounted

## FROM THE TRAVELLER'S NOTES

patrol was attacked by 200 blacks of the Nuer tribe. The Pyramid of Dengkurs, it will be remembered, was destroyed during the fighting early in 1928, the old ruins having become the stronghold of the Nuer wizard, Gwek Wonding. The attack of the Nuers was successfully beaten off; they left 18 dead on the field, amongst them Gwek Wonding, the magician whose influence caused the Nuer tribe in 1927 to revolt. Three other magicians were also killed. Pok Karajak, also a notorious medicine man, has unfortunately escaped. The mounted police are pursuing him...."

In vain I seek on my map the Pyramid of Dengkurs. I suppose it is somewhere near the mouth of the Sobat; perhaps those comfortable steamers pass it which go to the Uganda border and to those wonderful motoring roads. A pyramid! What pyramid? Who has been buried there, thousands of years ago: demigod, priest, or Ethiopian king? And wizards? What sorcery are they practising, what is this, what is still living there in those impenetrable swamps? What is yet possible in the Sudan? To-day still? To-morrow still?

*KHARTOUM: 25th January, 1929.*

Often and long I sit before the Mahdi's shattered sepulchre in Omdurman and think over the life of that man.

When the Mahdi died he was buried on the spot where his hut had stood; later on the Khalifa Abdullahi built a magnificent tomb over it, by far the finest and loftiest building in the whole country. Karl Neufeld, the German, who lived in such terrible chains in the Khalifa's prison, tells us that he was made to construct a model of the dome; he must have kneaded his curses into the clay. During the building of the tomb the Khalifa himself carried bricks up and down. For every stone one laid Allah would give a whole palace in Paradise! This monument stood there for more than ten years, a resplendent landmark, hard by the Khalifa's house. Thus Lenin now reposes by the Kremlin. From all Africa come devout pilgrims to this holy place, even from Arabia, from every land of Islam.

# THE MAHDI OF ALLAH

On the day before the battle of Kerreri, Sir Herbert Kitchener saw the white dome from the heights of the Jebel Surgham; the great spear projecting from the centre of the crescent-shaped ornament on the top of the dome was sparkling in the sunlight—a splendid target for artillery. As the Sirdar gazes at the lofty tomb his howitzers, previously sent up to Halfaya on the west bank, open fire. The third lyddite shell pierces the dome.

.    .    .    .    .

The English bursting in found the tomb shot to pieces, the dome smashed. I have seen the photos which one of the war correspondents made. In the interior there was still a finely worked lattice round the grave; but it, too, was all twisted and split up, and people were tearing souvenirs from it.

But the ground-plan still remained; a ruined tomb, but still a tomb with a body in it. Now I am sitting in front of an empty shell; only parts of the outside wall are standing, and behind there is a last sorry remnant of the once magnificent dome; everything is dust-grey and shabby and forlorn.

By order of Lord Kitchener, a few weeks after the occupation of the town, the dome—which was already unsafe through the heavy shelling—was pulled down, and the tomb reduced to its present ruined condition; the Mahdi's body was first disinterred, and then destroyed. All this was done publicly, in order to show the people that no miracle had occurred, that the Mahdi, whom they venerated like a divinity, that their so long-expected Mahdi had after all been a mere human.

But the Mahdi's head, which was found to be perfectly preserved and with recognizable features, was not destroyed with the body; it was sent, packed in a kerosene tin, as a trophy to Egypt. Winston Churchill relates that the British proconsul in Egypt, Lord Cromer, eventually had the Mahdi's head buried in Sudanese soil near Wadi Halfa; others aver that it was preserved in some medical institution in England. Who knows what really happened to it?

THE MAHDI'S TOMB, IMMEDIATELY AFTER THE
CAPTURE OF OMDURMAN

# FROM THE TRAVELLER'S NOTES

Head for head. The Mahdi had Gordon's head on a spear outside his tent.

. . . . .

The courtyard of the tomb may be entered by a door which the tourists' guide unlocks. Native Sudanese are not allowed to enter the courtyard, only we foreign sightseers.

Whenever I go near this tomb—and I visit it often—I always see what I am now seeing again: dusky Arab men, who pray on the step of this locked door.

To-day there is a magnificent Bedouin from the eastern desert, one of those Hadendoa who, under Osman Digna, fought so long and bravely for Mahdism. He is wearing nothing but a coarse cloak; his long hair is not covered by any turban, but has been worked with an ointment of mutton tallow into innumerable thin strands. This is why colonial slang calls these people the Fuzzy-Wuzzies.

He is very brown and strong and savage; a sturdy young fellow. He cannot have known the Mahdi, he is too young.

Before this tomb, which has been ruthlessly destroyed so that it should no longer be a holy place, I now see this young man, this Sudanese of to-day, prostrating himself. His sandals he has laid aside; his forehead touches the ground. Now he reaches out with his long aristocratic hand under the doorstep of the closed door of the tomb. I see now for the first time that this doorstep has been hollowed out; many, many worshippers have stretched out their eager hands until they touched the sacred soil that is beyond the step. Now the hand scratches the earth, comes back filled with dust—and the young Bedouin rubs the sacred dust into his face; it is the ablution with sand that the Koran has permitted.

Now he begins his prayer. The iron face of the man from the great desert is shining with earnestness.

. . . . .

Empty graves, I reflect, do not deter faith, nor do unfulfilled prophecies shake the trust in a prophet. Nothing of what

Mohammed Ahmed promised has been accomplished: that he would live on until he had conquered the earth for Islam, that even before the death of the Expected Mahdi, the Son of Mary, Jesus, would return for the Day of Judgment.

But the unrealised promises of prophets only give nourishment to desire, and faith is born of desire. Religions do not die.

This one, I see, never has died. This man from the desert who is praying there before that desecrated and empty grave, shows me that this old story of the Mahdi is not yet by any means ended.

I resolve to tell this tale once more, with every detail, without inventing anything. And, if I can, I want to be fair to the Mahdi. Until the present only his enemies have told his story. But I want to think all the time of that desecrated tomb and of the earnest face of this praying man from the African desert. I want to tell the truth—and not to offend this inspired young worshipper.

. . . . .

I hear him pray, and I know what he is saying. Even an unbeliever will know this prayer, which is the Fatt'ha, the opening sura of the Koran:

> "Praise be to Allah, Lord of the worlds! The Compassionate, the Merciful! King on the day of reckoning. . . ."

I am speaking this sura under my breath, in my unbelieving language. The afternoon sun is blazing over Mohammed Ahmed's tomb; my roving eye sees the African town, hot, yellowish, like the desert, and the boundless desert on the horizon.

> "Guide Thou us on the straight path, the path of those to whom Thou hast been gracious, with whom Thou art not angry and who go not astray."

# THE MAHDI OF ALLAH
## THE STORY OF THE DERVISH MOHAMMED AHMED

# THE TOWN

THE STORY of the Dervish Mohammed Ahmed begins half a century ago in the hot town of Khartoum on the Nile and in the country of the Sudan.

. . . . .

"When Allah," say the Arabs, "made the Sudan, he laughed."

Rather a grim joke of the Creator, this land between desert and swamp. The Sudanese Nile flows in several streams out of the great lakes of Central Africa. In the Sudan they unite with one another. When it enters the country, the Nile is prodigal with its water, pours it into many channels, into lakes, morasses, drenches and soaks through the soil until it is soil no more, only a jumble of reeds and mud, buzzing with tropical flies. The elephant trumpets in the tall swamp-grass, and huge black men, long-legged like herons, stalk about here and there and hunt the elephant.

Then the Nile enters a region of steppes. The Nile has all at once become niggardly, gives to its banks only little of its water. Yellowish grass, a dried-up vegetation, mimosas, acacias—this is the realm of the antelopes and ostriches and nomadic shepherd tribes. Close to the banks of the Nile and its tributaries, which in the rainy season are often full of water, a patch of stronger green, a tropically luxuriant forest, grows here and there, a field of *durrha* or the like. Though almost nowhere is there a really luscious fruit, a bright-coloured flower. But dust there is everywhere, flies and midges and scorpions wherever you step.

This country, full of sun and thirst, flat and miserable all over, just fertile enough to nourish a not very numerous population on its enormous surface, is belted round by naked, staring deserts. Deserts like moon-landscapes, deserts like ghost-hills and dead plains! The earth is nowhere else quite so lifeless, quite so barren as between Egypt and the Sudan. The Nile flows through this land as though its water were not wet and were not able to moisten the soil.

Thirst, thirst, thirst of the Sudan, which makes men there burning hot, in desire unbounded and eager, parched even to the depths of their souls!

. . . . .

It is almost as though Nature had wished to lay down a zone between Egypt and tropical Africa across which the Mediterranean peoples should not pass. Beyond those dreadful swamps, which are full of wild beasts—elephants, lions, hippopotami, and crocodiles—is good land, rich land. From the territories on the border of the Sudan since antiquity the richest treasures have always come forth: ivory in measureless quantities, ostrich feathers and precious gums. The sturdy negro nations have always formed inexhaustible reservoirs of valuable slaves, from the earliest times onwards. Ever since men can remember, columns of shackled negroes have been driven across the steppes of the Sudan: slaves for the building of the pyramids of the Pharaohs, slaves destined for the household of the Queen of Sheba, slaves for Mohammed the Prophet, and slaves for the Virginia plantations. Jeremiah spoke of the negro slaves from the land of Kush; Napoleon, when he was in Egypt, bought two thousand Sudanese blacks for his army; for all through the ages there have been armed negro slaves. They make the best of soldiers. Already in the tombs of the Pharaohs whole battalions of little black dolls have been found, symbolizing the negro soldiers of the Egyptian armies. And each one of these negroes in the course of centuries has been driven in chains or in the heavy yoke right across the Sudan; and the Bedouins have done the driving. This Sudanese soil has been more terribly drenched with the bloody sweat of human beings than any other soil in the world.

. . . . .

The Sudan is the "Other Side" to the Arabs; across the Red Sea they reach it easily. Through all the centuries the sons of the desert have swarmed from Asia to Africa. Since the Prophet sent out his people to conquer the earth, the Arabs have been the masters of the Sudan. There they have mixed with ancient and mysterious tribes; African languages that were spoken when Rameses was king can still be heard in the Sudan in the mouths of people who call themselves Arabs. There are Nubian Arabs and arabised Berbers and Arab tribes that have become negroid. No matter; the Arab in the Sudan has remained Arabian, a nomad, a trader, a robber. Here and there on the river he might settle down like the fellah peasant of Egypt, reaping his dates or his *durrha*. But mostly he is, in this country, the rover of the desert of the times of the

Prophet, a caravan guide or a caravan plunderer. He bears the sword, the spear, and even wears chain-mail and an iron helmet, like the ancient Saracen that he is. These are not your Arabs of the Mediterranean lands who have become half European. They are the same Arab men whom Mohammed led against the whole universe: primitive barbarians, strong and cruel, heroic in battle, ardent in the harem, intent on war and booty, fanatical in their faith and in superstition. They abhor a Christian, and since the first Khedive of Egypt, Mehemet Ali, conquered the Sudan, they reckon all these Turkish pashas and Circassian beys from Cairo as unbelievers. The Turk—the "Toork," as they say—is not only the oppressor, but has even been contaminated by Europe; he is an associate of Christians.

Meanwhile, in the south, in the elephant country, the negro lives on, remains a creature of the primeval forest, a cannibal sometimes, always an elephant hunter. The negro hunts the elephant, the Arab hunts the negro, and all are hunted and harassed by the Turk.

Such is the Sudan of the seventies, when the story of the Mahdi begins.

.    .    .    .    .

The corner between the White Nile and the Blue Nile is shaped like an elephant's trunk. For a century there has stood here the town which is called Khartoum, which means "elephant's trunk."

The Khartoum of the seventies—more of a canker than a city. The Viceroy of Egypt sends a Pasha into the Sudan so that he may raise taxes from the blacks. The Pasha is in a hurry; he is dreaming of his fine

KHARTOUM IN THE TIME OF GENERAL GORDON
From a contemporary drawing

## THE TOWN

country seat in the Delta, or perhaps of a trip to Paris and the opera dancers. In the meantime he resides in a palace of brick on the banks of the Blue Nile. This house is two stories high; from the roof one can see far around, and watch caravans coming in from the desert and slave ships sailing down the Nile.

Then there are one or two official buildings, wide-sprawling and dirty. Barracks there must be, a court of justice, a gaol, a revenue office. In these houses the bored effendis of the provincial Government sit whiling away the time, Turks or Circassians most of them, a few Copts and Greeks and Levantines. The people call everybody who wears a fez "Turk."

The Turk of Khartoum is pallid yellow or pallid green. He bears the climate badly, the heat, the fever. The Turk knows better things than this dismal exile: Alexandria, Cairo, Beyrouth, Stambul. As soon as the Turk gets rich, he goes back there and lives in bliss. Here in the Sudan, in the meantime, the black girls of the harem are some consolation.

The powerful bey and the Christian trader—they live in a few superior houses built of bricks; others inhabit tiny cubes of baked mud and clay, which are crowded in large numbers round a courtyard. On the banks of the Blue Nile are the gardens of the rich. Camels and black slaves turn the water-wheels which raise the precious water into the groves of date palms. Inland, up towards the market, there is only one street at all resembling a street. The simple minaret of the mosque dominates it. The Greek merchant's shop has a sheltered verandah; under it, in front of the shop, you may see the Greek as he sits with his friends and customers drinking *mastika*. One or two Europeans walk along the only street, bored and perspiring. An explorer going to the market to buy some provisions for his bearers and cotton cloth as a trading article for negro princes. A priest from the Austrian Mission. In front of the little Arab café some soldiers of the garrison are taking it easy: Anatolian bashi-bazouks, irregulars, each of whom has a kourbash hanging from his wrist. Now and again one also catches sight in the narrow street of some beautiful horse which is trotting towards the Governor's palace; seated upon it is a kind of godlike being, all bedizened with medals and gold lace, with a golden scimitar, with a weary yellow face beneath the crimson tarboosh: some pasha, some bey. But most of the people in this street are deep dusky-brown or black, Arabs and negroes of a hundred tribes.

. . . . .

Already the town of the elephant's trunk is the great market for half Africa. From the West, from Kordofan and the borders of the Sahara, caravans arrive with gum. Down the Nile come steamers and sailing boats bringing, from the innermost lands of the equator, ivory, ostrich feathers, and the hides of wild animals; below in the reeking hold of the sailing barques black slaves are stowed away, packed close together, and bound up like lifeless bundles. Everybody knows that in Khartoum and sees it, though not the Government, which has been ordered from Cairo not to tolerate the slave trade any longer—that disgrace of an otherwise enlightened century. The *dahabeeyahs* land quite near the Governor's house; in broad daylight the corpses of the dead negroes are thrown into the Nile. Such and such a percentage of the wares is

## THE TOWN

spoilt in transit. If half remain alive, then business has been quite good. In the *zaribas*—the fenced-in enclosures in the trading stations of the south—the human cattle has been kept until it could be forwarded. Now it is driven, young men and women and children, across Khartoum, then on through the desert to the Red Sea, and finally to the slave markets of the East. The slave dealer pays a percentage to the Pasha, the Pasha who officially is supposed to be stamping out the slave trade.

In Khartoum everybody owns a slave, one at least; no Arab mud house so poverty-stricken that a naked negress be not squatting on the doorstep grinding corn. Cannibals from the equatorial swamps can be found in Khartoum, and negroes from the farthest corners of Africa. An unspeakable town of huts straggles shapelessly into the aridity, into the dust of the desert; a town of flat roofs or of pointed cones of *durrha* straw. In the tortuous lanes between hut and hut there are everywhere deep holes, in which refuse and carcasses are putrefying. The Governor from his palace roof and the muezzin from his minaret look right down on all that dark throng, on the senseless congestion of the black town.

· · · · ·

The Mosque—a fortress of Islam on the frontier of Heathendom. Through the throngs of the market the mufti passes, a superior being, with a splendour radiating from his capacious turban. The sheikh of some Dervish order is honoured as much as the Governor-General; the mean folk even kiss the hands of the *fikihs*, ragged teachers of the Scriptures and reciters of the Book and writers of charms, zealots who wander with staff and bowl. In the courtyard of the mosque one sees them squatting in dozens. There are Moslems from many lands among them, from Morocco and Tunis and others who wear conical caps of lamb hide, Shiite heretics from Persia, who reject the Sunna. The Red Sea, that separates and unites the great sects of Islam, is near. All the doctrines of the Moslem world come hither, to this mustering-place of races, Khartoum. The austere fanaticism of the Wahabites, who forbid every enjoyment of life, and the mystical surrender to God, absorption into God, that is taught by the Sufi order; and that new and ardent faith of the Senussi monasteries, in the West of the Arab world: all that mingles in Khartoum. In Cairo, forty-four orders of Dervishes are known; in Khartoum there are more: strange ones, that have their own rites, spiritual exercises which lead to ecstasy, to the melting of the soul into Allah. Obscure magic, age-old African superstition has here leaked into Islam. The *foggara*, that is "the poor ones," the Dervishes, are priests and teachers and physicians and wizards. Their begging-bowl is filled with millet meal and sour pap by people who themselves are hungry. To the low people the Dervishes are holy men, but even the magnificent pasha will call them of an evening into his courtyard illuminated with festive lamps, so that they may recite from the Koran to his guests, or else, in the way that they know, by dint of singing, dancing, and whirling round, fall into those frenzies, into those wild ecstasies which are pleasing to God and for man a way into His spiritual world. Out of the thousand noises of the hot African town rises distinctly the tom-tom, tom-tom of the Dervish drums, an intoxicating rhythm, in which lies a magical power.

## THE YOKE

ONE DAY, about the hour of the noonday prayer (the whitewashed minaret was jutting up into a sky glittering with heat and throwing no shadow on the glowing earth)—there was a throng around the mosque, larger than usual; they were waiting for a procession that was to come out from the house of God.

.   .   .   .   .

A dispute had been going on during these days in the quarter round the mosque, a scandal, such as the pious always enjoyed.

A young Dervish, one Mohammed Ahmed, son of Abdullah, had openly revolted against his master, the great Sheikh Mohammed Sherif!

Mohammed Sherif, descendant of a most holy house, stood at that time at the head of that great order of dervishes the "Sammaniya Tarika," which means "The Way to God as the Saint Es Samman has shown it." Mohammed Sherif, whose ancestors had long possessed the saint's prayer-carpet, was himself a saintly man. After him his young son was to inherit the prayer-carpet and the mystical gifts of Sheikhdom. This boy was growing up, the ceremony of circumcision was going to be celebrated, and the happy father, Sheikh Mohammed Sherif, had long in advance invited all the members of his order to the town: they were coming in from the farthest provinces, through which they had been wandering with staff and bowl. The Sheikh had made it known that on the day of the festival even the most godly and the most ascetic would be allowed to enjoy themselves: music and songs, goodly fare, even the spectacles of worldly lust, were not to be wholly forbidden—the dances of dancing-girls and of dressed-up boys.

. . . . .

The crowd outside the mosque which was now waiting for the pageant in the sullen heat was talking with relish (for everybody liked that kind of thing) of the scandal which had resulted: before all Khartoum, before the solemn assembly of *fikihs* and Dervishes, the privileged favourite disciple of the Sheikh had openly contradicted him—his saintly master. What God had forbidden—debauchery and worldly pleasures—not even the Sheikh of the Sammaniya might excuse!

Sheikh Mohammed Sherif, mightily angered, had then called the presumptuous young zealot a traitor, a perjurer. He had expelled him from the Order as a man who had violated the great oath of obedience.

"Yes, Mohammed Ahmed is the name of the young fellow," explained, in the waiting crowd, the townspeople who knew all the gossip of the mosque, to some strangers, travellers from the desert. "Mohammed Ahmed, son of Abdullah. He comes from Dongola."

. . . . .

It was time for the procession to arrive. Great splendour was expected, a great show. The Bedouins from the eastern desert crowded nearer to the gate of the mosque; they stood there, leaning on their tall

## THE YOKE

lances, while the tallow dropped from their ornamentally greased locks.

The procession was now approaching out of the mosque. The first to come was the barber who was going to perform the circumcision of the boy. His slave, a huge negro from Kordofan, almost naked and black as a moonless night, carried the barber's professional symbol, a sort of stand, called "heml," somewhat in the shape of a wooden cabinet resting on four legs and decorated all over with pieces of looking-glass and brass ornaments. The black giant had lifted this tall object above his woolly head, so that the glass and the polished metal were glittering high in the sunlit air. The master barber, a Nubian from Dongola, light brown and oily, sank his turbaned head piously upon his breast; his importance was obvious to all. Around him were the musicians: men with kettle-drums and others who carried oddly shaped wind instruments. The music was silent, for there was a large group of *fikihs*, teachers, and reciters of the Holy Book, walking in disorder behind that barber's palladium, chanting a hymn in praise of the Prophet. Next came the boys of the Koran school, marching briskly in rows of four, schoolmates and friends of the little boy whose day of honour this was. Specially clean were these dark-skinned youngsters, and dressed up in new shirts and caps. They, too, sang with the rest, in a great tumult:

"Bless, O our Lord, the Perspicuous Light! The Elect, the chief of Apostles! Thou art a light above lights!"

"O Mohammed," sang the chorus afterwards, "Thou art a sun. Thou art a moon. Thou art a light above light! O Mohammed! O my friend! O Thou with black eyes!"

"O nights of pleasure!" sang, shrilly and quite alone, a small boy, black as a raven and all stiff in his caftan which he must have borrowed for the festival, for it was too long for him. He was the *arîf*, that is, the head boy of the Koran school, and was very dignified. His high voice sounded above all the noise, even that of the drums, which were now rumbling again.

"O nights of pleasure! O nights of joy! Pleasure and every desire, among friends assembled!"

. . . . .

The drums of the procession were heard in the interior of a small house, one of those cubes of baked mud. Here two men were crouching near to each other, curiously occupied: one of them was putting the *sheba* upon the other, that is, the yoke which was fastened to recalcitrant slaves.

The young Arab who was being tied to the yoke was a lean fellow, in a Dervish frock of rough cotton frieze, with a girdle and a skull-cap of palm straw. He had a birthmark on his dark face, and on each cheek three parallel slits, such as are used as distinguishing marks in different tribes. This face, framed in a deep black beard, wore an altogether peculiar smile, always a smile, even now, while the man was being fastened up in such a painful manner.

This young Dervish was Mohammed Ahmed, the Dongolawi, the disciple who had mutinied against the Sheikh of the Sammaniya, and had been excommunicated by him. He was causing his relative, in whose house he now was, to lay that dreadful yoke upon him as a sign of repentance and expiation.

. . . . .

## THE YOKE

The *sheba*—the murderous cross of torture to which the Arab slave driver during the endless desert marches used to bind the negroes who might try to escape. Nobody escaped who bore the *sheba*. But many would die, miserably strangled by it.

A heavy wooden fork, cut from a stout branch of a tree, was placed on the throat in such a manner that the slave's Adam's apple was compressed into the narrow corner. The two ends of the fork were bound together behind the neck with thongs. Then the long handle of the fork was lifted up until it touched the outstretched right arm of the prisoner.

Hesitatingly and almost in tears, Mohammed Ahmed's cousin (who was a stout, elderly person, a well-to-do man of affairs, engaged in the trade of hiring out camels, with a stately turban above his pock-marked face) accomplished the last manipulation, which gave the finishing touch to the torture of the *sheba*. Mohammed Ahmed's denuded right arm—a strong sinewy carpenter's arm—was tied with thongs of fresh antelope hide to the branch. The thongs would dry and shrink, and would then cut cruelly into the flesh of the arm. But even worse: the prisoner who had the *sheba* on his neck could never let the arm tied to the yoke drop, not for a moment, otherwise the wooden fork would press into his throat and throttle him.

．　．　．　．　．

The cousin himself was trembling all over. He was not so learned in holy things, not so versed in the Koran and the traditions as Abdullah's son, Mohammed Ahmed, of whose saintliness he was certainly a little proud—only, was it seemly that one of the blood of the Prophet (on whom be the blessing and the prayer!) should, even though it were voluntarily and for the sake of devout penitence, assume the infamous yoke of the heathen negro brute? "For," said the cousin, "it is almost certain that our family is descended from the Prophet, through Fatima and Ali, her husband. We have indeed a right to the title of Sayids!"

While the cousin was saying this and winding the thongs round the arm of the young Dervish, he was feeling a little superior on account of his majestic bulk, his greater age, his position as the master of that house.

Up to then he had spoken in Arabic, but now he dropped into the ancient Nubian dialect of Dongola, which was the real native tongue of both of them: "Consider, O son of the Sayid Abdullah. . . . Out of my love I warn you; for were not our fathers like brothers? Even a strong donkey, consider, will succumb to an immoderate thrashing."

Suddenly he stopped. The young Dervish, with the yoke already round his throat, the rod of torture strapped to his outstretched arm, had begun to sing a litany, which none might dare to interrupt, the sequence of the ninety-nine "Most Beautiful Names," or Attributes of the One and Only—Allah.

In the frame of its beard the face of Mohammed Ahmed was smiling calmly; nobody could see on it the torture which he had already begun to suffer by his own penitent will. The large eyes were half-closed. The lips, full but not negroid, allowed the magnificent teeth to be seen, and a curious V-shaped aperture between them, which was considered a great and mysterious sign. Who knows if the eternal smile of this strong face was not intended always to show this fate-telling sign?

A CIRCUMCISION PROCESSION
From the painting by Leo Diet

## THE YOKE

Mohammed Ahmed had struck up the holy singsong with the aid of which the Dervishes work themselves up to the highest pitch of ecstasy. Rapidly and endlessly he recited, again and again, the Beautiful Names, the exalted Attributes, in the Arabic of the Holy Book:

"Er Rahman, er Rahim, el Kerim, el Halim, el Bassir, es Semia, el Qadir, el Ghafir, el Hamid, el Mejid, er Rashid, el Queyyum. . . ."

"The Compassionate!" chanted the man in the yoke.

"The Merciful."
"The Generous."
"The Clement."
"The All-seeing."
"The All-hearing."
"The All-powerful."
"The Avenger."
"The Forgiver."
"The Laudable."
"The Glorious."
"The Straight."
"The Unchanging. . . ."

A horrid gurgling interrupted the litany. The young penitent, being yet inexperienced in the bearing of the suffocating yoke, had let down his tired right arm ever so little; now he thought he must choke.

. . . . .

The procession passed through the narrow streets of the town towards the house of the Sheikh. Everywhere were standing African people, gaily showing their ivory teeth in their dark faces; the tassels of their red tarbooshes swung to the rhythm of the music.

Childishly the crowd was enjoying the noise of the drums, the waving banners, the perfumed smoke of frankincense and aloe, benzoin and sandal-wood, that were smouldering in silver kettles carried at the sides of the procession. Boys were swinging the incense burners on long chains; the tinkling of silver mingled with the music. Other boys, walking in the parade, sprinkled rosewater out of silver scent bottles on the spectators' clothes, or poured essence of orange blossoms over their burnouses. Negro slaves carried ponderous silver vessels which contained hot coffee of the best Abyssinian kind, sweetened with honey, and perfumed with costly ambergris. O enjoyment, O felicity! Now and again an obliging cup-bearer took one of the exquisite little silver and porcelain cups from the big tray and filled it for this or that person among the spectators, some distinguished man who could be expected to give a baksheesh for it. Nobody refused to do so; everybody's face was smiling. Sombre dignity disappeared from every wrinkled forehead. The marching rhythm of the drums had gripped them all; all were happy, and at the rear of the procession veiled women were heard raising their shrill cries of jubilation.

. . . . .

Only the *muttahir* might perhaps have felt a little nervous, the little hero of the ceremony to be performed. The ten-year-old boy, who was thin and quite yellow, had been strangely adorned, and was mounted on a donkey; two of his little school-fellows marched on the right and on the left, holding the donkey's reins. A third schoolmate walked like a herald before the donkey; on his neck the *muttahir's* writing-tablet had been hung by a handkerchief; it was covered from top to bottom with beautifully executed Arabic characters, pious verses which the master of the Koran school had carefully written as a specimen of his great learning.

The little boy who was going to be circumcised was sitting on the donkey, somewhat scared but very proud. On his little yellow and black head they had wound a big crimson turban, a man's turban; but otherwise he had been adorned and dressed just like a girl. This had to be done on account of the evil eye which was sure to be lurking somewhere on the way. The evil eye would see the girlish finery and would be so astonished that the magic power of its look would be broken; certainly that evil look would not find the face of the boy at all. Furthermore, this face was hidden behind an embroidered handkerchief, which the boy pressed firmly to his cheeks the whole time. And finally, so that no preventive measure might be neglected, the mother of the boy was walking behind the donkey, deeply veiled and with a great tinkling of ankle-rings, and was sprinkling salt behind him into the donkey's tracks.

While she was thus walking, sprinkling salt and preventing every evil, the veiled principal wife of the holy Sheikh was continually uttering shrill cries, always on the same piercing note, and behind her were walking, shapeless in their wrappings, the other women of the Sheikh's harem and the women of all the relatives, one and all joyously shouting:

"O nights of pleasure, O nights of joy! And every desire, among friends assembled! O Mohammed, thou my friend!"

## THE MAHDI OF ALLAH

In the very middle of the procession there was, as it were, a walking island of sheer dignity and solemnity and quite a different rhythm of murmured litanies: it was a closed group of Dervishes. The great "Sheikh et Tarikat," Mohammed Sherif, was riding upon a beautiful Arab horse, surrounded by the disciples and followers of the Sammaniya order. Many of these people were waving flags, embroidered with religious sentences, others were reciting monotonously. Mohammed Sherif, unmoved and as if frozen with earnest self-importance, rode past, did not look to the right or to the left. He was already an elderly man, his long beard was quite grey. He was dressed in his very long caftan and in dark-red pointed babooshes. As a sign of the highest and most worshipful dignity, his broad turban was of green material. The crowd on the way was pressing forward, in order if possible to kiss the holy man's foot or the hem of his robe.

. . . . .

In the house of the Sheikh the preparations had already long been completed. Lanterns and multi-coloured little lamps adorned the large courtyard, where the couches and seats of honour had been arranged, with a profusion of carpets and costly brocades. Rose sherbet had been prepared, sherbet made of liquorice root and sherbet made of sorrel; whole sheep, stuffed with spices and fat currants, awaited the dusky fingers that would tear them to pieces; bread cakes had been baked from *durrha* dough; the dancing-girls were putting on their paint and their trinkets; Karagoosh, the jester, was already arrayed in his motley and ready to perform; the reed-flutes lay at hand, and the tambourines and the pumpkin-drums of the southern negro tribes. Everything was in order, and the black servants of the house, in festive white gowns and fine new caps, were waiting, merry and highly excited, before the outer wall that enclosed the cluster of low cubical buildings, the home of the holy Sheikh. Already from afar the drums of the procession could be heard, and from all sides people were running up to see it arrive. But then something happened—a sensation; the crowd shrank back in awe at the sight of a tall lean fellow, who suddenly was there; nobody had seen him come. He was carrying a huge slave-yoke, he was almost naked, and his long uncovered hair, his beard, and his powerful shoulders were covered with ashes. Silently he passed through the throng; he was strangely rigid, perhaps because of the yoke, or because he did not want to shake the ashes off his head. People made way for him; he squatted down before the entrance of the house. In doing this he did not try to prop the yoke against the wall; he crouched forward over his meagre legs, which he had drawn under him, and carried the arm which was fastened to the wood stretched out as if in a spasm. The tortured hand, above which the thongs were cutting into the wrist, held with bloodless fingers a rosary of coarse wooden beads. The lips of the penitent were murmuring ceaselessly the litany of the ninety-nine epithets of God, and again once more the ninety-nine. And those lips kept smiling, kept smiling all the time.

The shadow of the man in the yoke, as it fell clear and sharp on the long wall, was like the shadow of a crucified man.

·     ·     ·     ·     ·

The servants of the Sheikh's house had at once recognised this individual; soon the whole crowd of spectators knew that this was the audacious one, that disciple, the Dongolawi, who had dared to contradict the Sheikh and had been cast out by him. Ah, so now he was repenting! Lying down there in the dust at his master's doorstep!

An excited murmuring rose up round the young man in the yoke. It was strange that nobody should begin to mock the humiliated one, that nobody should start throwing dirt, that hardly a single broad negro's mouth should be grinning. They all only looked at him full of awe and dismay, as he lay there. Some strong influence was going out from that man, an indefinable magic; perhaps it was that perpetual smile. A slave woman of the Dinka, with an ivory pin stuck in her upper lip, stepped up quite close to the prostrated man. Her right hand grasped a naked baby that was riding in a strange way on her hip. Her left arm, adorned with many copper bangles, was hanging down, so that the hand almost touched the Dervish's turbanless head. The black girl breathed in deeply and ecstatically, as though she were inhaling an entrancing perfume.

Then the drums and the flutes were plainly heard.

· · · · ·

As the festive procession came near the house it lost its orderliness and solemnity. The lively group of boys broke out of the ranks; they pressed forward towards the door. For now there was going to be great fun: the customary song in honour of the schoolmaster. So excited were the boys that they scarcely noticed the penitent, the man with the yoke.

## THE YOKE

The *arif*, the head boy of the Koran school, sang out first and the others repeated the doggerel verses after him:

> Praise be to God, the Mighty Creator,
> The Sole, the Forgiver, the Conservator.
>
> He knoweth the past and futurity
> And veileth things in obscurity.
>
> He knoweth the tread of the black ant
> And its work when in darkness vigilant.
>
> He formed an exalted heaven's vault
> And spread the earth over the ocean salt. . . .

They all sang it together, in time. Then the rhythm became quicker and merrier:

> May He grant this boy long life and happiness,
> To read the Koran with attentiveness;
>
> To read the Koran and history's pages,
> The stories of ancient and modern ages.
>
> For this youth has learned to write and read,
> To spell and cast up accounts with speed. . . .

Now the vivacious little dark-brown boys began to shout at the top of their voices and to dance round the *fikih*, their schoolmaster, who was standing in their midst, dignified, in his dark-coloured robe with long sleeves. He made a sign to them to stop: Sheikh Mohammed Sherif was just dismounting from his horse, and what followed was intended to be heard by him especially; the *fikih* had practised these verses with the children; they were most important.

> His father, therefore, should not withhold
> A reward of money, silver and gold.
>
> Of my learning, O father, thou hast paid the price;
> God give thee a place in Paradise!

Then the rejoicing broke forth unrestrained:

> Our fikih has taught us the alphabet:
> May he have every grateful epithet!
>
> Our fikih has taught us as far as "The News":
> May he never his present blessing lose.
>
> Our fikih has taught us the Sura "The Cattle":
> May he never be the subject of scandalous tattle.
>
> Our fikih has taught us as far as "The Cow":
> May he ever be honoured in future, as now.
>
> Our fikih——

The sing-song of the boys suddenly broke off, smothered by a murmuring.

. . . . .

Sheikh Mohammed Sherif has come to his door and has noticed the prostrated penitent. With an imperious gesture he lifts his hand.
A heavy silence falls. The sun is burning. A hawk is circling high in the air above Khartoum.

. . . . .

Had the desperate young penitent murmured words

of repentance? Had he begged forgiveness, confessed his fault, the sin of heresy? Nothing was heard.

Only the answer of the holy Sheikh was heard. His voice was shrill with wrath, his eyes beneath the green turban were red with passion.

"Miserable Dongolawi!" he shouted uncontrollably.

"A traitor!" he roared, and kicked his foot against the prostrate man, so that his big red baboosh quivered. "He does not fear God and rebels against his master!"

His voice changed, became whining: "O Mussulmans, he is splitting the firm staff of Islam! O Believers, how true is the saying, 'A man from Dongola is the Shaitan in human shape.'"

The head of the Sammaniya Tarika stretched out his arms with tremendous pomposity, so that the voluminous sleeves of the white robe were spread wide like wings:

"Mohammed Ahmed Ibn Abdullah! Be off with you, for you are not forgiven!"

. . . . .

A long time after the guests of the festival had disappeared into the house, the man with the yoke stood up. His smile remained frozen upon his bloodless lips.

# THE ISLAND

The young Dervish whom the Sheikh of the Sammaniya had driven from his threshold lived thereafter for years on the Island of Abba in the White Nile.

.   .   .   .   .

On this wooded island on the edge of the negro country there dwelt a man from Dongola, Ahmed Sharfi. With him were living the sons of his deceased nephew. This dead man, who had been called Abdullah, or rather the Sayid Abdullah—for he had always upheld his right, as a descendant of the Prophet, to bear that title—had been an excellent boat-builder, and skilled in the building of large and small river-craft and of water-wheels, such as are used on the banks of the Nile to water the fields. The four sons of this man had also learnt this trade. The family came from the Egyptian border, from Dongola. Since the death of Abdullah the sons had made their home with their uncle on Abba. The eldest was called Mohammed, then came Ahmed, then Mohammed Ahmed; the youngest, Abdullah, was a posthumous son. The brothers of the Dervish Mohammed Ahmed were simple and strong fellows, well skilled in their deceased father's trade, which on Abba also they plied successfully. Everywhere up and down the Nile the barks of acacia-wood which this gifted family knew so well how to build, were renowned. Mohammed Ahmed,

## THE ISLAND

too, like his brothers, had learned the carpenter's trade and had practised it, even as a Dervish, for the brethren of the Dervish orders were not forbidden to carry on secular professions. But now that the wanderer had come back to their island, the uncle and the brothers would have been willing and glad to provide for him, even if he should not have wished to work at all. For them he was the scholar, the saint, the pride of the family; no doubt he was going to prove and assert the family claim to their venerable descent from the Prophet of Allah. The best hut in the hedged-in settlement in which the uncle and his nephews were living was set aside for the use of the saint of the family.

.   .   .   .   .

No monastic rule forbids a Dervish to marry. This one had two legal wives, who were both named Fatima, and were both his cousins, one the daughter of a paternal uncle, the other of his uncle on Abba. But Mohammed Ahmed did not live in his hut with his wives; they only came to him daily to the cave-like hole in the Nile bank where he was living like a hermit. They came, two chastely veiled figures, talking together like sisters, down to the hole, kissed the hands of their lord and filled his wooden begging-bowl with *durrha* porridge or dried fish meat.

This was how Mohammed Ahmed lived. He wore on his body nothing but a shirt of rough fabric. If it were torn, then the wives had to sew it up with patches; if it were dirty, they had to wash it carefully. Never would he tolerate any uncleanliness near him or about him. He had a plaited girdle of palm straw and a skull-cap of the same material. In that attire he could often be seen working in his uncle's fields. Then he would toil like a negro slave. He would tend camels and donkeys; or else he would help his brothers on the wharf; he knew well enough how to wield the carpenter's axe.

Yet he was not working for his living or because he was asked to do so: he wished only to prove his humility to himself. But most of the time he would be sitting, far from his people, a stranger to his people, in that lonely cave amidst the bushes of the riverbank.

．　．　．　．　．

Before the entrance of the cave he had built a shelter, just four stakes thatched with palm leaves. There, in the shade, stood his *angareb*, the native couch made of a wooden frame and hide thongs which in the Sudan even the poorest people possess. Here the Dervish used to dream away the hours that were not given up to prayer or to the endless mystical exercises by which he was trying to mortify his body and to tire his soul, so that it might surrender entirely to God and be absorbed into the Divine essence.

Sometimes weeks would pass before he emerged into the light of day out of the dark hole in which he was praying and singing and fasting. Then again there would come days when he would have to rest, to collect strength and to dream.

．　．　．　．　．

Under the straw roof he reclined and looked upon the flowing Nile. The Nile was his oldest friend, his real home. On an island like this Mohammed Ahmed was born, on Darar Island, near Dongola, in a village

## THE ISLAND

built with the baked mud of the Nile, under the date-palms. The melancholy song of the water-wheel on the river-bank, raising the water out of the Nile, was his earliest memory. The Nile near Dongola, now idyllic, flowing between green orchards and cotton-fields, now rushing stormily in cataracts between the rocks—that was the first experience of this man; it was as though the Nile were flowing through his arteries, dark, ancient, mysterious, dangerous, fecundating, devastating. His father, the boat-builder, had been wont to carry him, almost as an infant, down to the water with him; before he could walk he had been swimming about in the Nile with other naked children; later on his father had made him a tiny boat and he had paddled it along with his little hands.

Always the Nile had been most intimately bound up with his life; and it was so, too, when his father later took his family up the river to Khartoum and Kerreri, where the boat-builder had carried on his trade until his untimely death. Mohammed Ahmed could not separate in his mind the picture of his father from the Nile. He saw him half-naked in the shallow water, as he repaired a damaged boat, or on the wharf with the axe in his hand.

. . . . .

But the father of Mohammed Ahmed had been no ordinary man, satisfied when he had worked enough to obtain the necessary food. He had been almost as well-versed in the Koran and the Traditions as any *fikih* or learned scribe. Never had he missed one of the five daily prayers, and he had taught his children to recite the suras. And he was never tired of asserting again and again what the peasant people at home were never ready to believe: that there was something peculiar about his ancestors and himself, an incredible and wonderful sanctity. His forefathers, he said, had not always dwelt on the Nile; they had come from the East, with the host of the Arab conquerors, from Medina, the town of Mohammed the Prophet, and they had been themselves of the Prophet's progeny, descendants of Fatima, Mohammed's daughter, and of his cousin Ali. Together with the first sura which he had learnt to recite, Mohammed Ahmed had had to repeat an exalted, an almost divine line of ancestors.

"I am the Sayid Mohammed Ahmed, son of the Sayid Abdullah, son of Fahl, who was the son of Abd el-Weli, the son of Abdullah, son of Mohammed, son of the Haji Sherif, who was the son of Ali, son of Ahmed, son of Ali. Son of Hasb en-Nebi, the son of Sabr. . . ."

The boy had learned all the names of the ancestors. The father of the ancestral Sabr, some time in the dark centuries, had been Abd el-Kerim, then came Husain, Aun-Allah, Najm ed-Din, Otman, Musa, Abul-Abbas, Yunus, Otman, Yaqub, Abd el-Kader, Hassan el-Askari. . . .

"Son of Ulvan," the boy was taught further, "the son of Abd el-Baqui, son of Sakhra, son of Yaqub, son of Hassan es-Sibt, who was the son of our Lord, the Imam Ali, son of Abu Talib, who was the Prophet's paternal uncle. . . ."

When he pronounced the more than sacred names of the Khalifa Ali, of Hassan the Martyr, and of that other Hassan, called El-Askari (from whom it is said that the twelfth Imam of Islam is to descend, the Expected One), tears of pride came into the eyes of the boy. Those were his ancestors—although the other boys mocked him if he said so. Yes, he was the Sayid Mohammed Ahmed, Ibn es-Sayid Abdullah, a "Sherif" of the house of the Prophet, on whom be blessing and peace. . . .

Perhaps it was this that had impelled the boy to such diligence in the *medressas* at Kerreri and Khartoum, where he squatted at the feet of the *fikih*, learning to read and to recite the sacred texts. At nine he could recite by heart all the endless Koran; he was then considered a young wonder; his mother was proud, and his uncle, and his brothers. . . .

. . . . .

The hermit of Abba, on his couch near the entrance of the cave, was dreaming now of his later years when he had been a pupil of greater masters, of godly sheikhs: Sheikh el-Emir, in the riverland between the two Niles, then Sheikh Mohammed el-Kheir at Berber. How much study, how much fasting, how much hard and menial work all day, what vigils and prayers, and prayers and vigils at night!

Until one day he had examined himself, full of tremulous doubts, to test whether he could now be worthy to become a servant and a pupil of that great saint of God, the head of the Sammaniya Tarika—Mohammed Sherif: the same who, after so many years of loyal service, in the end had driven him from his doorstep like an unclean dog. . . .

As soon as his thoughts had drifted to that, to the ghastly shame of that day, Mohammed Ahmed would more than once retire into that gloomy cave which he had dug as a refuge against these very thoughts, and commence again those exercises which were a joy to him as well as a torture; they were more than prayers and more than mortification: hidden in them was a magic that lent power, conjured the Invisible Ones, compelled mystic Beings to come and help, might even, perhaps, prevail upon God. . . .

There was one of these ceremonies, called the "Riada": the ascetic penitent, clad in clean clothes and fasting severely, repeated for days and days two of the names of Allah: "Ya Kerim, ya Rahim!" "O Thou Magnanimous, Thou Compassionate!" Not arbitrarily; certain numbers of cabbalistic import governed the repetitions of prayers and gestures. Twenty-one times (after the morning prayer) the one hundred and ninth Sura:

"Say, O ye unbelievers, I worship not that which ye worship, and ye do not worship that which I worship; nor will I worship that which ye worship, nor will ye worship that which I worship; to you be your religion; to me my religion."

This twenty-one times, then all the ninety-nine names of Allah, three times, then only the two names —ya Kerim, ya Rahim—again and again, without the slightest pause, until far into the night, only interrupted by the most indispensable functions of the body; but in between at a certain hour had to come the prayer for the Prophet, one thousand times ("God bless and save the Prophet!"). Sometimes a certain formula was recited that was very mysterious: the worshipper lay prostrate with his forehead in the dust; then he again pronounced the two Names as many times as corresponded to the number of letters forming them. . . .

Day and night, day and night. The worshipper was nourishing himself frugally with dried grapes, a little flour, oil, and vinegar. During the whole time perfumes

## THE ISLAND

had to be burning near him in a special perfuming vessel: benzoin, ambergris, and other and more secret drugs that produced a heavy-smelling vapour. The devotee, intoxicated by those perfumes, by his own weariness, by the name of Allah, by his singing voice, by the swinging of his head, might finally see visions. Unknown Ones would come to him; he had forced them to descend; they were compelled to serve him. Shapeless Beings from another world, Resplendent Ones or Dark Ones, would suddenly emerge; voices would begin to talk; they were saying prodigious things. . . .

.   .   .   .   .

Those secret voices that talked to him restored to the humiliated Dervish his self-confidence. And more: after a time this man who had worn the yoke began to feel his neck free again and to raise his head.

Now he came out of his cave again, into the open. The people of Abba, who until then had looked upon this mysterious person who had crept into a hole in the ground only from a distance and with a certain horror, now sometimes found him seated beneath the big acacia tree, where the village folk used to gather in the shade. He was always allowed the seat of honour near the trunk; there he sat, on a sheepskin. In his hand he held a rosary; his patched Dervish shirt was wonderfully clean; round his skull-cap there was a turban cloth of resplendent whiteness; one end of the cloth hung over his cheek and touched his black beard, which was carefully anointed. Whoever came near to him—but very few dared—perceived a perfume that emanated from the smiling man. Was it the perfume of those mystic flames in his cave, or was it the odour of sanctity? For people now began to believe the hermit was a saint.

First a superstitious awe caused the island people to stay away. Also it was not befitting to interrupt a godly person who was praying the prayers of the rosary. But soon the friendly smile of the man conquered the children. Tiny naked toddlers, brown Arab boys without a stitch of clothing on their bodies, and negro children from the Shilluk village, all swollen-bellied and woolly-headed, came on long spindle-legs to stare at him, and finally played their strange little games near him without fear. That gave the women of Abba the first excuse to come as well. Young girls and old hags, black women and lighter coloured ones, veiled ones and naked ones, stood on the edge of the clearance where that huge tree was and looked with wide eyes, ecstatic or giggling, at the beautiful saint. For the first time they observed certain signs which he bore on his person: the gap between his front teeth, a certain birthmark on his right cheek—signs that meant a great deal!

. . . . .

The Island of Abba lies on the great waterway to the negro lands of the South. The steamers which the Pasha sent from Khartoum to Fashoda, to the newly opened-up equatorial provinces, passed by it, and likewise the sailing barks which brought ivory and tragic cargoes of miserably penned-up slaves from the factories of the big Arab traders in the negro country. The caravan road from Lake Chad, along which, from Bornu, Wadai, and Dar-Fur, the pilgrims journeyed to Mecca, crosses the White Nile not far from Abba. The township of Kawa on the eastern bank, opposite the island, was an important harbour and trading place; from here and from Abba the steamers obtained from the forest the wood for their furnaces before entering the woodless region of the swamps. So it happened that Abba, though inhabited by only a few people, by peasants who had fled from the Nubian villages around Dongola before the tax collector, and some huge Shilluk negroes, whose villages of conical huts begin here—that Abba was visited by numerous strangers. Boats put in: big *dahabeeyahs* and the unwieldy cargo barks, called *nuggars*. It was known that on Abba was living a family of shipbuilders, who were able to repair leaky boats; and how often would a boat be damaged on the sandbanks or mangled by some furious hippopotamus! Also it was well known by now that a new holy man was living on Abba. The sailors would go ashore to see him as he sat under the tree; many of them would ask him for a miracle-working amulet. Was it not common knowledge that the words of the forty-sixth sura, written by a cunning hand on a plank of the ship, would always prevent the vessel from foundering? If the holy *fikih* wished, he would write on the plank: "In the name of Allah, swim away, ship, and cast thy anchor! Verily the Lord is most merciful, most compassionate!" If he wished he wrote on a leaden tablet: "Ya Rahim, ya Rahman"—which, infallibly, would fill the net with fish, if you put the tablet into it.

Was not this "Abu Falja," the "Father of the V-shaped gap," as they all called him in common, bound to know the formula that is written with rose-water upon a strip of gazelle skin which you fix on your flag before a fight or put into your captain's turban? An Arab from Khartoum, journeying upstream to

Zubeir Rahamet, the biggest slave hunter of the upper Nile, would call at Abba and ask the holy Dervish for this talisman which he wanted to carry with him when attacking negro villages. A sheikh of the Baggara Bedouins in the south would desire the famous charm to help in catching escaped slaves.

Each one of these visitors brought with him some gift, sometimes a sheep or a basket of *durrha*, sometimes even ivory or fine garments or Maria-Theresa dollars. The smiling young Dervish under the big tree would listen to everyone, would say a pious word to everyone, would even give to this or that person a copper case in the interior of which there was a verse of the Koran; but he scarcely professed to possess miraculous faculties: "All the strength and the power is with God!"

And all the gifts he divided amongst the poor of Abba. This is why they called him "Zahed"—the Renouncer.

. . . . .

For a long time already the wooded islands in the Nile had been a place of refuge for fugitives whom the Turk was hunting. The Turk, the "Toork"—that is what the Egyptians were called throughout the Sudan, for their pashas and beys were mostly of Turkish origin, although many of them were Syrians and Christian Copts, and even Europeans. The Toork was every fair-skinned person with a tarboosh; you could never rightly know whether he was, as he would pretend, a Mussulman, or an unbeliever, as was often whispered. However, the Toork was always the wicked enemy of the Sudani—tyrant, oppressor, and extortioner.

The Dongolawi whose date crop the Pasha had seized, or the Jaali whose camels had been impounded, escaped to Abba. A Baggara Arab whom the bashi-bazouks had threatened to torture in order to find out where his cattle were hidden in the woods, fled hither. The bashi-bazouk! The Anatolian or Arnaut mercenaries of the Pasha were plundering the entire Sudan. With their Remington rifle and their kourbash, the formidable whip made of hippopotamus hide, they would come and demand not only the legal taxes, but tenfold; then, besides, black slave girls for themselves, the fattest of food, and many pots of *merissa* beer. Those who refused they flogged; or they spread a shackled man naked on the soil baked by the midday sun. If some virile Arab tried armed resistance, then his thorn *zariba* or his village of tents was set upon by the Bazingers, half-naked heathen blacks in the Pasha's pay, who as war provender were in the habit of carrying bleeding bits of human meat in their cartridge-boxes, but were armed with the best of rifles and trained to fight. That was what the Turk was doing in the Sudan.

. . . . .

More and more often the ascetic of Abba heard those despairing and angry voices: "Toork! Toork!" Did they mingle in the drunken dreams of his ecstatic prayers? After days passed once more alone in his cave, fasting more strictly than ever, once he recited to the circle of those who thronged around him under the tree those Suras of the Sacred Book that promise the victory of the Faith, and predict the misfortune that is the unbeliever's lot.

Soon, perhaps, he said mysteriously, the hour was coming. A Saviour, an Avenger was to be expected. With God alone was the knowledge!

## THE STORK

A PADDLE steamer is sailing up the Nile. On the fore quarter-deck, at a table covered with books and cigars and writing material, sits Charles Gordon. It is hot, but it is not uncomfortable here. Gordon is writing a letter to his sister Augusta.

"Chinese" Gordon, as they call him, has been almost everywhere, but he has never been in Africa before. Now he is going to Gondokoro as Governor-General of the new equatorial province.

A nice province! Nothing but fever and mosquitoes and slave-hunters. But Charles Gordon does not know it yet. Though he may have his forebodings.

.   .   .   .   .

He is smoking furiously; a small, slight man of forty, with whiskers framing a healthy red face. He is wearing the undress uniform of a Colonel of the Royal Engineers; on top of it an Egyptian tarboosh. He is writing and writing all the time; he likes it. Sometimes he will get up in the middle of a sentence; he has remembered that he wanted to search for some text in the Bible. The Bible is lying next to him, with a book-mark in it that Augusta has embroidered—green silk with yellow checks, and inside the green squares smaller blue ones: those are the tartan colours of the Gordon Clan.

He is always searching for Bible texts, is Charles

## THE STORK

Gordon. From time to time his light-blue eyes, in which there is a will, scan the Nilotic landscape; then he throws away his cigar and takes a new one. He is just a little jumpy, is Gordon. His concentration is ardent and vigorous, as long as it lasts; then suddenly it will cool off, and what just now has been the most important thing in the world has become quite insignificant.

Charles Gordon sighs a little. It is a strange thing, but his mood is not quite what it should be to-day. Then he yawns, then goes on writing, in his curly but legible hand, to his sister Augusta in England.

"Your brother's title is now 'His Excellency General Colonel Gordon'—(it seems an extraordinary mixture)— 'the Governor-General of the Equator'; so no one can or ought to cross it without permission of His Excellency.

"But the day before your brother had his trousers off, and was pulling the boat in the Nile, in spite of crocodiles, who never touch you when moving.

"We left Khartoum amid a salute of artillery, and are now steaming up the Nile. . . . We see a great many crocodiles. They lie out on the sand every evening and look glistering in the sun. They are dreadful-looking creatures as they lie, with their mouths open, basking. There are also a number of little birds about them always.

"The steamer is very slow: only four miles an hour against the current, which is about two knots. The black and white Danube storks are in thousands on the banks, with pelicans and all sorts of storks, from the little egret to the immense great bird with a huge bill who sits perfectly stationary. I saw some hippopotamuses to-day, but it was only their noses—

they were in the middle of the river. Troops of monkeys come down to drink, with very long tails stuck up straight like swords over their backs. They look most comical. The banks are thickly wooded, and the country quite flat. The trees are either gums or tamarisks. We have passed some people who wear a gourd for a headdress, and also some Shilluks who wear no *head*— or *other*—dress at all. . . ."

Charles Gordon stops, reads what he has written, knits his brows. There is that thing about the storks. . . . Strange birds, storks—very mysterious! He has always been interested in storks. During his official journeys on the Danube he saw so many of them. This is the country to which the Danube storks fly in winter.

Colonel Gordon hesitates. Should he tell Augusta about those storks of yesterday? Last night. The thought is troubling him a little.

.   .   .   .   .

This highlander, this Colonel of the Royal Engineers, Charles George Gordon, is living a life full of colour. He has taken part in the Crimean War. Then he was in China, and was present when Lord Elgin destroyed the Summer Palace in Peking. Later on a Chinese Messiah arose, one Hong, who declared that he was the Son of God and that he was going to found the Kingdom of God, Taiping. But, on the Taiping rebels proceeding to menace the European Settlements of Shanghai, Captain Gordon was made General of a fantastic militia called by the Chinese the "Ever Victorious Army." Gordon's friend, the great Chinese Li Hung Chang, has declared ever since that the Scotsman then saved the Chinese Empire, so they

## THE STORK

called him in England "Chinese" Gordon. After that he went home again, commanding the Royal Engineers at Gravesend, and completing the defences on the Thames. Then he went to represent Britain in the Danube Commission at Galatz. From Galatz he visited Stambul, where he met Nubar Pasha, the Egyptian Prime Minister. And now he was going up the Nile to Gondokoro. Nubar wanted an Englishman for a Governor of the Equator, so that people in Europe should not always say that Egypt was doing nothing to prevent the slave trade. So now Gordon, His Excellency Gordon, Colonel in the British Army, General in the Egyptian Army, is going all alone into that wild country of the swamps, into that vague province which presumably exists up there.

For he has started off (this is so like him) without waiting for his staff, for his troops, for the provisions he has been promised. And which never arrive. Nothing arrives, and nothing goes right, and nothing is in order. These Egyptians, he is beginning to realise . . .

Gordon frowns. It is strange, but he is not quite at his ease to-day. Those storks of last night . . . He has such presentiments.

Of course, he is trusting in God. He is a believer, is Charles Gordon. Now it seems clear enough to him that no hazard, not Nubar Pasha, but God himself has chosen him to redeem Africa, to wipe the disgrace of the slave trade from the face of the earth. The dispensation of Providence is so visible; certain texts of the Bible (which Gordon is always investigating) prophesy the greatest things. Strange that no exaltation should be forthcoming. . . .

Is it, perhaps, because he has seen Cairo and the

Egypt of the Viceroy Ismail Pasha? What a foolish system of Government, and what corruption! The Khedive, choked with debts and childishly infatuated with all the baubles of civilization, is submitting to bloodsuckers, and is himself sucking the blood of the nation; Cairo reeks of putrefaction and Paris perfumes.

And Khartoum! With a nervous feeling of disgust Gordon thinks of the days which he has just spent there, as the official guest of honour of Ismail Ayub, the Governor-General of the Sudan. To be sure, the Pasha had been the very paragon of Oriental politeness; he had bothered Gordon quite enough with receptions and parades and salutes of guns and with the most dreadful thing he knew on earth—big, formal banquets! But Gordon is well aware of the fact that in reality the fat Pasha, with whose assistance he is supposed to struggle against slavery, hates him, and that every single *effendi* in Khartoum must in his heart hate a European who may perhaps really be going to take this struggle seriously. What has made them all so fat, indeed? Why, the profits of the slave trade, in which they participate. "Whatever these pashas and beys will be able to do against me on the sly," thinks Gordon, "they most certainly will not neglect!"

"Never mind," thinks Colonel Gordon immediately, changing from gloomy foreboding to the most optimistic hope, "they won't all be against me! There is that splendid fellow, Abu Saud, whom I am going to make my lieutenant on the Equator. Everybody in Khartoum warned me against him; they say he is such a frightful scoundrel, and that I ought never to feed in his presence in case he should poison my dinner! Poor Abu! I am so sure they are running him down because he is a decent fellow. He is going to help me, and I trust him; he is going to become a great man in my province. And then there is another good man waiting for me in Gondokoro—Rauf Bey. Things will work out all right. I am going to clean up this Augean stable. These man-hunters, these sellers of widows and orphans, these extortioners, these masters of bloody caravans, the slave merchants, and negro-killers—I shall extinguish them all from the face of the earth!"

. . . . .

"Only," thinks Gordon, suddenly veering round like a sailing boat in a changing wind, "only is it possible? Could I really do anything useful in this awful country?"

The colonel has left the table and is now standing near the railing looking at the river. Everything is peaceful and quiet, perfectly still, except that from below in the quarters of the native crew comes a subdued long-drawn-out Arab chanting. Gordon looks at the river and the banks; sees a boat with naked jet-black fishermen in it, and among the trees a village of huts shaped like haystacks. But as a matter of fact the wandering eye of Gordon is searching for storks. Although he has been thinking of other things, it is most curious how storks have been occupying Gordon's mind since yesterday evening.

All at once he goes back in haste to the table and sits down, energetically. His healthy face between its side-whiskers is even redder than usual, there is a misty look in his pale-blue eyes; he is quite excited as he takes up his pen again and at last unbosoms himself. He is like that—he must always write down every experience on paper. He writes to Augusta:

"Last night we were sailing along slowly in the moonlight, and I was thinking of you all, the expedition, and Nubar, etc., when all of a sudden from a large bush came peals of laughter. I felt put out; but it turned out to be birds, who laughed at us from the bushes for some time in a very rude way. They were a species of stork, and seemed in capital spirits and highly amused at anybody thinking of going up to Gondokoro with the hope of doing anything. . . ."

Charles Gordon stops writing, turns the sheets of his long letter, inserts the date that he had forgotten: March 27th, 1874. He must remember this date.

The sing-song in the steerage drags on. The ship's crew and the native servants are now accompanying the monotonous chant with a rhythmic clapping of hands. Gordon is not listening, but he hears in spite of it. His spirit is overclouded. This superstitious premonition that has taken hold of him is growing stronger, more definite. His blue Nordic eyes are losing themselves in the distance. His ancestors in the Scottish Highlands could foresee everything, had second sight. . . .

* * * * *

With a jerk Gordon comes to himself again, lifts the book from the table, his little Bible, and opens it at the place where the book-mark is inserted, the piece of silk in the colours of the Gordon tartan. How many times since yesterday night had he read that passage?

JEREMIAH viii. 7:

"Yea, the stork in the heavens knows her appointed time. . . ."

THE STORK

What time? What has been "appointed"? What did this stork know, why did it laugh so horribly?

. . . . .

Gordon pulls himself together. He puts Augusta's book-mark carefully back between the pages of Jeremiah; but he turns the leaves back farther and seeks the passage in Isaiah which he wants to read over once more, because he imagines he sees in it a description of his present journey and a mysterious prophecy, relating to himself personally. Since he has been travelling in Egypt, Gordon has been using the Bible as a guide-book. Where could the Nile country be better described than in the Bible? Even now, this stretch of the Sudanese Nile——

Colonel Gordon's lean, sunburnt hands turn the leaves. ISAIAH xviii. 12:

"Woe to the land shadowing with wings," he reads. "Woe to the land shadowing with wings, which is beyond the rivers of Ethiopia. . . ."

Colonel Gordon nods his head. Everything is there, everything is mentioned, has been known beforehand. The "land shadowing with wings" is, of course, the swamp country on the upper Nile, "beyond the rivers of Ethiopia"—of the Sudan. Shadowing wings of the myriads of mosquitoes! He reads on:

". . . that sendeth ambassadors by the sea, even in vessels of bulrushes upon the waters."

Nowhere is the voice of prophecy clearer, Gordon feels. The "vessels of bulrushes" are those small rafts made of *ambatch* reeds in which the Shilluk negroes are accustomed to navigate the Nile. Everything is written down in the Bible! But now:

"Go, ye swift messengers, to a nation tall and smooth,

to a people terrible from their beginning hitherto; a nation that meteth out and treadeth down; whose land the rivers divide!"

Gordon stares into his little Bible; he does not quite understand this. The nation that is "tall and smooth" —that could be, must be, the giant Sudanese negroes, with their hairless bodies rubbed over with oil. But what are they "meting out" or "treading down"? Should it not say: "trodden down,"—this nation of slaves?

Charles Gordon sighs a little, because it is very hot now and because he cannot understand the passage in the Bible. But the end of the chapter, he consoles himself, sounds very beautiful and full of hope. Of this "tall and smooth nation" between the rivers, meaning the negroes whom he is going to liberate, the negro tribes of his new province between the headwaters of the Nile, it is said that from them "shall a present be brought unto the Lord of hosts . . . to the place of the name of the Lord of hosts, the mount Zion. . . ."

Only partly intelligible, maybe, but certainly an auspicious prophecy! Gordon closes the book (but the book-mark which projects from it reminds him of storks!). He tries to believe in his heart that this is a great promise, addressed directly to him; yes, he is going to redeem these enslaved people, these downtrodden people—though how, he does not know. . . .

He closes his eyes and immediately sees pictures: Savage, armed men surround peaceful villages; then the assault; huts burning, men murdered, women dragged away, youths marching across the desert with the yoke upon their necks; skeletons lying in the track of the sinister caravan; the lash and the slave market.

## THE STORK

Charles Gordon knows that he cannot live on and stand that.

. . . . .

Again and again he finds himself standing by the railing with his telescope, examining the banks, to see if there are any storks.

Sometimes he hides it from himself; he just wanted to know where he is now. What is the name of this village on the bank? Of this island? The river-map of the Nile which he has, the one by Manuel, is pretty bad. Gordon is making notes and sketches for a new map which he intends to draw up. From Khartoum, he notes, 160 miles to Kawa. That was that harbour and wood-yard. The place of last night lay almost opposite to it, that island where the storks in the bushes——

He looks at Manuel's Nile chart in order to find out what the island is called. Perhaps there is no name to it. Yes, for a wonder.

The island on the shore of which the stork had laughed (the stork that knows the appointed time), this completely unknown island in the White Nile is called—the Island of Abba.

# THE BOWL

THE TRAVELLERS who had been to Abba spread the news of a new wali who was living there; wali means "one who is near to God." Already students wandering with staff and bowl were travelling from distant places to visit him. Yet he was still only a Dervish who had been cast out from his order, driven from the path and one who was not authorised to lead others. Now his story reached the ears of the Sheikh El Koreishi, who was living out his old age in great sanctity not far from Messalamieh. This Sheikh El Koreishi was the spiritual head of a group of Dervishes who obeyed the rules of the Sammaniya Tarika and yet did not profess allegiance to the sheikh who excommunicated the hermit of Abba. The pious ones in the land hotly debated the question as to which of the two groups was conserving the Sammaniya doctrine in its full purity. Consequently there prevailed the most cordial jealousy between El Koreishi and Mohammed Sherif.

One day El Koreishi sent one of his Dervishes to Abba and invited the former favourite of his rival to come to him on the Blue Nile. He wished to give spiritual preferment to the man who had been expelled from the path of Dervishdom; he promised him the very highest dignities of his following. He was to become nakib or even khalifa. Mohammed Ahmed at once prepared to follow this call and to go in pilgrimage to his new master, in order to swear the oath of allegiance.

## THE BOWL

But just then there arrived in Abba another messenger: from Mohammed Sherif! The Sheikh who had once kicked his babooshes against the humble young Dervish lying in the dust, must have learned now that not only had he won honour, but also that El Koreishi was making up to him. And immediately Mohammed Sherif sent to his former disciple a large diploma, very beautifully calligraphed: The brethren of the Sammaniya were thereby given notice that the name of Mohammed Ahmed had again been written on the rolls of the order, that he had been granted the privilege of enrolling novices and that he was authorised to take part once more in the ceremonies of the order.

To this messenger Mohammed Ahmed gave a hard answer: "The wretched Dongolawi," he said, "does not wish to discredit his former master." Then he hastened to Messalamieh, kissed the aged El Koreishi's trembling hand, and received his blessing.

From now on he wandered much through the land, with the begging-bowl and the iron-tipped staff.

· · · · ·

The Sudan is full of the wandering, pious persons who are called here the "foggara," the "poor ones," in India, fakirs, and in Persia Dervishes. They roam about alone or in groups, men of many countries of Islam, some of them coming from a great distance. To fill the bowl of a Dervish is a duty that nobody may neglect; but in return the begging monks make themselves useful as teachers, magicians, priests, and doctors of the populace. They are the scribes; an inkstand is always in their girdle. They know how to write those salutary formulæ that are afterwards washed off with water, so that this inky water may be given to a sick person to drink. They write on little rolls of paper the most powerful suras of all, the sixth, the eighteenth, those passages that lend sure protection: "But God is the best protector and He is of all those who are merciful, the most compassionate," "And a guard against the rebel, the Shaitan." Women will enclose these strips of paper in leather or copper capsules and fix them upon their foreheads or on their children's wrists. The names of the Seven Sleepers of Ephesus, written down in a special manner, and the names of Allah and of the Prophet, enclosed in amulets, will procure fortune and happiness for whoever carries them, and guard him from the evil eye.

The wandering Dervishes write these formulæ, pray by the sick, preach in the mosque, squat in the midst of the children and teach them to gabble the "Fatt'ha"; in return the women fill their begging-bowls with *durrha* and *dukhn*, with millet and maize, with a kind of stiff porridge, with wild honey and sauces made from dried antelope meat. The stranger a Dervish's behaviour, the more welcome he is in a Sudani village. Some of them Allah has disturbed in their reason, so that they must rave and drivel. There are those among them who wind snakes round their necks or feed on scorpions, and others who go about with firebrands in their armpits or drive thorns and nails into their bodies. They wear various kinds of garments, according to their origin and their order. The turban of one has to be black, the other wears the pointed lambskin cap of the Persians. One is serving Allah rather by dancing; the other, by wild howling. But all of them carry the begging-bowl.

## THE BOWL

Mohammed Ahmed met his fellow Dervishes in many places where religious festivals were being held: in the house of some wealthy man or in some village where they were celebrating the anniversary of the saint who was buried there. Before the dazzling white dome of a tomb, or at night by a smouldering fire, he would sit with people who had come from the Hejaz or from Maghreb. There would be discussions about the doctrine of the Wahabites, who rigidly forbid tobacco smoking and reprehend carnal joy, as well as the worship of the saints and oral tradition. Other men came from the monastic communities of the Senussiya in the far west of Islam; they had knowledge of certain wonderful hopes. The holy Sheikh of the Senussi had announced in the Oasis of Jerhbub that the day of the revival of Islam was near, the day when it would conquer the earth. Somebody, they said, would suddenly be recognised; perhaps he was already there—he, who had come to accomplish these things. Was the Dervish of Abba listening? The seer of visions in his cave? Still more was he drawn towards the men in the lambskin kalpaks, the Persian Dervishes who often came across the Red Sea into Africa. In Turkey and in Egypt they usually disowned the fact that they were Shiite heretics; they pretended to be good Sunnites, exiled on account of their faith. In the Sudan they would talk more openly. When they glorified their Shiite martyrs, Hossein and Hassan, was not Mohammed Ahmed strangely moved, did he not think of the deep roots of his descent, of that family tree that his father used to make him recite: "The Imam Hassan, son of Ali, the son of Abu Talib, who was the Prophet's paternal uncle"? But the Persians spoke also of another Hassan, called El-Askari, from whose stock the Hidden One was to spring, the twelfth Imam, the great hope of the faithful. And in Mohammed Ahmed's line of ancestors was also Hassan El-Askari.

．　　．　　．　　．　　．

Among the Persians who carried their begging-bowls through the Sudanese villages, the Sufi were very numerous. Most of them would probably belong to the lower degrees of the great mystical community, to the common herd that is shepherded with words. But was not some old Dervish, some opium-smoker and hashish-swallower in miserable rags—was he not, perhaps, under his rags and under his dreamy lethargy, a Sufi of high degree, a "urefa" who believed he was justified in regarding himself as divine? A dreamer of those last magnificent dreams of participation in God? Did not perhaps the Dervish Mohammed Ahmed learn from some Sufi sage the innermost secret of this mystic doctrine: that for one of the *Illuminati* it is even permissible to lie, that he is not obliged to practise what he teaches to the lowly ones, that there exist degrees of virtue that change according to the different grades by which knowledge and intellect are ascending to the Godhead; and that the uppermost grade may dispense with virtue, dispense with truth, dispense with goodness—because the saint is soaring upwards into so much higher regions. . . .

Did the Dervish Mohammed Ahmed ever listen to such hashish-talk? Was he allowed to learn of such opium-dreams?

．　　．　　．　　．　　．

The villagers would invite the pious wanderers

A SUDANESE VILLAGE

Drawn by W. H. Fischer from a contemporary photograph

## THE BOWL

to the anniversaries of saintly men, of whom there was sure to be one buried near every village. Then in the evening little lamps would be hung from all the huts and the villagers would assemble to listen to a renowned *fikih* reciting suras. Sometimes Mohammed Ahmed would recite the whole Koran in a single night, before the marvelling villagers; it was very meritorious to be present and listen. Or there were assemblages of Dervishes who had come from near and far, with multi-coloured banners, with a crowd of wives, of musicians, of torch-bearers, because near the domed tomb of a saint or in the house of some powerful sheikh a prayer festival was to be celebrated, called "zikr." Then the Dervish of Abba was one of those who sat in the wide elliptical ring at night, in the light of a blazing fire, while the flutes shrilled ceaselessly and the Dervish drum rumbled a monotonous and fascinating tattoo. First came a long prayer, reverently spoken by one individual, then an endless, ecstasy-provoking chorus of those squatting in the ring:
"Allah! Allah! Allah!"
And "*La ilaha illa 'llah!*"
"*There is no god but God!*"

.    .    .    .    .

The Dervishes sit close together in a long chain. The drum sets the rhythm and their frantic cries sound like one common voice. Whenever they have said "Allah!" each of them throws his body to the left; after another "Allah," to the right, quicker and quicker, in a giddy rhythm. "Allah, llah, llah!" quicker and quicker; and hollower, until the noise becomes like a roaring of wild beasts, a "*hu! hu! hu!*" which means "He"—"He, He, He!"

And "Allah!" and *"hu!"* and "Allah, *hu*, Allah!" They fling their heads forward with every "*hu*"; turbans and skull-caps fall from long hair, from dishevelled locks that are whipping the earth; and then "*hu! hu!* Allah!" on and on, to the wailing of the flute, to the beating rhythm of the drums—tom-tom-tom, tom-tom-tom—till the endlessly ejaculated syllables dissolve into a hoarse moaning, till the blood stuns the reeling brains, blinds the eyes and fills the ears with a strange buzzing, in which unearthly voices drone. The body of the howling Dervish is losing its gravity, the soul is becoming free to melt into HIM, who is HE, *hu! hu!*—Allah!

. . . . .

One of the brethren, a Chosen One, is then seized by the Spirit. Suddenly he breaks away from the ring, staggers into the centre; his moaning becomes a muttering, he suddenly talks with words that none can understand; some Unknown Being, some good jinn, has taken possession of him; he spins round like a whipped humming-top, utters shrill sounds and finally collapses, groaning, in a heap.

More and more often now it was Mohammed Ahmed who appeared in the centre of the Dervish ring, into whom the spirit entered, who spoke with tongues, a Chosen One, an instrument of the Invisible.

. . . . .

The Dervish Mohammed Ahmed carried his staff and his begging-bowl, his beautiful smile and his fervent words through all the Sudan. Especially in the Gesireh river country, between the two Niles, and on the Abyssinian border, he became well known. In the widespreading and shapeless towns of huts he preached in the mosques. Already a holy radiance surrounded his ever-smiling and bearded head; here and there the people began to say that he must be the "Kutb," "the axis of sanctity," which is what the legend of Islam calls a mysterious being that emerges, once in every age, to be the guiding axis of all the spiritual world; all the other holy ones, the godly walis in the lands of the faithful, take their direction from him. The Kutb is seldom recognised; he comes and disappears; every one of the pious beggars at the city gate or by the well might be the Kutb. . . .

And amongst the Kutbs of all ages there is again one, a Kutb of Kutbs, a Being who never dies. He has drunk of the Fountain of Life, like Elijah of the Jews; he lives on until the Day of Reckoning. This is "El-Khidr." A thousand legends tell of him, not one of them like the other, so that only a hazy outline of this mystical personality is distinguishable through so many tales.

. . . . .

And who was he, what was he, the "father of the V-shaped gap," the man with the birthmark, who was called Mohammed, like the Prophet, the son of an Abdullah and, they said, of an Amina, like the Prophet, and certainly of the Prophet's blood?

Wherever he passed, excited people kissed the hem of his dress. Especially the womenfolk raved about him. He was among the sons of men of a strange beauty, a paradisaical perfume floated round him. He distributed the rich gifts which the faithful brought him at once among the needy and only kept for himself what his bowl would hold; he was the Renouncer, full of bounty and kindness.

And then one would hear a wonderful voice, talking fiercely.

.   .   .   .   .

He spoke to the dark and fanatical people of the Sudan about the misery of the times and about hope and salvation. The people felt that they were suffering. Now a Voice had arisen that knew how to tell it to them. A frightful burden had been tolerated too long; tyranny unparalleled was devastating the land. But then the extortioner, the tax-gatherer, the bloody bashi-bazouk, the insatiable Pasha in his palace—they all acted in the name of the Viceroy in Cairo, who in his turn represented the Padishah in Stambul. And the Padishah was the Khalifa, the successor of the Prophet, the head of Islam! Should one not obey *him*? The ulema told the people every day that they should.

And now a man had arisen and said that the Turks were not true believers. Although they might confess, according to the formula: ". . . and Mohammed is the Apostle of God"—yet their life and their doings proved that they had not the Faith. A drinker of wine, a glutton, an oppressor of the Moslem—such was the Turk!

.   .   .   .   .

The orator vomited the hated word as if it were poison. For a moment his smile was darkened, his voice seemed to rumble like thunder, the listeners clenched their fists; like a rolling of drums it echoed amongst the crowd: "Toork! Toork! Toork!" And then a gesture of the preacher softened the excitement. "God," he said, "is going to destroy his enemies. But do not you yourselves live like the enemies of God? Are you not drinkers of millet beer? Do not your women wear ornaments of gold and silver? Do not you hold festivals with sinful pomp? Circumcisions? And weddings?"

"Whoever dresses like the Turk, whoever lives like the Turk, he is like the Turk!"

. . . . .

"The Way," said the pious orator mysteriously, "the Way along which I will guide you leads through six virtues. And there are three vices which you must avoid. Practise these virtues:

>Humility.
>Meekness of Spirit.
>Little Food.
>Little Water.
>Endurance.
>Visiting the tombs of holy men.

"And, ye Moslems, avoid the three vices: Envy, Pride, Neglect of the Five Prayers. He who is stained by any one of these vices cannot be a soldier in God's army!"

. . . . .

So he spoke again and again, in many places. He spoke to the tortured, to the despairing. From this one the tax collector had but yesterday taken his last she-goat, from that one he had collected the same tax for the third time; the effendi had stolen this man's fields and the bribed kadi had denied his right to recover them. Turk! Turk!

The dark, the sullen, the hot-headed folk of the Sudan listened to that inspired voice, saw those magical eyes, inhaled the perfume of that man; and suddenly, with lightning suddenness, with dream-like suddenness, the realisation burst upon them—that there was a redemption, a salvation. One would have to throw off some minor sins, the most cherished, the commonest ones, it was true, but it seemed all at once so easy. No more *merissa*, starting from to-morrow. The ankle-ring that black Aisha wanted was sinful! The pilgrimage to the tomb of the holy sheikh had been put off too long. Easy sins, simple sins! All around the preacher tears of contrition were flowing. From to-morrow onwards, yes, no more merry dances—especially not on the day of the next circumcision ceremony! But then, if one had avoided three vices and strenuously practised six virtues, if one followed the teaching of the saint of God, then there was a WAY! A mysterious, difficult, wonderful Way! Whoever possessed the six virtues, but not the vices, whoever did not live like the Turk, he would be a fighter in the army of God!

"For, hearken, there is a God, there is a Way, there is an Army, there is a Guide."

. . . . .

"Allah! Allah!"
And "Turk! Turk!"
The first murmuring before the storm. Drums here and there, but still muffled.

Mohammed Ahmed, the preaching, wandering Dervish, returned for a time to his cave on Abba Island, to more fasting, praying, and visions.

# THE HERO

Like a sudden whirlwind, Gordon Pasha, the Governor-General, was rushing to El Fasher.

All Dar-Fur was in full rebellion; the province, which had only recently been conquered and united to the Egyptian Sudan, had had enough of the Egyptians and had revolted. For five centuries the land of the Fur had been an independent nation, not badly ruled by its Sultans. Then, all at once, in the year 1875, Zubeir Rahamet, with his armed slaves, fell upon Sultan Ibrahim. Zubeir, an Arab of the Jaalin, was the biggest of the Sudanese slave-hunters; on the Upper Nile he owned those great *zaribas*, in which he penned up the stolen blacks. The young savages whom he caught he used to arm; he possessed a regular army and the Khedive in Cairo was beginning to fear it. In order to dispel his master's distrust, Zubeir embarked on this war against Dar-Fur; he conquered the invaded land and placed it at the Khedive's feet. The Khedive pretended to be grateful and invited him to come to Cairo; there, as a reward, he was to be invested with the Government of Dar-Fur. The ancient trick of Oriental cunning defeated the barbarian: when he arrived at Cairo he was seized and not permitted to go back to the Sudan. As a consequence two separate revolts broke out in Dar-Fur: a rebellion of the inhabitants who wanted back their independence and who had a prince of the old royal house for their leader, and a rebellion of the slave-hunters. Suleiman, the young son of Zubeir Pasha, fortified himself in his brigands' stronghold, Shakka. But between the two rebellions there raged a bloody war; the Egyptian garrison of the towns was besieged now by one of the rebel parties, now by the other, and against both alike they showed themselves helpless and cowardly. It became obvious how feeble was the Egyptian rule in the Sudan.

.    .    .    .

Thereupon Gordon Pasha suddenly appeared on the scene. Now, three years after the night when the stork had laughed, he was no longer Governor of the Equator; a short time before, the Khedive had given over to him the government of all the Sudan. Gordon had just been in Khartoum, where he had been formally invested with his high office; then he had mounted a camel and had ridden, with a tiny escort, like a madman to Dar-Fur.

In the city of El Fasher ten thousand Government troops had allowed themselves to be besieged by the rebels. Gordon relieved them with two hundred horsemen. When he arrived everything was at once all right; the rebel sheikhs craved his pardon. "You ought to pardon me!" said Gordon. He knew well what the Turkish rule meant to them.

In those daily letters to his sister, which constituted his diary, he once wrote, after a victory, when 160 of the enemy had fallen: "My allies have three men wounded, one, I fear, mortally. I am sorry for the 160 and I am sorry for the three men. I wish people could see how dreadful is the suffering of human creatures—I mean those who wish for war. I am a fool,

I daresay, but I cannot see the sufferings of any of those people without tears coming into my eyes. . . ."

Soon everyone knew how good this Christian pasha was, how he could pardon and pity. Only towards his own people he was sometimes relentless. He had a *kaimakam* (lieutenant-colonel) of the Egyptian troops shot because he allowed himself to be bribed by the enemy. Another, who had conspired against him, he sent into a harsh exile. What was the use of it? He had nothing but traitors around him. He was always trusting, and always being deceived, even by his closest confidant, his secretary, a black man called Ibrahim. The pasha, the British colonel, made this negro his friend; he believed in him, liked him, made him presents—and then discovered one day that Ibrahim had received £3,000 from the slavers, to whom he was communicating Gordon's plans. The fellow had to be sent to Khartoum in chains. What was the good? They were all alike!

With bitterness Gordon remembered his experiences with his officers. There was that rascal Abu Saud, whom he had taken with him three years before to the Equator. He had trusted this one too, even in spite of warnings. That was the worst scoundrel of all, a beastly, treacherous cur. And another too, up there in Gondokoro—Rauf. This one he had sent back to Cairo, and there he told calumnious lies to the Khedive about Gordon. And now this Rauf stood in the highest favour at the court of the Viceroy.

All the effendis were like that. Robbers, thieves, bribed judges, oppressors of widows and orphans. And with their help Gordon was to redeem this poor country!

.   .   .   .   .

A feeling of despair seized Gordon. He was quite alone, he could rely on nobody. The officers were a cowardly mob, the troops not much better. Wherever he showed himself in person, his cause was successful; if he turned his back, everything was again lost. Anger was driving him mad. He stormed about the country, almost without escort. He rode and rode on his camel, alone, across those awful deserts. This was a deplorable country: flat steppes and sand and thorny bushes; there were scarcely any wells; only a little rain-water was stored in the hollow trunks of the Adansonia trees. Everything had been devastated by the wars; the slave-drivers were exceedingly audacious; on his rides Gordon met their caravans everywhere, or found the human skeletons that marked the trail of the slave caravans. He punished the robbers, had them lashed or shot, freed the shackled women and skinny children. And then? He could neither feed nor clothe these people; they were far from the villages from which they had been stolen; and, if Gordon did not want them to starve miserably, he was forced to allow some neighbouring Arab tribe to take them on as slaves.

On one occasion he discovered that his own body-guard, marching with him, were secretly taking along with them a handful of blacks, with the object of selling them.

.     .     .     .     .

But what a country! To think that wars were waged over it! Gordon, the Bible student, read:

KINGS iii. 9: "And they made a circuit of seven days' journey; and there was no water for the host nor for the beasts that followed them."

ZUBEIR RAHAMET PASHA, THE GREAT SLAVER

Yes, it was just like that in Dar-Fur. You wandered about the country, you rode miles and miles, you didn't eat, or drink, or sleep, you manœuvred among the water-holes. And there was not a single person in the country who really desired the Egyptian rule. Did Gordon desire it himself? The mere sight of a bashi-bazouk made him sick. Nevertheless, he restored once more the province to the Khedive in Cairo; the rightful heir of the ancient Sultan, Prince Harun, he chased back into the desert, although he knew it would be better if he received the kingdom back instead of the Egyptian beys or the slavers who were going to rule it.

These slave traders, led by the young son of Zubeir, were gathering round Shakka. They had excellently equipped negro troops. If they revolted openly, everything was lost. How feeble was the hold of Egypt upon the Sudan! To-day Prince Harun, to-morrow Suleiman, son of Zubeir. Each rebel that rose up was more powerful than the Khartoum Government. Gordon was still there, of course; he knew that he could remain master of the country, somehow. But, he thought, ought he to stay on there for ever? For what sins had he merited such a punishment?

. . . .

Gordon learned one day that young Suleiman was camping with six thousand men near Dara. He decided to talk to the youngster himself. He suddenly set off, rode seventy miles in a single day, and such was his impatience and the swiftness of his famous camel, that he left his escort far behind. He was now all alone in the desert; the head of his poor camel was covered with horrible flies which drove the animal to still greater speed.

Gordon, his red face covered with flies, was carrying on a conversation with himself, or with God—it is practically the same thing:

"A sack of rice jolting along on a camel would do as much as I think I am doing. Who am I? My success until now has been due to a series of flukes. Only to the world it seems different. I am such a fraud. Am I clever? Am I efficient? I know that I cannot do anything. But I do thank God for using me as His instrument and I look forward to my rest...."

. . . . .

"If I could stop this slave traffic," Gordon went on thinking, "free those caravans of their lean phantoms, those starved children on the road, then I would willingly be shot this night. But where is the hope? Now comes the question: could I sacrifice my life and remain in Kordofan and Dar-Fur? To die quickly would be nothing to me, but the long crucifixion that a residence in these horrid parts entails appals me. Shall I stay and crush the slave-dealers? It is a worthy cause to die for. Yes, if the death were speedy, but oh! it is a long and weary one and for the moment I cannot face it!"

. . . . .

The lonely rider halted his camel and looked round at those mournful steppes. Nothing to be seen but some thorn bushes on the horizon—and swarms of flies. Gordon, tormented to the point of fury, hit out at the flies, then suddenly dropped his arm. It was no use. Hopeless!

No use! Hopeless! This was revolving in his poor, tormented brain. The man would like to slide from the camel and remain lying there for ever, on that hardbaked earth, beneath that thorny skeleton of a mimosa bush.

Little dark thoughts were fluttering round him, tormenting like the flies:

"The Sudan cannot be saved for Egypt, it is but a question of time...."

.   .   .   .   .

He sat on his camel, motionless. All at once he became feverishly energetic and drove the beast on to run. The slave-dealers! One could not allow oneself to die as long as the slave caravans were winding through Africa!

The Egyptian officers of the Dara garrison could not believe their own eyes when in the evening the Governor-General arrived, completely alone, and covered with flies. Only at night, when Gordon was peacefully sleeping, did his escort appear. In the morning he put on his Turkish marshal's uniform, a gorgeous array of dazzling gold galloons and Grand Cordons, and, in spite of the heat, donned over it his golden cuirass, a precious gift from the Khedive. Then the little man, all ablaze with gold, rode forth again; only a few bashi-bazouks in gala dress escorted him into the walled camp of the slave-dealers, the rebels, the robbers.

While he was waiting to be admitted, astonishment and confusion arose. What could it mean? The Pasha himself? And practically alone?

Young Suleiman, son of Zubeir, had six thousand men in his camp. Why did they not simply make an end of Gordon? But the calmness and self-assurance with which he suddenly appeared and spoke and gave orders cowed these people at once. Zubeir's son, a nice-looking lad of twenty-two years, in a blue velvet riding-jacket, he thoroughly trounced, pointed out to him the results of his disobedience, his rebellious action, and the devastation of the land, all those human bones that were lying about everywhere. In his angry and abominable Scotch Arabic, Charles Gordon said all this, with eyes glaring and a mystical radiance emanating from his cuirass, from the authority of his high office, and from that of his master, the Viceroy in distant Cairo. The dumbfounded assembly of man-stealers he ordered instantly to come to Dara, to be tried there with all formality in the public divan. The son of Zubeir trembled in his blue jacket. While Gordon was still in his power and should have been afraid for his life, this boy looked so miserable that Gordon already began to pity him. "A spoiled child!" he thought. "Brought up in the midst of obsequious people and slaves. He has a bitter time of it before him, before he realises the nothingness of the world! Of course, a good shaking would do him good."

At once Charles Gordon thought of a fitting Bible text:

"And David said, Deal gently, for my sake, with the young man. . . ."

"I will try to do so, if I can," thought Gordon; but, for the time being, he kept a wrathful face.

· · · · ·

The youngster, now completely tamed, refused to listen to the sullen old Bedouins around him, who would have liked to cut the infidel in pieces there and then. Gordon drank a glass of water, and then returned slowly to Dara. Scarcely had he arrived, when young

Suleiman, fascinated and obedient, with his councillors, joined him; the erstwhile rebels squatted round Gordon in a circle and assured him, striking the ground with their foreheads, of their fidelity and repentance.

As long as Gordon remained in Dar-Fur, peace was maintained. But as soon as the Governor-General went back to Khartoum the rebellion broke out afresh, worse than ever. Young Suleiman became a danger to Egyptian rule; Gordon, now beside himself with fury, threw all his pity to the winds. He sent his best helper, the Italian Romolo Gessi, against the son of Zubeir and his slavers and ordered him to use ruthless severity. After many fights, Gessi conquered, and young Suleiman, who had been captured, one morning was executed.

But that was no use either. Nothing was any use.

## THE FRIEND

An Arab of the Taaisha tribe, Abdullahi by name, started out one day on a pilgrimage to a holy Dervish of whose fame he had heard.

The Taaisha tribe, in the land of Fur, is a part of the great Baggara race; they are the herdsmen who roam far and wide through the southern steppes. The formidable Taaishi horsemen were much feared in the negro villages as slave-hunters.

This Abdullahi, who was on his way to Abba, was the son of a certain Mohammed Adam (called Tawrshein, which means "Ugly Ox"), a God-fearing person, who was well skilled in reading the omens that can be recognised in the figures in the desert sand. Before starting on any *razzia*, the Bedouins would come to him to ask him if the plundering expedition would be successful; also he recited to them the Terrible Names so that they could gain power over the enemy's arms. Abdullahi was one of his four sons. He had not his father's knowledge of the Scriptures nor any learning, but he was a warrior honoured by his tribe. When Zubeir Rahamet invaded Dar-Fur and subjugated the land, Abdullahi fought against him. In the battle he was taken prisoner; but Zubeir spared his life.

Soon after, Abdullahi's father died, and on his death-bed he urged his son to go on a pilgrimage. He was to visit a certain holy man who lived in an island in the Nile.

## THE FRIEND

Abdullahi, the Taaishi, tramped barefoot behind his donkey, which carried his water-bag. He walked like this, armed with his spear, through many wide lands; never had he imagined that Allah had made the world so big. On the way he passed through settlements of foreign peoples who hated the Baggara—who called them robbers and odious cow-stealers.

When he came near to the Nile and to Abba, he learned that the Sayid Mohammed Ahmed had left the island again. He had gone to Messalamieh to bury the sheikh of his order, old Koreishi. Abdullahi the Taaishi drove his donkey on until they came to Messalamieh.

．　　　．　　　．　　　．　　　．

After the death of his old sheikh, Mohammed Ahmed became himself the head of his order, the "Master of the Prayer-carpet," as it was termed. It was now his duty to build, with his own hands, the dome of the tomb over the body of his spiritual father.

The old man was buried on the very spot where he died. Mohammed Ahmed and his many disciples who accompanied him formed bricks of mud and built the cube-shaped sepulchre that later would be crowned by a whitewashed cupola It was pious and meritorious to do such a work, and from all sides the Moslems streamed in to spend a few days kneading clay or carrying dried bricks, in the midst of many prayers and recitations of suras of the Koran. Mohammed Ahmed himself worked with his hands, and thus Abdullahi saw him for the first time, as he stood by the half-finished wall of the mausoleum, a bucket full of clay at his feet, stopping up cracks between the bricks.

The Bedouin, having arrived at the tomb, first

greeted the deceased: "Peace be with thee, Sheikh!" Then he slowly walked round the grave, reciting the Fatt'hah the most holy opening sura: "Praise be to Allah, Lord of the worlds, the Compassionate——"

The worshipper took care to say "amen" at the end; the Archangel Gabriel himself had taught the Prophet never to omit this word after that sura. Then Abdullahi the Taaishi, having accomplished his circuit of the tomb and probably not knowing any other sura to recite, squatted down in the shadow of the wall and stared for a long time at Mohammed Ahmed, who was at times working ably with his clever carpenter's hands, at times addressing the crowd that surrounded him wherever he went. He was smiling all the while. Abdullahi, who dared only look at him from a distance, thought he smelt a wonderful perfume that was wafted from him, which made him glad and elated. For a long time Abdullahi the Taaishi sat there, quite shy and trembling.

. . . . .

Abdullahi, son of Mohammed, was tall, lean and bony, a little older than Mohammed Ahmed, a real Bedouin with a hook nose. His face was light brown and marked by smallpox, his beard scanty. The Dervish shirt, sewn with big patches, which he was wearing, was none too clean; like every Baggara he was much addicted to the eating of clarified butter, so that his clothes were always greasy with it.

Only when the sun went down and the time for the evening prayer was near did he tear himself away from this spell, this rapture, this patient gazing, and go near to the saintly one. With lowered eyes he uttered his petition; he would fain swear the oath of allegiance and become the disciple and servant of Mohammed Ahmed until the end of his days.

The two looked firmly into each other's eyes. The smile of Mohammed Ahmed brightened up like a glowing fire into which fresh fuel is thrown. Slowly he nodded his head.

．　　．　　．　　．　　．

First the holy sheikh bade his new disciple bring water and a prayer-carpet and perform the religious ablutions. Then the two men stood face to face, in a circle of pious onlookers, and interlaced their hands in a special manner, generally used only in the engagement ceremony between a man and a woman. The long sleeve of the sheikh carefully veiled the locked hands, like a secret.

Now Mohammed Ahmed bade the Bedouin repeat the words he was going slowly to recite to him. First, a confession of sins:

"I beg forgiveness of God, the Great . . ."

Abdullahi had to say this three times. Then:

". . . than whom there is no other deity, the Living, the Everlasting.

"To Him I turn with repentance, His mercy I implore, His forgiveness, and exemption from the fires of Hell."

"Dost thou turn to God with repentance?" asked Mohammed Ahmed now, with a kindness that charmed the disciple.

He answered, after the sheikh had first recited the phrase:

"I do turn to God with repentance; and I am sorry for all my evil deeds; and I determine never to relapse."

And now, trembling, Abdullahi the Taaishi kissed the hand of his master, which was still a little splashed with clay, and said with a loud, robust, fervent voice the words of the great oath:

"I beg favour of God, the Great, and of the noble Prophet, on whom be the prayer and the blessing, and as a guide to God, praised be his name, I do choose my lord, the Sayid Mohammed Ibn Sayid Abdullah, having resolved never to swerve or separate from him, God be my witness. In the name of God, the Great!"

Three times he repeated the oath. Then both together they spoke the Fatt'hah. They were bound to each other for ever.

.    .    .    .    .

When the building of the sepulchre had been completed and the whitewashed dome could be seen from far off, Mohammed Ahmed returned to his island. He rode on a donkey, and his people walked behind him, a numerous and rather noisy retinue. But before the donkey walked Abdullahi the Baggara, carrying a large black banner inscribed with verses from the Koran, which he could not read.

The banner was heavy, the way was long, and Abdullahi's sandals were badly worn. He limped a little and seemed to be suffering. Nevertheless, envious looks were cast at him from behind. The followers of Mohammed Ahmed were mostly Danagla, men from Dongola, from his own tribe, often his blood relations. On the Blue Nile some Arabs of the eastern desert had joined them. Amongst all these camel Arabs, Abdullahi the Baggara was the only one who smelt of cattle, and they hated him, if it were only for this. His dialect sounded foreign and consequently ridiculous; his customs, which were different, were considered coarse and brutal.

## THE FRIEND

How could the holy sheikh put his banner into the filthy paws of that fellow! They said it openly in the presence of Abdullahi, round the evening fire. He, one amongst many, merely clenched his fists; he could not answer that all the Danagla were thieves, that they stank of camel dung, and that it was well known that every one of them was a Shaitan in human shape; for by saying so he would offend his master, Mohammed Ahmed, who was also from Dongola.

. . . . .

Not once during the days of the march did Mohammed Ahmed speak to the Bedouin. Although he was carrying the banner, he was still the least of the brethren; the time of his probation was not yet over. An elderly Dervish, called Ali, had been given the task of instructing the novice. He found him of quick understanding, but absolutely unteachable. Instead of meditating on the attributes of the Prophet, he would consider how the Turk could be vanquished, how so many Baggara horsemen should be enlisted, armed with lances or with matchlock rifles. In the evening, by the camp-fire, Ali tried in vain to make of this man a Dervish whose spirit would melt into the divinity. Only when they spoke of the Sheikh, of Mohammed Ahmed, did Abdullahi experience ecstasies, something like spirituality. At such moments he would allude mysteriously to certain secret things of which he knew; his father, the geomancer famed among the Baggara, had told them to him, as he lay dying and with his last strength bade his son set forth to the Nile to join the Dervish Mohammed Ahmed. For this man, the dying father had said, this man was——

"What?" old Ali asked eagerly.

But Abdullahi became silent. Things would soon be seen. The time had not yet come to talk about that.

. . . . .

On the way, as he walked before the marching procession, laboriously stepping out under the load of the heavy banner, to the beating of the Dervish drum that ceaselessly rumbled behind him, Abdullahi sometimes felt, yes, he distinctly felt on his bent back, like a caress, the gaze of the man whose banner he was carrying on before. He did not turn round, he did not dare to, but he straightened himself up, he forgot his aching feet, and that those Danagla, sons of dogs, were always so vilely offending him. He would like to go on and on, on and on like that, through the whole Sudan, through the whole world, with the black banner of Mohammed Ahmed, before which the infidels would tremble yet and the Turk bow down to the ground.

. . . . .

When they had reached Abba, amid much shouting, firing of volleys, and beating of kettledrums, the novice Abdullahi was given a little peaked straw hut near to the big one in which Mohammed Ahmed now usually lived, for he only went into his cave for frequent self-castigation.

In this small conical hut Abdullahi fell very sick. An attack of dysentery consumed him, made him terribly weak. The old Dervish, Ali, nursed him, with some kindness; otherwise no other human being entered the hut.

One day old Ali took the water-bag and went to the Nile to fetch water—and never came back. Many days later Abdullahi learned that Ali had entered the water at a shallow place and that a crocodile had seized him by the leg.

Abdullahi, on his Sudanese bedstead in the little hut, waited long for the old Dervish and, with still more yearning, for that water; then everything melted away into the heat of fever. The sick man was quite alone and forgotten, and yet the noise of the village floated into the hut. More than once in his fever dreams he heard the gentle voice of his holy master; perhaps he was sitting outside beneath the roof-shelter and talking to the crowd around him.

Abdullahi lay there, he knew not how long. Had a day passed? Had a week passed? It must have been towards evening; it was getting dark. Outside somebody was singing:

> My heart is troubled with love . . .
> O thou gazelle from among the gazelles of El-Yemen!
> I am thy slave without cost.
> O Mohammed . . .

. . . . .

Abdullahi heard the song and felt sad, because now he was going to die, he knew it. He felt he wanted to go outside, to shout——

He was quite weak; only his hand moved, and the bed creaked under his weight.

Suddenly Mohammed Ahmed was standing in the hut. Behind him one of his wives, the daughter of his uncle, Mohammed Sharfi, entered. She was carrying a gourd, out of which a vapour was rising. Mohammed Ahmed took the gourd from her and stepped up to the *angareb* on which the sick man was lying. Smiling, he sat down on the edge of the bed. Abdullahi was unable to move, but his senses were wonderfully alert. The coarse gown that the holy one was wearing seemed so white, it was shining through the darkness of the hut; the coloured patches that were sewn upon it were shimmering like gems. And now the sick man closed his eyes, he could not bear the splendour. He smelt heavenly perfumes.

He awoke from the swoon into which he had fallen. He was quite happy, quite strong, only he could not speak. The friend who had come to him was sitting by him. He handed him the gourd, in which there was *medida*, a pap made of flour and hot butter.

Now Mohammed Ahmed was talking with his wonderful voice: "Drink this and trust in God!"

Abdullahi the Taaishi trusted in his holy friend even more than in God. He felt the bowl on his parched lips, he drank, he was already well, he knew it, he was already strong. . . .

He sat up with a sudden jerk; his eyes were wide open and were emitting a strange light. He said with a loud voice what he had so long been thinking, that which his dying father had confided to him:

"*Thou art the Expected Mahdi!*"

# THE VISION

THE MAHDI? The Expected Mahdi?

A miracle had happened on the island of Abba. The dying man who had risen from his death-bed went about and announced: "The Expected Mahdi has appeared at last! He has healed me!"

The Mahdi himself? Was Mohammed Ahmed neither the Kutb nor the Khidr, but the greatest of all? The one who was to come? The Mahdi of Allah? Could it be true? Until then people had not been willing to believe it, although whispers had already long been going round.

Before the hut of the holy sheikh the Moslems of Abba crowded together. He ought to come out, to speak to them, to tell them that he was the Expected One.

But Mohammed Ahmed was not in his new and spacious house. He had hidden himself in his hole in the river bank; there he was fasting long, bitterly, his prayers never ceased, he hardly slept, day and night were no longer divided, nor waking and dreaming, nor thinking, believing, hearing, and seeing. . . .

Over and over again he recited the ninety-nine magical names, the ninety-nine mighty Attributes of Allah: "Er Rahman, er Rahim . . ."

And most often, again and again, "El Queyyum"—"The Unchanging." That was a specially strong name, there lay in it a mysterious and compelling power.

## THE MAHDI OF ALLAH

For many days Mohammed Ahmed did not come out into the light—the man who had been called the Expected Mahdi.

.    .    .    .    .

For twelve centuries the peoples of Islam have dreamed of El Mahdi el-Muntazer, the expected Guide. The Koran, indeed, does not mention the Mahdi. In announcing the day of judgment the holy book only says that Isa, son of Maryam (He whom the unbelievers call Jesus), is going to appear before the Prophet Mohammed comes back to earth. Isa is a great prophet even in Islam, inferior only to Mohammed.

The Hadiths, which are the oral traditions from the times of the Prophet, since collected and written down, make veiled allusions to another precursor of the Judgment, a Mysterious One, "whom Allah is to guide"; consequently, the Guide. Mahdi means "the guided one."

He is to appear before Jesus descends upon the holy rock of the Temple of Jerusalem and before the Judgment is fulfilled.

Even before the Judgment, the Mahdi will achieve the World Empire of Islam. Wherever there are still unbelievers on earth, the Mahdi will conquer them and stamp them out.

The Expected Mahdi is to descend from the family of the Prophet. He is to be known by many secret signs. Certain marks he is to bear on his body; certain things he is to do, in certain places. For twelve centuries legend has been at work. The passages of the holy book are ambiguous, the doctrines of the various sects are divergent. Is the Mahdi the same as Isa? Or is he the Elijah of the Jews? Or is he the hidden twelfth Imam?

. . . . .

The doctrine of the Persian Shia knows twelve holy Imams, leaders of the prayer of the faithful. The first is Ali, son of Abu Talib, he who had wedded Mohammed's favourite daughter, Fatima. Of his blood and Mohammed's blood there are eleven more Imams. The eleventh Imam was called Hassan el-Askari. The twelfth Imam is named like the Prophet—Mohammed. They call him Mohammed el Mahdi.

Persian Islam has known for a thousand years that this twelfth Imam, the Mahdi, is still alive. For a thousand years he has been hidden in a cave. And he is to come back, like the Elijah of the Jews.

Again and again in the lands of Islam men have arisen, through the centuries, and have announced: "I am this twelfth Imam. I am the Expected Mahdi!"

The dynasty of the Fathimid Khalifas in North Africa was founded by a Mahdi.

Again and again somebody comes forward and calls himself the Mahdi. But still the world has not been conquered for Islam, still there are unbelievers. And still, as ever, the Moslems are waiting for him who is to complete the work of the Prophet.

. . . . .

Queyyum! Queyyum! "The Unchanging." Of the ninety-nine names of Allah, the one that the Mahdi is destined to inscribe upon his banner.

The worshipper in his gloomy cave repeated the name, quicker and ever quicker, with a thousand bows, jerks, spasmodic contortions, until his body was worn out and his soul strangely awake; until froth welled out from the praying mouth and the eyes were quite glassy and fixed and were seeing things. . . .

Dream of a sleeping man or apparition to a man awake? Sleeping or waking, the Dervish Mohammed Ahmed had always on his lips the one word, a storm, a frenzy of prayer:

"Queyyum!"

In the ears of the Dervish droned the echo of those words that a man had spoken:

"Thou art the Expected Mahdi!"

And one day, one night, in waking, in sleeping, he saw Mohammed, the Prophet of God, appear to him, in a green mantle, which shone.

. . . . .

Round the Prophet there was a great host of angels and of the holy dead. The beatified sheikhs of the Sammaniya were all there, the saintly founders and guardians of the Order. Lovingly El Koreishi was stretching out his arms towards Mohammed Ahmed. Behind him, countless and shadowy, were the pious dead, men of all the ages. The walls of the cave had vanished, and an infinite space could be seen, full of radiant spirits.

An expectant hush was reigning. The Prophet drew nearer. Now someone was by him; they walked together, hand in hand.

The dreamer knew who it was: "This is my brother, the Dervish Isa! Isa, son of Maryam. Why does he come? The Mahdi is to appear before him!"

Then, full and marvellous, the voice of the Prophet was heard, speaking to Isa:

## THE VISION

"Behold, this is the Expected Mahdi, whom thou must obey!"

And Isa, the son of Maryam, said: "I believe in him!"

And the voice of Mohammed the Prophet filled the space:

"If anyone believe not in him, he believes neither in God nor in me!"

.   .   .   .   .

The praying Dervish beheld a resplendent throne. Mohammed was seated upon it. Round him were four Radiant Ones, the first Khalifas of Islam.

The Dervish Mohammed Ahmed stood before the throne. And now the Prophet stretched out his hand, and easily and painlessly it penetrated into the Dervish's body until it touched his heart. And Mohammed Ahmed saw the heart in his own breast. It was quite dark, a human heart. But as the hand of the Prophet touched it, the heart of Mohammed Ahmed was instantly purified and white, and a light went out from it.

And then the Prophet descended from his throne; and he girded his own sword on Mohammed Ahmed, and said:

"The faith of Mohammed is with the sword!"

Then all the radiant spirits, all the saints of Islam, all the glorified people of Paradise, stretched out their hands towards the Dervish Mohammed Ahmed, who was now the Expected Mahdi and was to carry the Prophet's sword over the earth; and the cleansed heart of the Mahdi glowed like a great fire, and the voice of the Prophet Mohammed, all alone in the silent infinity, spoke:

"Behold, thou art created out of the effulgence of my innermost heart!"

"Behold, God has given to thee the signs of the Mahdieh; they are the birthmark on thy cheek and the separated teeth!

"Behold, a banner of light is with thee; and Azrael, the Angel of Death, will carry it wherever thou goest!"

The Dervish Mohammed Ahmed, who was the Expected Mahdi, knew, without turning round, that behind him, towering behind the throne, stood One, a Shapeless One, a Boundless One, a Vague One, who held above him a giant banner of sheer light, and one word was written upon it:

"Queyyum!"

And the Mahdi of Islam knew that he had to go forth into the world with the sword of Mohammed, and that wherever he stepped the Angel of Death would follow him.

. . . . .

On this island of Abba in the Nile there was, besides the Arab settlement, also a village of negroes. They were fishermen of the Shilluk tribe, gigantically tall, slender, completely naked and unconvertible heathens. They wore their hair at the back of the head, in a curious matted disc, shaped like a spade; an ostrich feather was plaited into it. They oiled their inky-black bodies and wore arm and leg rings of copper and ivory. They were very skilful fishermen and knew well how to navigate their little rafts on the Nile, spearing the big shad with long barbed spears.

On a certain Friday, fear and astonishment reigned in the conical straw huts of the negro village. The island was swarming with strangers, who had suddenly landed. Were those Arabs, perhaps, preparing some *razzia*? Were they planning to surround the Shilluk

## THE VISION

village by night and kill the trusty warriors with their fire-arms? Did they want to shackle the young boys with leg-irons, to drive the women and children with hippo-whips out of the burning village?

Nothing else could it mean, that so many Arabs had assembled together on Abba. A *razzia* began like that.

A certain number of Shilluks, with shields and long spears, stood as scouts in the deep shadow on the edge of the forest. They stood, as always, only on their left leg and propped their right leg against it in a peculiar way. They watched, attentively and without understanding, what was going on in the place of worship.

. . . . .

The place of worship of the Arab settlement was a clearing not far from the huts. The trees of the forest looked into this open-air mosque; whenever it was quiet one heard the birds screaming, and the monkeys chasing each other. This was a day in the rainy season; it was not actually raining, but the steaming air was full of moisture.

In the sacred clearing were sitting hundreds of men, in orderly rows, each upon his piece of carpet or a skin. One could see the white robes of the Danagla, the many-coloured silk garments of several sheikhs from Dar-Fur; men from Kordofan also were present and warriors of the Southern Baggara, fellow tribesmen of Abdullahi. Wandering students from far-off Bornu had come all that way, as far as this place, clad in goatskins; and even from the deserts on the Red Sea several Hadendoa had arrived, Bedouins clothed in coarse home-spun cloaks and without turbans, their hair glued in many tresses to the skull. All these men spoke many different dialects and between them was tribal hatred and scorn.

But all of them had the same faith, and the Turk was their common enemy.

The Shilluk warriors saw them sitting there; they were quite still. Each one had bared his feet and laid his weapons down beside him. Sometimes, while one person was addressing them, the squatting men bent their foreheads to the ground. Then it was as if a wind were playing over an orderly bed of white and dark flowers.

The Shilluk scouts with their sharp eyes could recognise the preacher who was talking to the strangers. Yes, that was the smiling man out of the hole. But he was a good man! Perhaps he was not going to steal any children!

.   .   .   .   .

The Dervish Mohammed Ahmed, surrounded by those who had come to hear a great message, began, first quietly, in the usual tone of the leader of prayers, of the Imam pronouncing the Friday sermon. He spoke so low that the noise of the birds almost drowned his voice.

"In the name of God, the Compassionate, the Merciful!

"Praise be to God, the Creator, who has made man from the earth and given him an excellent form, who has called him to obedience, knowledge, and worship and has promised abundant reward to those who are pious and bear affliction with patience——"

The preacher's voice grew louder.

"Praise, much praise be unto God who has revealed

# THE VISION

the light of His truth to His faithful who were in darkness.

"Blessing and peace be on our Lord Mohammed, from whom the rays of light were spread about to enlighten those chosen to be faithful!"

. . . . .

Near the preacher a man stood up, known to many—Abdullahi, a Taaishi of the Baggara. He lifted up a black banner, with Arabic characters sewn on it. Those who could read, read:

"O Thou Living One, Thou Unchanging, Thou Glorious Fountain of Mercy!"

And:

"There is no god but God and Mohammed is the Prophet of God!"

The black men of the Shilluk shrank more fearfully against the trees which were hiding them. That man with the banner had suddenly shouted out something, something unintelligible. And now the crowd jumped up, the men seized their weapons, they were all shouting.

But the man in the centre stretched out his arms. Everything became perfectly still. The voice was saying something. The waving sleeves cut the air like the wings of a bird.

The Shilluk scouts looked with big round negro eyes at those Arab strangers who were jumping, yelling, weeping, exulting, writhing, kissing the earth, the dust at the man's feet! What witchery was being worked? What new danger was brewing?

. . . . .

The Dervish Mohammed Ahmed had said to the assembly:

"I am the Expected Mahdi. He who believes not in me, believes neither in God nor His Prophet!"

. . . . .

In their hiding-place the Shilluk warriors did not understand those words, yet they trembled. Most certainly this uproar in the clearing, these cries, these brandished weapons signified death for black men, burning straw huts, and women-folk carried off.

The people in the place of worship were shouting, raving. But now into the midst of them stepped the man whose will was strongest, he who had already had been found worthy to carry his master's banner. Abdullahi, the Baggara, tall and erect, with his flag in his hands, dominated the confused crowd. With imperious gestures he commanded silence.

And then he cried out, so that he could be heard far off, for the first time, the creed of a newly born faith. The hundreds repeated it after him, loudly and solemnly: "There is no god but God. And Mohammed is the Prophet of God. And Mohammed, the Mahdi, is the successor of God's Prophet!"

. . . . .

In later days those indescribably excited people would tell in all the Sudan that behind the Mahdi they had seen a second banner raised up, a banner made of sheer light, which a Shapeless One, a Boundless One, a Terrible One was bearing aloft.

# THE WARNING

In February 1881 Romolo Gessi—Gessi Pasha, Gordon's best officer—returned from the Gazelle River. After Gordon had gone back to Khartoum, Gessi had fought the slave-hunters on the White Nile and he had shot that pleasant youngster in the blue riding jacket, the son of Zubeir.

Many *zaribas* had this sturdy Italian with the greying black beard destroyed, many slaves had he liberated and armed. And then the slaves in their turn had hunted down the slave-dealers and murdered them. A melancholy business, setting people free!

Now Romolo Gessi was worn out and sick. He wanted to go home. He had a presentiment that he would now die very soon.

When he arrived at Khartoum he found another Governor-General in place of his friend Gordon. The Khedive had recently recalled Gordon, in none too kind a manner. The Governor-General now was that Rauf, the man whom Gordon had turned out of Equatoria and sent back to Cairo. There he had spread slanderous reports about Gordon. And now he was sitting in Gordon's place, in Gordon's palace. And the right-hand man of His Chibouk-smoking, Harem-loving Excellency was none other than that second worthy whom Gordon had had to expel ignominiously from the Equator Province—Mohammed Bey Abu Saud.

Both of them hated Gessi as an ally of Gordon and because he had waged war against the slave trade in real earnest.

.   .   .   .   .

Before Romolo Gessi started for Cairo (where he was to die suddenly, the poor, brave old fighter for the cause of freedom), he wrote, to the editor of the magazine *Esploratore*, one of those travel letters which have made him famous all over Italy.

"I found Khartoum after an absence of three years very different from when I had left it. Fine buildings along the river-bank, luxuriant vegetation, new law-courts, a garden to the Government Palace. To a man arriving from the swamp lands of the Nuer and the Shilluk, all these things cause a certain wonder, even to one accustomed to the great cities of the world.

"It is the European colony which has transformed this region, instructing the people in the art of making bricks and lime and cutting stone, and proving to them that the most unpleasant places can be rendered habitable, and life therein supportable. The Catholic Mission was the first teacher, later on the Maltese Del Bono, then various Arab, Copt, and Greek merchants, and now there is general rivalry in building houses provided with all the comforts of European civilisation.

"Monsieur Marquet, a Frenchman (Romolo Gessi told the *Esploratore*), already sells every variety of goods: conserves and foodstuffs, manufactures and stationery. Other shops are resplendent with ornaments, lamps, and chandeliers. You can hardly buy better things in the best Milanese shops. The gum business is flourishing. The outlook for our Italian trade is bright. Already the Società Commerciale di Milano——"

Yes, civilisation had begun. There were consuls of the Powers in the growing capital city of Khartoum. There was Herr Martin Hansal, Consul of His Majesty the Emperor of Austria. (He had lots of black servant girls, seven or so. The Austrian colony, of which he was the head, consisted of the missionary priests and the tailor Klein. This latter subject of His Austrian Majesty was, however, permanently drunk.) And there was the Consul of the Basileus of the Hellenes, no mean dignitary! The town, in fact, was swarming with Greeks. The Greek ladies were all loaded with ornaments, so much was business prospering.

Almost every month a new consul arrived or a new firm was established: exportation of gum, ivory, or senna. It was true that all the officials had to be bribed, but that scarcely diminished the huge profits.

.   .   .   .   .

Since that troublesome Gordon had been sent to the devil, everything in the Sudan had settled down so beautifully. Otherwise the Khedive Tewfik in Cairo had many worries: the National Party was pestering him, Colonel Arabi Pasha threatened to throw him off his throne, the European creditors were becoming a nuisance, an English interference was to be feared— only in the Sudan was the Egyptian Empire flourishing. The sultanate of Dar-Fur had now been conquered, the faithful Rauf Pasha was sending large revenues, and, above all—enlightenment, the victory of civilisation! Even the Anti-Slavery Society in London had nothing more to grumble at.

## THE MAHDI OF ALLAH

In Khartoum, indeed, the big *dahabeeyahs*, laden with shackled slaves, could now hardly cast anchor at the riverside quay opposite the Pasha's Palace, not even if there were high Government officials on board. The slave trade was no longer as safe and easy as it used to be.

Hitherto the Arab tribes in the Sudan had paid their taxes out of the sale of slaves. But now the country was full of white Idealists like Romolo Gessi who were combating the slave trade in the provinces. Oh, they were indomitable fellows!

Dr. Eduard Schnitzler, a native of Oppeln in Prussia, under the name of Emin Bey, was at present Governor of the Equatorial Province. Like Gordon before him, he imagined he would be able to prevent the stealing of negroes.

In the newly conquered province of Dar-Fur, Slatin—Rudolf Slatin of Vienna—had become Governor-General: a smallish gentleman, very young, astonishingly energetic. It was a marvel how he was whacking those Bedouin rebels!

And explorers were striding about all over the country and exploring. Wilhelm Junker, a Russian German, went up and down the Nile, once into Central Africa and once back again. And Roman Catholic missionaries came into the Sudan, and more and more Greek traders.

But the bashi-bazouks with their hippo-whips raised all the money that was needed for the wages of the white Idealists and for the reforming governors. And the explorers had escorts who requisitioned by force everything that was wanted from the inhabitants. And the traders had their methods, too. . . .

• • • • •

## THE WARNING

The bashi-bazouk in his capacity of tax collector would come down on the Arab sheikh. In former times the sheikh would first simply have set upon a negro village and then sold the negroes. But now so many slave transports were lost. The risk was becoming too considerable.

So the Arab hunters after a *razzia* preferred to kill the black heathen and to search much more thoroughly than usual for the ivory buried under the huts and the cattle hidden in the woods.

And in the end the revenue was collected all right. The bashi-bazouk extorted it from the Arab, the Arab stole it from the negro. Finally the Egyptian Pasha and the European Idealists got their nice little salaries safely.

Everything being so quiet and peaceful in the Sudan, Rauf Pasha (who was not a very warlike person) was able to discharge whole masses of negro soldiers. It was such an economy. The former soldiers formed bands and roamed through the country, robbing the people. If anything were to happen, these would be excellent recruits.

But for the present everything was quiet.

. . . . .

Everything, indeed, was perfectly quiet and peaceful, except for a squabble which was going on amongst the priests in the mosque at Khartoum. What was the matter with them? They were usually amiable people, fat, and loyal to the powers-that-be. But now they refused to keep calm. Some great arch-heretic, apparently, was causing every green turban to wag. Some new Dervish on an island in the Nile. A saint or something. The wrangling never ceased. In the midst of their rising prosperity the Greek traders heard far too much bazaar-talk about this Dervish.

But for the consuls of the Powers he had not yet any official existence, and the Governor-General went on smoking his long pipe and discharged a few more troops.

 .  .  .  .  .

One day, however, the holy Sheikh Mohammed Sherif, the head of the Sammaniya Tarika, paid a visit to the Governor-General's Palace.

The Governor-General, Rauf Pasha ("hokmdar" is the Sudanese title), came out to meet the old man on the threshold of the audience chamber—such was the honour due to the Sheikh. The Sheikh saluted: "Peace be with you!" Then he sat down in the place of honour, drank several cups of coffee, but refused, so great was his self-denial, the pipe that a negro slave tendered him. Rauf Pasha (who had been obliged to don his full-dress uniform and was sweating in it) sat there, toying with his rosary, and wishing that his reverend visitor would soon go away again. Rauf Pasha was, certainly, as good a Moslem as any, but what did he care about a row among a lot of Dervishes? There was, it seemed, some complaint. Some crazy *fikih* or other——

"He is splitting the staff of Islam!" said the Sheikh darkly.

The oily Pasha smiled, showing his sympathy. His eyelids fell down above the pouches under his eyes. He was blinking. He would like to go to sleep. A single word woke him up:

"Mahdi!"

 .  .  .  .  .

The sleepiness of the Pasha was all gone. Now

## THE WARNING

indeed he was listening, and not thinking any more, between whiles, of that newly purchased Abyssinian slave girl (who was like the full moon, like a gazelle). If this mad Dervish was not pretending to be merely one of the usual saints, El Kutb perhaps, or even (for aught he cared) El Khidr in person—but the Mahdi, then the matter was serious. A Mahdi had always meant rebellion and bloodshed. If it was reported to the Khedive in Cairo that there was a man preaching that he was the Mahdi——

Rauf Pasha hurriedly questioned the Sheikh. Who was this Dervish? Were his adherents numerous? Were they armed? But the old Sheikh was stroking his beard, he was not to be interrupted by questions. Slowly he talked on, complacently intent on showing his own theological learning, the strength of his orthodoxy.

For a long time, it seemed, the Sheikh had pondered the question whether this *fikih* Mohammed Ahmed was a heretic. His doctrines were not authorised by the texts of the Koran, nor did they correspond to the oral traditions as recorded in the Hadiths. Long ago this man had begun, like a hypocrite, to oppose permitted, even sacred things; for example, a celebration so acceptable to God as a circumcision. . . .

How then could he be the Mahdi? That he was of the blood of the Prophet he himself asserted, but all the knowledge was with God, and his family had hitherto been considered insignificant. How could he be the Mahdi? Had the signs been accomplished that are enumerated in the book called "Hadik en-Nadih," of Abd el-Ghani of Neblus, and in the book of Shaani, "Keshef el-Ghummah"? Had the Euphrates dried up at all, and had the golden hills revealed themselves beneath it? Had anybody seen the arm in the clouds which is supposed to point to the earth when the Mahdi appears?

Finally the Sheikh et-Tarikat produced a sheet of paper; he had, he said, composed a writing, in verse of course, in order to demonstrate in it all the wickedness of this person. Everything was stated in it: how he feigned to be a god-fearing person, when he first came to Mohammed Sherif as a disciple—when was it?—yes, twenty years ago, in the year 1277 of the Flight....

The Sheikh unfolded the paper and read the poem out, in the traditional chanting tones, himself fascinated by the classical beauty of his own verses; in the Arabic the last word of each line invariably ended on the letter "R" throughout the whole most artistic poem.

He read:

.    .    .    .    .

"He had come to me in the year seventy-seven, in a place called the Sultan's Hill on the shore of the Nile.

"Craving to reach the straight way through me.

"The path of guidance he did tread sincerely;

"On the path of laudable works he did show his zeal.

"So I exalted him above others; I foreboded not the end.

"He was living with us, taking upon himself every duty,

"Such as grinding corn, watching by night, gathering wood, everything arduous by which humility can be proved.

"How he fasted! How he prayed! How he recited!

## THE WARNING

"From the fear of God his tears were ever flowing.

"How he said the 'Allahu akbar!' from the time of the evening prayer all through the night until the morning prayer. . . ."

. . . . .

At the end of every verse, when the Sheikh had pronounced one more rhyme on "R," the Pasha nodded his head in order to show his appreciation and his great refinement. He had to listen (for nobody would dare to interrupt such a recitation) to many more such verses, all of them gracefully rhymed on "R." The verses went on to tell how the piety and good example of Mohammed Ahmed had won over many people to him; but that then two devils had got him into their clutches, namely Shaitan himself, and another one, a devil in human shape, a certain Bedouin. . . .

The old Sheikh related how Mohammed Ahmed had suddenly sent a strange message to him:

"He had said: 'I am the Mahdi! Yes, the Mahdi is thy son,

" 'He, whom thou didst cherish and honour in this world of dust.

" 'So stand up with me for the victory of the Faith,

" 'And let us kill those who are not obedient.' "

. . . . .

Yes, and the false Mahdi, declared the Sheikh, in perfect verses rhymed on "R," even offered to his beloved teacher the throne of the Sudan if he would follow his guidance!

"But I said to him: 'Forgo thy intention, for by God it is wicked and leads to perdition!'

"But the Shaitan spoke to him: 'Proclaim thy message without fear.

"'For truly thou art victorious on the land and on the water.'

"Then he inclined to love Empire and Violence, saying:

"'I am like water, of a cold nature;

"'But if it is heated it is like raging fire. . . .'"

. . . . .

"And so I pronounced a decision against him!" The old Sheikh was reading this out in a thundering voice, his eyes flashing.

"And so I pronounced a decision against him: In heresy and in error!"

After this anathema the real intention of the whole poem became clear enough; the reverend Sheikh wished to denounce certain persons. Always in rhymes on "R" he told the Governor-General that he, Mohammed Sherif, had already warned the Government official, the *kaimakam*, whose duty it was to enforce the law on the Island of Abba, but——

"And I had advised the *kaimakam* to seize him.

"But he merely sent me a message: 'Leave this most holy man alone!'"

(The Governor-General understood these verses perfectly well. Here was a person who was quite capable of sending even to Cairo a few magnificent verses containing a well-rhymed denunciation of the *hokmdar* of the Sudan. . . .)

. . . . .

As soon as the old Sheikh had finally gone, Rauf Pasha sent for his most trusty assistant, Abu Saud.

## THE WARNING

Mohammed Bey Abu Saud was, perhaps, a little too much of a scoundrel even for a high Egyptian Government official in the Sudan of the 'eighties. In the Equatorial Province, before Gordon fired him ignominiously, he had been superintending the abolition of the slave-trade, and simultaneously administering the enormous *zaribas* which he owned and chartering slave ships. Even now, if rumour did not lie, he often successfully did business with the southern slave-dealers for his master, the Pasha.

He entered, executed a great salaam, touching his forehead and breast with his hand. The Pasha received him with no particular signs of favour.

"What fikih is that on Abba? Why haven't you told me anything about him?"

Abu Saud apologised abjectly. He called the Pasha "Saadar"—"Your Felicity." Who was he, Abu Saud, that he should have dared to fill the ears of His Felicity with nothingness? Yes, there was, indeed, one Mohammed Ahmed living on Abba; some called him a Sayid. Yes, a preacher of sermons. Yes, some malcontents gathered round him. It was said that some of the Arab traders who had been unfortunate in conveying slave caravans had taken refuge with him. The Felicity knew that the Mohammedan faith allowed and even ordered the enslaving of the heathen and of the foes of God. This Dervish was preaching, maybe, against the most excellent Christian governors whom His Highness, the Khedive, sent into his provinces.

Abu Saud told all this in a low voice, looking firmly at the Pasha, who was blinking his eyes a little uncertainly. Then the Pasha came to a decision:

"I must see this fikih. As you know him, go to Abba

and fetch him here. Use persuasion; you know how to do it...."

Abu Saud, in a servile attitude, his hands hidden in his sleeves, said, as smooth a snake and with a look darting and pricking like a snake's tongue:

"And what is the Felicity planning to do to the Dervish, if he comes?"

"*Ma shaa-llah!*" said the Pasha. "What God wills will be done!"

· · · · ·

With an ambiguous smile Abu Saud went to carry out the Pasha's orders. He travelled to Abba; with flattering words he was going to invite the Dervish to the capital. While he was still on his way, many rumours filled the town. Suddenly everybody was talking about this Mahdi. "The false Mahdi," people said. "The impostor of Abba." All the *ulema* of the Mosque were hostile to him. They easily proved from the old books that he must be lying. But one very young *fikih*, a student of theology, on his way up the Nile to Cairo (where he intended to study in the school of El Azhar) was publicly heard to say, in the courtyard of the mosque in Khartoum: "This sheikh in Abba has the birthmark which is the seal of the Mahdieh, and between his teeth he has the gap. Furthermore, it is known that the great Senussi, just before he died, prophesied this very year of the Hegira, that the Expected Mahdi was to appear."

The young heretic was driven with blows out of the mosque. But among the populace many were murmuring.

A caravan from Kordofan which was carrying gum to Suakin was resting in Omdurman, opposite Khartoum, and the news spread: this Dervish, the false Mahdi, had recently travelled through Kordofan and very many there believed in him; they said that he was indeed the Expected Mahdi. The women of several Arab villages had found hens' eggs, on which characters were written. The learned ones, the *fikihs* who were teaching in the schools, had read the letters: there it was written that Mohammed Ahmed was the Mahdi.

All Kordofan had seen him. From village to village he had journeyed, in a patched shirt, with an iron-tipped staff and an earthenware bowl. With the great ones, the emirs and the tribal sheikhs, he had had long and secret confabulations. Those who had been taught to read were reading a pamphlet which he had written. He said in it that he was the Expected Mahdi, descended from the Prophet by twenty-nine descents, and that all the faithful ought to do penance and go to the Jehad, the Holy War.

A man in the caravan had the pamphlet. Rauf Pasha ordered him to be put in irons.

. . . . .

Abu Saud returned, alone. He went to the Pasha, with lowered eyes. No, he had not been successful. He had not been able to persuade this Dervish to come with him to Khartoum.

"We were, O Felicity, in his hut. Abdullahi the Taaishi was there and Ahmed Sharfi and Hamed, the brother of the Dervish. He was sitting on his *angareb*, in a patched gown and with a Meccan skull-cap. I said to him: 'Master, come with me to Khartoum, so that our lord, the hokmdar, may honour you!' He was silent. I said: 'You must come with me.'"

Abu Saud stopped. The Governor-General looked at him angrily.

"Well, and what did this dog of a Dongolawi answer?"

"O Felicity, he jumped up, he beat his breast with his hand:

"'What! *Must?* By the favour of God I am the lord of this land; and this is the sword with which the Prophet has armed me!'"

# THE FLIGHT

On a hot evening during the rainy season two companies of Egyptian infantry, each under the command of a *saghkolaghasi*, an adjutant-major, landed on the island of Abba. The steamer *Ismailia*, which had brought the Government troops, remained in the middle of the river, well out of range of any possible shot. On this steamer was Abu Saud, whom Rauf Pasha had sent to fetch the rebel Dervish, this time by force. Abu Saud was not a fighting man and would never have landed at night-time and in a mist on marshy islands where enemies were waiting.

But how did he know that they were waiting?

. . . . .

Perhaps one or the other of the two effendis who commanded the soldiers would also have been glad enough to have waited till morning. But they were terribly jealous of each other; neither of them could endure that the other should have the honour of catching the Dervish alone. The Pasha had promised promotion to the one who brought him in—promotion to the rank of *bimbashi*! Each of the two already saw himself with a major's epaulettes, and as the superior officer of the other.

The companies landed in disorder, because they were trying to forestall each other. It was a close, steaming night; the darkness reeked of stagnant water.

THE MAHDI OF ALLAH

Apart from the cautious man on the steamer, Abu Saud, nobody knew the island.

It had been raining for weeks; the soldiers sank in in the darkness, could not see where they sank, fell into puddles, remained stuck, lashed by the reeds.

Silence had been ordered. Only a clinking of arms could be heard now and again, a hideous sucking noise of water and mud, a half-stifled cry.

Silence again. Then, suddenly——

.   .   .   .   .

Out of the long grass something white leapt up. Abdullahi the Taaishi yelled out, "Allah!" and swung a huge sword. An awful trumpeting, the sound of a hollowed-out elephant tusk, rent the silence. Then shouting and volleys. The two companies were firing aimlessly into the darkness and hitting each other. Then those savages were upon them, armed only with spears and clubs, but many, many of them. A well-prepared ambush.

How could the Dervish have known that the soldiers were coming? How could Abdullahi have collected in good time all those helpers, men of the tribes between the two Niles, men of the Kenana and of the Degheim who believed in the Mahdi and were ready for the Holy War?

On this day, before the steamer came, the Mahdi had preached to them. Mohammed the Prophet himself had promised him a victory, in a great vision. A victory without weapons, with sticks alone; yes, even with reeds and straw the Turks could be slain.

And now it had happened—the miracle. The miracle of God for His servant, the Mahdi.

.   .   .   .   .

## THE FLIGHT

But from where had Mohammed Ahmed obtained knowledge of the coming of the troops?

Could it be that the cautious one on the steamer, Abu Saud, knew about it? He had told the Governor-General what he had talked about with the Mahdi when he had been to the island for the first time. But what had he whispered to Abdullahi after that?

Could it be that the friend and mercenary of all the slavers of the South, the friend of the owners of thorn-hedged negro-pens, of the masters of sinister death-caravans, of the leaders of bloody *razzias*—that Abu Saud had not viewed the rise of a rebellion with displeasure? All those British, Austrian, and Italian pashas and beys had, after all, at last become a nuisance to the slavers.

Could it be? Abu Saud with his steamer, which had a gun on board, made no attempt to intervene in this nocturnal battle. A few desperate swimmers who had escaped the Dervishes on the shore and the crocodiles in the water brought the news on board that all was lost. At once Abu Saud gave the order to return to Khartoum as quickly as possible. Only the indignation of the ship's captain induced him to wait a little longer to see if any more fugitives would come.

On the island, between the dark trees, a great scurrying and flickering of torches could be seen. Somewhere in a clearing a huge fire was blazing. And tom-tom, tom-tom, tom-tom-tom went the kettle-drums all night long.

No more fugitives came on board. As soon as it was morning, the *Ismailia* steamed slowly upstream, to take the news of what had happened to Khartoum.

Tom-tom, tom-tom-tom! The island was full of noises, full of cries. They were still searching for, finding and murdering the wounded who were hiding in the reeds. Mutilated corpses were everywhere, stark naked. Arab boys of the island village were looking for scattered arms in the tall grass. Somewhere behind the huts, in the deepest shadow, a drinking-bout seemed to be going on; the shouting sounded like milletbeer. Or was it the drums that were making those people so drunk?

The biggest kettledrum, the copper one, was rumbling in the clearance where the great fire was burning. Towards that spot processions of warriors were moving from every part of the island. A herd of naked prisoners was being driven in. The booty was brought in, the captured firearms were piled up in a great heap. The Turkish flag with the star and crescent, which had been captured, lay in the mud beside the weapons. High above it, in the light of the fire, waved the black banner of the Mahdi.

But had not the believers, the victors of that night, seen with their own enraptured eyes another banner, woven of sheer light, that a shapeless monster held up behind the praying Mahdi?

.　　.　　.　　.　　.

All at once it became very still round the blazing fire. Only the drums on the river-bank were sounding on—tom-tom-tom: the message of the Holy War going out into the night.

In the illuminated circle of the camp-fire Abdullahi had risen. His sword was still bared; he was soiled with blood. With a grand gesture he pointed towards the Mahdi, who now stepped forward, in a shining white gown with many-coloured patches. His turban gleamed.

The Mahdi smiled; he spread out his arms. He spoke to his friends.

"O ye Ansar!" he said.

He paused, his smile beaming upon them. And they shouted for joy. He had called them "Ansar"—"helpers." With one word he had consecrated and sanctified this savage rabble. Ansar—that was the name that Mohammed the Prophet had given to his first companions, his friends of Medina. The mere word was a promise of paradise and of delights unspeakable. . . .

. . . . .

"Ansar!" said the Mahdi.

And the wild crowd, the bloodstained fighters, men drunk with the sound of the drums, men of many tribes, semi-negroes from the Gesireh and Bedouins from the edge of the Sahara, yelled out, driven crazy by that single word:

"Death to the Turk!"

. . . . .

In the middle of the wide circle the prisoners were standing, the soldiers of the Pasha, quite naked and defenceless and dying from weariness. A cry of rage was raised against them; weapons began to dance. The unbelievers! The heathen! Infidels, who did not believe in the Mahdieh! Toork! Toork! Toork!

Abdullahi, with flashing eyes, sprang between them, the kourbash hanging from his wrist. Already they had learned to obey him. With a murmur they shrank back. The captive fellaheen, whose yellow skin had become quite grey with fright, prostrated themselves before the Mahdi. He looked at them, smiled, and in kindly tones spoke the sura of the Koran which ordained that pagan prisoners should be the rightful booty of the faithful, and their property as slaves.

"And we have the message of the Prophet," he preached to the captive soldiers of the Khedive; "we have the message," he said (and as he talked his smile showed the significant gap between the fine teeth), "that whoever doubts our Mahdieh and denies and contradicts it is an unbeliever, and that his blood will be shed and his property will be booty . . ."

And with his gentle smile he recited another sura of the Koran, which ordered the slaughter of conquered unbelievers and the enslavement of the surviving ones: "Then off with the heads, and fasten the fetters!"

After the Mahdi had spoken this grim sura, he paused for a moment; then he said smilingly that he would be willing, after all, to pardon the soldiers, if they repented.

Then they all came and kissed the dust at his feet. Each one walked up separately and laid his trembling hand between the dark hands of the Mahdi and pronounced the new creed:

"There is no god but God. And Mohammed is the Prophet of God. And Mohammed the Mahdi is the successor of God's Prophet!"

. . . . .

Whoever did not believe in the Mahdieh, even if he believed in Allah and the Prophet, was an unbeliever and would be delivered to eternal torment. Hundreds of the Ansar of Abba swore that they had seen the

## THE FLIGHT

flames of hell suddenly shoot out from the dead body of a Turkish officer.

.   .   .   .   .

Before sunrise, Abdullahi the Taaishi—they said already: "Our lord Abdullahi, the Khalifa of the Mahdi" —announced an order to the Ansar: they were to prepare for immediate departure. Great indeed was the victory of the faithful—said the Khalifa—and henceforth none would resist the Ansar; but it was decreed that, like Mohammed, the envoy of God, Mohammed the Mahdi also had to accomplish a flight, to Mount Masa.

This was the twelve hundred and eighty-ninth year after the Hegira of Mohammed. With this new Hegira the new age of Islam began.

.   .   .   .   .

Tom-tom, tom-tom-tom; everywhere on the banks of the Nile, in Sennar, in Kordofan, the drums of the Jehad were beating. The Mahdi was marching on the western bank of the river. As yet his band of fighters was small; arms and horses were lacking. Only the Mahdi was mounted, on a mean Abyssinian nag; Abdullahi, his Khalifa, walked at his side. More than once danger threatened. Here and there some Egyptian garrison had been alarmed. Once a certain adjutant-major had the chance to capture the Mahdi, only he had not the pluck to do it. Giegler Pasha, the German Governor of Kordofan, heard that the rebel was not far from El Obeid, his capital. An old colonel of the garrison, Mohammed Pasha Said, was sent out with four companies to attack the insurgents. The old pasha arrived in the neighbourhood of the camp where the

Mahdi was resting with his tired, sick, and half-starved followers—made no attempt to attack them, but waited in idleness for three days and then retreated back to El Obeid. The soldiers told each other mysteriously that the old man was troubled in his conscience. Did he, perhaps, himself believe this Dervish to be the Expected Mahdi?

Mohammed Ahmed continued his march and arrived in the Tagalla Mountains. The Sultan of the Shilluk negroes, who hated the Egyptians (they had treacherously captured his father and let him die of starvation in their prison), sent the Mahdi a big gift of *durrha* and a warning: he was not, he said, safe where he was; he ought to go farther into the interior.

After wandering about for a long time, weary and plagued by fever, the Mahdi's little army arrived in the Nuba hills. Here, on Mount Gadir, there had been for a long time a sacred place, a rock on which the Prophet was said to have once reposed.

Here Mohammed Ahmed pitched his camp, thus finishing his flight. An old legend told that the Expected Mahdi was to come from Mount Masa. This was the name of a hill in distant Maghreb, in the Atlas Mountains. But Mohammed Ahmed had seen a new vision: the real Jebel Masa, on which the Mahdi was to appear, was not in the Atlas, but precisely here; it was, in fact, that big rock close by their newly pitched camp. He had learned this in his visions.

Soon the entire Sudan knew that Jebel Gadir was actually the legendary Mount Masa, and that the Expected Mahdi, as prophesied, had appeared there. Jebel Gadir—that is, Jebel Masa—was the terminus of the new Hegira; from it radiated the new salvation.

# THE MOUNTAIN

Dar Nuba, the highlands of the black Nuba people, stands out picturesquely from the dreary plains of Southern Kordofan: a system of mountain ridges between which are beautiful valleys, not dry "wadis" in which there is seldom any water, but "khors," through which mountain torrents rush the whole year round; a dense, tropical vegetation fills them, the trees grow to an enormous size, the jungle is full of wild animals. This rugged region contains more than a hundred hills, of varying height. Jebel Tagalla is the name of one, another is called Jebel Delen, another Jebel Gadir

Although a country full of monkeys and elephants can hardly be compared with the Southern Tyrol, a young Tyrolese who was then living here, the Rev. Father Joseph Ohrwalder, from Lana, near Meran, was reminded of home by these Nuba highlands. He was only twenty-five and had not been with the Sudan Mission very long. He had landed at Suakin at the beginning of 1881 with Bishop Comboni and two other missionaries; for a few weeks he had stayed at the Austrian Mission House in Khartoum (which had such a beautiful garden), then his fellow-countryman, Rudolf Slatin, who had recently been appointed Governor-General of Dar-Fur, and was proceeding to take up his new post in that province, had taken Father Ohrwalder with him part of the way. The young priest was destined to work in the new station which the Austrian Catholic Mission had just established in the Nuba hills. From El Obeid, the capital of Kordofan, the priest had to travel alone, and the dreary region of the steppes was not pleasing to this Tyrolese mountaineer. But he was charmed by Dar-Nuba and the station at Delen. Here there were hills, verdant forests, and rushing waters!

Father Ohrwalder found his work pleasant, too; being a completely simple man and consequently a good one, he was ready to get on well with everybody and to do his share of work without grumbling. Between him and the superior of the Delen Mission, Father Bonomi, there was perfect understanding. Both took a delight in energetic and efficient handiwork. The provisional buildings of the Mission had to be extended, for there was already a growing colony of converted blacks living in the Mission; new accommodation had to be created for them. Father Ohrwalder tried his hand with success at baking bricks; with great pride he was soon able to show two thousand excellent bricks which he had made with the aid of his black assistants. Meanwhile his superior, Father Bonomi, with the help of Brother Mariani, the carpenter of the Mission, had brought into existence the very first mule-cart ever seen in Kordofan; now it was possible to cart bricks and palm-wood and excellent lime from the Saburi mountain.

.    .    .    .    .

Father Ohrwalder also liked his new charges, the Nuba blacks. They were, it was true, perfectly naked, but, as the priest got to know, of very innocent morals. There was something peasant-like about them,

FATHER OHRWALDER

which pleased the man from the Tyrol. They did not have to do much cultivation—just a little maize: the woods were packed with fruit. But they kept cattle and goats and made good butter. Perhaps on a holiday they would drink a little too much *merissa*. On these festivals they would dance, not the men alone, as is the custom everywhere else in the negro country, and the women among themselves, but boys and girls together, as in the Tyrol. Notwithstanding the absence of any kind of dancing costume, the good father did not see anything too shocking in these dances. Yes, he was fond of his Nubas!

They were half Mohammedan, half heathen; their religious chief, who was also their paramount ruler, was called the Khojur. Whatever this Khojur might be thinking in his heart of hearts about the Christian mission, he knew that it meant a valuable protection for the little Nuba community. Since olden times the Nuba had had wicked enemies, these were the Baggara, the wild nomads of the plains. Again and again they would invade the mountain valleys, rob the cattle and drive the people away as slaves. But now, on account of the mission, there was in Delen a small garrison of Government troops, and a tolerable calm prevailed.

Until April 1882 Joseph Ohrwalder lived in Delen as in a peaceful paradise. Then all at once wild rumours burst into this quiet tropical mountain world.

.   .   .   .   .

Not very far from Jebel Delen, on which the mission stood, rose a somewhat higher hill, Jebel Gadir—and there, so it seemed, a whole swarm of people had suddenly settled down, some crazy Dervish with his followers, a horrible swindler and hypocrite, who was making out to the blacks that he was who knows what, a kind of saint, in fact more than that, the Messiah. . . .

From the start the Roman Catholic missionary must have hated the Dervish Mohammed Ahmed. Soon, indeed, he had every personal reason for doing so. For this strange neighbour was disturbing the peace. Already the blacks, yes, the baptized blacks of the mission, had begun to grow unruly. Among themselves they no longer talked of anything else but this miraculous man, Mohammed Ahmed. Whoever or whatever he might be, one thing was at all events certain: that he possessed the mighty Tebrid talisman, which, as was well known, would change enemy bullets into water, so that they dropped harmlessly off the charmed body of the fighter. That, of course, must be true, for how could his adherents otherwise have vanquished the troops of our lord in Cairo?

The priests of Delen corrected their blacks lovingly: that was superstition! But just then terrible news came to Delen: the Mudir (Governor) of Fashoda, Rashid Bey, had tried to annihilate the Gadir rebels—and had himself been annihilated. A German, Berghof (a former photographer, now inspector for the suppression of slavery), had been with the troops when they fell into the ambush in the jungle. They had not even had time to dismount from their camels! The false Mahdi had captured a quantity of arms, ammunition and stores of every kind. That the Mahdi's prayers made his adherents bullet-proof was now proved beyond a doubt. It was heard in Delen that people were flocking to him from all sides. The Baggara tribes were coming; one of their people, who

## THE MOUNTAIN

was with the Mahdi, had summoned them. Escaped slaves and slave-hunters, whom the Government was now threatening to throw out of employment, were joining, and so were the black soldiers whom the thrifty Rauf Pasha had just discharged because everything was so peaceful.

The pious missionaries of Jebel Delen saw one after another of their cherished flock go over to the Mahdi. In the Mahdi's camp there was rich spoil to be divided, and, besides, it was not dangerous to fight for one who had the Tebrid talisman.

. . . . .

In the rebel camp on Mount Gadir (which they persisted in calling Mount Masa) nobody doubted the miracles of Mohammed Ahmed. For now he was only called "Mohammed the Mahdi on whom be the blessing and the prayer." This pious formula had until now belonged to the Prophet only. But were not Mohammed the Prophet and Mohammed the Mahdi similar in every respect, or even the same? Both had to flee, the Prophet to Medina and the Mahdi to Masa. Just as the Ansar had rallied in Medina around the Prophet, to fight for him, to conquer for him first Arabia, and then half the world, so the new Ansar were first going to conquer the Sudan for the Mahdi and then achieve the world empire of Islam. It had been written.

. . . . .

The savage warriors who flocked from every side to the Mahdi did not doubt. In the battle against Rashid all the Turkish bullets had turned to water! From the spears of the Ansar destructive flames had been seen to shoot out against the enemy!—and a mystical banner had been seen, made of sheer light!

Also the news was spreading that, on the steppes, birds' eggs had been found and, in the forests, leaves on which the name of the Mahdi was clearly written. The scholars had been able to read it.

From afar came enthusiastic followers. The Baggara came, Abdullahi's fellow-tribesmen. Three of his brothers were in the camp town of peaked huts that had sprung up on the hillside. The people of Dongola, countrymen of the Mahdi, came in crowds to share his fortune and his spoils. Between them and the Baggara much jealousy was rife from the start, but the Mahdi maintained peace and concord among the Ansar. The leader's strong will was making of this savage rabble an army, a people, a state.

.   .   .   .   .

As Mohammed the Prophet had done in Medina, Mohammed the Mahdi organised the Bedouin hordes on Mount Gadir. At the head of the army, which was first to wrest the Sudan from the Turks, and later, no doubt, conquer Cairo, Mecca, and the rest of the earth (only about the rest of the earth his ideas were somewhat hazy), the Mahdi placed his khalifas. As at the beginning of Islam there had been four great khalifas, companions and immediate successors of the Prophet, so Mohammed Ahmed wanted to have his four khalifas of Islam: one, who should correspond to the blameless Abu Bekr, the first khalifa of Islam, and three others who were to have the respective ranks of Imam Ali, Othman, and Oman.

The position of the first khalifa was given to Abdullahi. He was to command, in the army, his fellow-tribesmen, the Baggara; and he kept as his ensign the black banner which previously he had carried in front of the Mahdi. A young relative of the Mahdi, Mohammed esh-Sherif, received the second khalifate, a red banner, and the command of the Dongolawis, to whom he belonged.

The people of the Gesireh country between the two Niles were to be led by the fourth khalifa, Ali Wad Helu, a man of the Degheim who had fought with the others on Abba. But the third khalifate (that of Othman) the Mahdi did not confer on anyone of his Ansar. A letter was travelling across the great Sahara to the oasis in the west, where the great Senussi was living, the head of that powerful spiritual fraternity whose influence was so strong in the north of the continent. To him the Mahdi had offered the dignity of his third khalifate and the yellow banner, inviting him to join in the common war against the infidels. The answer could not be expected yet for a long while: the way across the desert is endless.

. . . .

In the camp, order was established. Each of the khalifas with his emirs and subordinate leaders moved into a special quarter of the town of huts on the hillside; in the middle stood the huts of the Mahdi himself. The man from the cave of Abba already needed several huts, for the number of his wives was increasing: it was good policy not to refuse the daughters of powerful sheikhs who were offered to him for his harem; also, as the leader, he had a right to part of the booty of slave-girls.

In the midst of the women's village that was growing up around him the Mahdi, still lean and ascetic, sat in his own hut dictating proclamations to his secretary.

"In the name of God," the scribe was told to calligraph, "the merciful and compassionate. And blessing on our lord the Prophet . . .

"From the servant of his Lord, Mohammed el-Mahdi Ibn Abdullah, to his beloved in God, the believers in God and in His book the Koran. . . ."

"Continue!" the Mahdi ordered his scribe Abi Saffiya, who was squatting beside him with a reed-pen and an inkstand; and he told him to write how the change of the times and the falling away from the faith had long ago distressed the righteous and the faithful. "Therefore," he dictated, "it is best now to abandon your homes and every aim of life for the revival of the true religion; and jealousy for Islam must not delay to possess the hearts of the believers.

"Now, my friends," wrote the Mahdi to all the tribal sheikhs of the Sudan and to the Government officials, "now, as to what it has pleased Allah in his eternal decrees to grant to his humble slave. . . . The eminent Lord Mohammed, on whom be blessings and peace, has announced to me that I am the Expected Mahdi. And in the hour of battle the eminent Lord will in person go before my hosts, as also the four Khalifas of Islam. And he gave me the sword of victory. Then said he, on whom be blessing and peace, 'See, thou art created out of the effulgence of my innermost heart.'"

The squatting scribe forgot to write and prostrated himself, quite carried away, until his brown forehead touched the earth in front of the Mahdi.

. . . . .

Many days the Mahdi remained in his hut, busy with the scribes. In many letters he announced his call. He spoke of the birthmark on his right cheek and said that in truth he was of the blood of the Prophet. "My father was a descendant of Hussein, on his father's and mother's side, and likewise my mother on her mother's side, while her father also was an Abbaside; and the knowledge is with Allah."

All the predestined signs had been fulfilled, the Mahdi announced. The wise doctors of the Khartoum mosque who tried to prove from ancient books that he was not the Mahdi, he answered with quotations from other learned books. "Knowledge of the Mahdi," the great Sheikh Muhiy ed-Din had written, "is like knowledge of the hour of judgment; and that hour nobody knows but God Most High." And Sheikh Ahmed Ibn Idris: "Fourteen folio volumes of the Savants of God have lied about the Mahdi." "But to me," said the proclamations of Mount Gadir, "the eminent Lord has said, 'He who doubts that thou art the Mahdi has blasphemed God and His Prophet.'"

"Peace be with you,"—the Mahdi dictated the ending. The writer sealed with the new square seal, on which the three lines were engraved, with many flourishes:

"There is no god but God."

"Mohammed is the Envoy of God."

"Mohammed el-Mahdi, Ibn Abdullah."

These letters went out, hidden in Dervish cowls and the shafts of lances and under the saddles of Bedouin horsemen, to be conveyed to every town and village of all the Sudan and far beyond. Those who could read, read them, and those who could not, listened.

Here and there, in every province, muffled at first, the drums of the Holy War were rumbling.

. . . . .

The Roman Catholic missionaries of Jebel Delen heard more and more often of their menacing neighbour, and what they heard filled them with pious indignation. This carpenter's son from Dongola seemed to them to be aping not only his own Mohammed, but also Jesus Christ—to whom he referred very often in his sermons and letters.

The reports that arrived at Delen related how this devil of a Mahdi was preaching his Sermon on the Mount, seated on the rock on which, according to a legend, the Prophet had already once rested.

And in his sermons could be heard, hardly mistakable, an echo of Christ's Sermon on the Mount. Did not the carpenter's son from Dongola also teach Poverty, Humility, Abstinence, Renouncement of worldy goods for eternal salvation?

"Brethren," preached the Mahdi on the Gadir mountain, "in His holy book God has commanded us to be pious.

"When you eat, eat for God, when you drink, drink for God, what you wear, wear for God, and what you ride, ride for God.

"You will please God by walking instead of riding. If you must ride, then ride on a donkey. Be not proud. When the Prophet's donkey became tired, he dismounted and walked behind with his servants as their brother. If the servant were sick, he mounted on his master's donkey, and the Prophet walked.

"God has said in his holy book: 'Let the worshippers of God walk humbly on earth!'

"And see: I myself am but a slave who has been commanded to bring back the book and the doctrine into the light.

"When you are favoured by God, kneel down and thank Him. But know that it is not on account of your virtues that you have been favoured, but because God is merciful and gracious."

. . . . .

Words of humility, of meekness. But nevertheless this new Sermon on the Mount preached wrath and hatred—and war.

"Follow not," cried the Mahdi, "follow not the example of your oppressors the Turks, who live in luxury and arrogance!

"This is a saying of the Prophet which has come down to us through oral tradition:

"'Tell my brethren, Live not in the way my enemies live, wear not what they wear; else you become my enemies, as they are my enemies!'"

. . . . .

To differ from the Turk, even in externals, was the paramount duty of the Ansar. One day the Mahdi, before the assembled army of the faithful, pointed, with an ecstatic gesture, to the *jubba* he was wearing, the rough frieze shirt of the wandering Dervish on which are sewn coloured patches as a sign of a beggar's poverty. In a great vision, said the Mahdi, the Prophet had revealed to him the profound relations which existed between this symbol of the patched *jubba* and the creation of Mankind:

"Man himself is made of rags; his head is a blue rag, the skin of his lips is a red rag, his teeth are a white rag, and his nails are yellow rags. Fourfold, said the Prophet, are the colours of the rags: white, red, black, and yellow."

Those were the four colours which the banners of the Mahdi's host displayed.

. . . . .

The religious doctrine of the Mahdi always meant first of all the army, and the Jehad.

If he preached the poverty that is pleasing to God, he ordered at the same time all worldly treasures to be laid in his great war-chest, in the common treasure-house of the army which he had founded.

And the patched beggar's dress, the mystical garb of humility, was turned into a military uniform. Very soon the young Arab warriors and the muscular blacks discovered that the Dervish costume, if properly girdled and sewn with the four colours in regular patterns, was even a smarter war dress than the Egyptian uniform. They wore a coloured skull-cap with it, or a turban, and wide trousers. That produced a garb of humility of which one could be proud.

. . . . .

The missionaries of Delen hoped for a certain time that this new kingdom of the Mahdi could not endure; he was much too severe, his doctrines forbade everything the Sudanis were fond of: *merissa*, smoking, fine clothes, gold and silver ornaments, even the usual head-dress of the women!

Were those childishly vain natives going to give up everything that had embellished their lives? The Mahdi prohibited songs and dances, every kind of music, unless it was the drums of Holy War! To ride

MAHDISTS IN PATCHED DERVISH JUBBAS

horses was not allowed unless it was in the army. The Mahdi was violently declaiming against those festivities which are so dear to the Sudanese. The usual buying of brides was an evil thing. From now on it was not to be lawful to pay more than ten dollars for a virgin on the wedding-day, and five for a widow. As gifts for the bride two dresses had to suffice, one girdle cloth, one pair of shoes, oil for anointing her, and some perfumes. A wedding banquet of dates and milk; nothing more was permitted.

. . . .

The missionaries of Delen thought that the Sudanese would not submit for long to such austerities; just as, at the same time, the learned *ulema* of Khartoum were quite sure that the dreadful heresies of this false Mahdi would be rejected by the true believers. Had he not abolished the four rites of Islam—those of the Malikites, the Hanafites, the Shafites, and of the Hanbalites? Only the way in which he himself was accustomed to perform prayers was to be the rule for all! He forbade the pilgrimage to Mecca, and even the visiting of the tombs of the holy, for, said he, the war of the faith was more necessary now than pilgrimages. He had the books of theology burnt and the law-books of the Sheriat cast into the river. But, worst of all, he pretended himself to be the Prophet's equal.

All this could not possibly last. The Dervish Sheikh Mohammed Sherif had proved it very clearly in his great didactic poem rhymed on "R."

. . . .

But the preacher of Mount Gadir knew what he was doing. Not by allowing things, but by forbidding them, are new religions created. Human beings are like that. By unheard-of commands and prohibitions the Mahdi distinguished his Ansar from the common herd; that is what they wanted, what they had longed for. This new faith interrupted the monotony of everyday life, changed everything; even the severity of the new laws was prized. A new costume had come, a new flag, a new hope!

. . . . .

While the Mahdi was preaching and writing proclamations, his first Khalifa, Abdullahi, busied himself with collecting arms, with the reports of his spies, with parades and equipment. In the whole Sudan, from Dongola to the Nile swamps, the drums of rebellion began to beat. Small drums, big drums, wooden drums, gourd drums, and the big copper kettledrum of the emirs:

"Tom-tom, tom-tom, tom-tom-tom, Turk!

"Tom-tom, tom-tom, tom-tom-tom, kill the Turk!

"We are destroying this world and creating the next!

"Tom-tom, tom-tom-tom, the faith of Allah is with the sword!

"They are not dead who fall in the Jehad; they are alive!

"Tom-tom, tom-tom-tom, Paradise!"

. . . . .

The echo of all these drums was dinning well into the ears of the missionaries of Delen; their own position was becoming more and more perilous; but they still went on hoping that the Government would soon be able to overpower the rebels!

Their hopes would have been diminished if the priests had known that at this time things were going topsy-turvy, not only in Khartoum, but also in Cairo. There Arabi Pasha, the head of the Nationalist Party, had just become Prime Minister and was driving the country into a conflict with Great Britain. The British fleet was already lying off Alexandria. The bombardment of this port and the landing of the British Army, which was to smash Arabi's "Nationalist Army" at Tel el-Kebir and occupy the country for many decades, were impending. These were not the times when the Egyptian Government could worry about the distant Sudan, send troops there, arms, even money.

In Khartoum, the Governor-General Rauf Pasha had finally been overthrown and his successor was on his way. In the meantime Giegler Pasha was Governor, a German, who had lived already too long in the Orient and was none too energetic. However, he understood what the noise of those drums from Mount Gadir meant; he understood the great danger of the Mahdi and sent an expedition up the Nile: six thousand men under Yussef Pasha esh-Shellali, an officer of poor Gessi's school. This man pushed forward and summoned the Mahdi to surrender.

The Delen missionaries breathed more freely. At last!

Emin Bey, already isolated in the swamps on the Equator, waited breathlessly for good news. They waited in Khartoum, waited in El Obeid.

Then the news came. In the dawn of 7th June, 1882, the Mahdi had attacked Yussef's badly fortified camp. Nobody knows what really happened, for hardly a single man of the expeditionary force escaped to tell the tale. All of them were dead, prisoners, or had deserted to the enemy. Yussef Pasha had been slain in his nightdress. All the arms, the provisions, and the soldiers' wives were in the hands of the rebel Dervishes.

.   .   .   .   .

Tom-tom-tom! Half the Sudan was now already in rebellion. Everywhere villages were burning; in the cities the Egyptian garrisons were being besieged. Everywhere they were killing the tax collectors, the bashi-bazouks. All Kordofan, all Dar-Fur had risen. The Bederia Arabs were slaughtering the people of Abu Haraz, the Hammada, the Jehena, the Hawazma were assaulting the town of Sennar, even on the shores of the Red Sea, the Hadendoa were becoming restless; one Osman Digna, an emir of the Mahdi, was inciting them to revolt, and on the very borders of Egypt the Bisharin were plundering caravans. Elias Pasha, a notable of El Obeid, sent messengers to the Mahdi telling him to come: the capital of Kordofan, they said, was full of spoil.

The Mahdi set out with his armies from Mount Gadir to besiege El Obeid. As in the rainy season a torrent will suddenly rush out of the parched hills of the desert, so the fanatical host of the gentle preacher dashed from Mount Gadir down into the plains....

.   .   .   .   .

Poor Emin Pasha! This is the beginning of your great African Odyssey!

Poor missionaries of Delen, poor Father Bonomi, poor Ohrwalder! One evening you hoped and prayed; the next morning you were awakened by Dervish drums and driven away as miserable slaves!

Even in Europe now they were hearkening to the war-drums in the Sudan.

# FROM THE TRAVELLER'S NOTES

# FROM THE TRAVELLER'S NOTES

*KHARTOUM: 7th February*, 1929.

My Nubian dragoman, Mohammed Sherkawi, in his best caftan with silk stripes, is standing, with an emphatic and somewhat oily humility, beside my seat. His black-brown hands he has clasped over his stomach, which attitude is befitting to his humility, but is also calculated to give prominence to his gold ring, in which a small diamond is set. Slowly and with perceptible unction he translates to me what the heavy and dignified man on the sofa wishes to tell me.

I am in Omdurman, in the extensive Arab house owned by the Sayid Sir Abderrahman el Mahdi, the posthumous son of Mohammed Ahmed. The son of the Mahdi has received me in a room which, evidently for European visitors, has been fitted up with rather stiff English furniture: it is a verandah, open in front, from which you go down a few steps into a courtyard. In this courtyard are drawn up, silent and grave, the servants of the house, numerous men in spreading white garments and turbans, swarthy Arabs and big negroes. The oldest amongst them have certainly served with the Mahdi. Now they are listening with a deep and reverent attention, as the son of the Mahdi tells me about his father's life.

. . . . .

Sir Abderrahman has invited me to his house, because he has heard that I am engaged on a biography of his father. He wishes to tell me himself about the Mahdi. Actually he has never seen his father; he came into the world twenty-two days after the premature death of Mohammed Ahmed. His mother Maqbula was (and is, for she is still living) of the ancient African royal house of the Dar-Fur Sultans.

## THE MAHDI OF ALLAH

The Mahdi had ten sons and ten daughters, borne by the one hundred wives and concubines in his harem. Of the sons only the two posthumous ones are alive to-day, Abderrahman and his half-brother, Ali.

The Sayid Abderrahman el Mahdi has been educated, after the destruction of the Dervish rule, under English protection. He has always supported the English Government in the Sudan by the great prestige of his name, and the King has bestowed an order on the Mahdi's son, and granted him a knighthood. So he is Sir Abderrahman. He is very wealthy, too. The island of Abba in the White Nile, where the Mahdi used to live in a cave, now belongs to his son, and he runs a huge cotton plantation there, using all the most modern methods. He still owns the cave as well, and often goes there to pray.

The son of the Mahdi is himself considered a holy person all over the Sudan and a great glory radiates from him, on account of his father, whom the Sudan has not forgotten.

As I see him here now, in the forty-fourth year of his life, he looks as the contemporaries have described the Mahdi, big, massive, with a deep black beard round his chin, with manly features and large dreamy eyes. His colour is rather darker than that of the Mahdi must have been, and approaches the deepest shade of old mahogany. Although the lips are very full, there is no trace of the negro in the cut of the fine Arab face. I look curiously at Sir Abderrahman's fine, healthy teeth, to see if he has got that gap between them, which seemed such a portentous sign to the Sudanese when they observed it in their Mahdi. But I do not see it.

Sir Abderrahman is wearing a long dress of a rich silky white fabric and for a turban a white shawl of incredible daintiness. Except for this turban his garb seems to me very much like the everyday dress of the Pope in the Vatican. On his feet he wears European patent leather shoes.

The son of the Mahdi has another house besides this one, a modern European villa in Gordon Avenue, Khartoum. Gordon Avenue! These are the jokes of history. This house here in Omdurman apparently has just this one reception room in

## FROM THE TRAVELLER'S NOTES

European style. Already in the next room, into which I am able to look through an open door, I divine the conservatism of the Orient. The wall which I see is covered with a Turkish carpet; on it is hanging a curved scimitar, all golden.

.    .    .    .    .

After the Sayid has entertained me in ceremonious fashion with lemonade and plum cake and strong tea, very European— my dragoman tells me that the son of the Mahdi is ready to give information about his father: I am to take notes. So I begin to write away, under Sir Abderrahman's vigilant eyes. From time to time he asks me, with much dignity, to read aloud what I have written down. He insists upon my taking everything down properly and accurately. "For," he says, "it is not known in Europe that my father was a good man. If the Khalifa had been as good as he, then the Sudan to-day would still be free!"

"Translate it exactly!" I tell the dragoman, sharply.

"Free," Sherkawi repeats.

.    .    .    .    .

Free? What does the son of the Mahdi mean? I look into his face and find it benign and impenetrable, just like the face of his father, which I also cannot penetrate; I do not know what there is behind that Dervish's smiling mask!

Between Sir Abderrahman and myself stands the barrier of language. I see very well that he would like to understand more directly what I am saying to him. Who might I be? Am I honest? Do I want to be fair to his father, the Mahdi? That I call myself a countryman of Slatin is not altogether encouraging. Slatin suffered so much through the Mahdi.

"Read it!" the Sayid begs, whenever I have written a few pages. He would like to make sure that I have noted it rightly. Then I take up a formal attitude and repeat what he has dictated, translating my German shorthand notes into English. The dragoman says it after me in Arabic.

First of all come the names of the twenty-nine ancestors

of the Mahdi, ascending to the Prophet. The Sayid Abderrahman thinks it important to impress upon me his illustrious descent. Then come details out of the life story of Mohammed Ahmed, some of which are not contained in the books. Eagerly I note down that the Mahdi since his youth had been a Sufi. This gives me a key long sought for. Many things can be explained by the fact of his having been a Sufi: traits in his character that otherwise would have been puzzling.

. . . . .

Whenever I have read a page and the dragoman is translating it, I gain time for thinking and looking about. Often my glance strays into the next room where that curved, golden scimitar hangs. At last the son of the Mahdi notices my glances.

"No," he says, "that is not the sword with which my father conquered the Sudan. . . ."

He explains that the curved scimitar in the next room belongs to his, Sir Abderrahman's, gala dress. He had worn it in London. Yes, he had been to London to pay homage to the King. An Oriental, in doing homage to his overlord, proffers him the hilt of his weapon. The King had touched the hilt of this golden scimitar and then handed it back to his vassal.

"But that is not the sword of my father!"

. . . . .

Suddenly I decide that I must manage to get a look at the actual sword of Mohammed Ahmed—that wonderful, half-mystical sword. Now I remember something I have read: when the Mahdi died, the Khalifa searched long and in vain for this sword. Aisha, the "Mother of the Faithful," the head wife of the Mahdi, had hidden it, to save it for the Mahdi's children.

In order to find out something about this sword I use a trick. I say casually:

"Oh yes, I know, the sword of the Mahdi is exhibited in the Khalifa's Palace. . . ."

I know very well that the weapon which I saw there is not the famous sword, that in that glass case in the Khalifa's house

## FROM THE TRAVELLER'S NOTES

there lies some sabre that the Mahdi is said to have lost in one of his very first fights against the Egyptian troops. But I pretend to believe that this shame had befallen the real sword of the Mahdi.

To prove that this is not true—now, it is my triumph!—the Sayid claps his hands. An old servant appears, kisses his master's hand. The Sayid gives an order and (my heart is standing still) the servant fetches a gleaming something, a tremendous sword, the very sword that Rudolf Slatin was thinking of when he called his book *Fire and Sword in the Sudan*: the sword that conquered half Africa and vanquished Gordon. With a great emotion within me I gaze upon it.

. . . . .

This sword of Mohammed Ahmed, although it is a straight one, looks very strange and barbaric. It is enormously long, its golden hilt is adorned with stars and half-moons; the sheath is also of hammered gold and decorated in the same fashion. Like that Dervish sword that the dealer in the hotel wanted to sell me, this one, seemingly, is flattened out towards the point into a wide rhomboid-shaped end. But as the Sayid draws the sword out of its sheath it does not look so exotic. Indeed, it looks like——

I jump up excitedly. I must see this sword from a shorter distance. I do not ask permission, I bend over it. It looks like the two-handed sword of a German lansquenet of the sixteenth century.

But I see an inscription in Arabic characters on the blade. "A verse out of the Koran?" I ask. "No," says the Sayid, "those are the names of my mother's ancestors, the Dar-Fur Sultans: Sultan Zakkaria, Sultan Ali, Sultan Mohammed el-Fadl. . . . For this sword has been a dowry of my mother, it has been in the crown treasury of the kings of Dar-Fur——"

I am not listening any more. "And this?" I am almost shouting with excitement.

### THE MAHDI OF ALLAH

Beneath the Arabic text on this blade I have seen a clearly engraved relief, an armorial bearing long familiar: the double eagle of the old Holy Roman Empire of the German nation! And now, with staring eyes, I read, on this sword of the Sudanese Mahdi, Gothic letters of the sixteenth century.

Below the imperial double eagle, beautifully engraved, are the words:

VIVAT CAROLUS V.

And further down, in German:

ROEMISCHE KAISER.

. . . . .

At that moment I know what an extraordinary, what a wonderful meaning this must have. I feel certain that it cannot be otherwise: I am holding in my hands the sword of a German warrior, some Crusader who accompanied Charles V on his ill-fated expedition against the Algerian corsairs and who fell on the battlefield. Or else this German knight (for this is a nobleman's sword) was taken prisoner and ended his life miserably as the slave of some Mussulman. What happened to his sword then? What fate may this magnificent weapon have had, what epic adventures—whilst, starting from Algiers, then slowly, slowly, in the course of three hundred years, it wandered through the Sahara, from one half-savage sheikh's tent to another, until at last it came into the treasury of the black kings of the Land of the Fur. . . .

Allah! What an enthralling romantic adventure is Thy world's history!

. . . . .

Immediately afterwards I find myself in a fantastic situation, giving a private lecture on German history to the son of the Mohammedan Messiah of Africa. For the Sayid Abderrahman wants to know exactly what this inscription signifies. Could it be that I am the first German speaker to have seen it again

FROM THE TRAVELLER'S NOTES

after so many centuries! The double eagle is known all over the Sudan from the stamp on the Austrian Maria-Theresa dollars which are still in circulation in this part of Africa. But "Roemische Kaiser"! Why Roman? It is difficult to explain, so I say, briefly, that the Pope of Rome had bestowed this honorary title upon the German kings. At this the Sayid nods. That he understands. He has, of course, heard of the Pope in Rome.

. . . . .

And now I do some questioning. The son of the Mahdi knows the history of his part of Africa better than I do.

So his mother, Maqbula, was of the house of those black kings who for five centuries ruled in Dar-Fur on the border of the Sahara. Her father, Sultan Nurein, was the brother of that great King Mohammed el-Hassin. After him reigned Sultan Ibrahim and Hassib-Allah, but in the late 'seventies the slave-dealer Zubeir Pasha suddenly and in peace-time attacked the Empire of the Fur, to conquer it for Egypt.

I take notes for myself.

. . . . .

While I sit like this opposite the Mahdi's son and write things in my notebook, I picture to myself mentally a scene which once must have happened.

A man, who perhaps looked exactly like his son here (no portraits of the Mahdi exist), is sitting in a tent or more probably in a round hut with a conical roof. Clean matting covers the floor. The smiling Mahdi is sitting on an *angareb*, a wooden bedstead, strung with elastic hide thongs. No, the Mahdi could not have looked then like his son is now. He was younger at that time, still lean from his fasting, and he was still wearing his mean Dervish dress.

Outside, I imagine to myself, lies the camp of the rebellious band that is besieging El Obeid. Up to now the Mahdi has achieved nothing but a local revolt. He has not yet occupied any of the more important towns of the Sudan and large parts of the country have not as yet declared for him. Perhaps the whole movement would remain a mere riot against the tax collectors, a fanatical outburst of religious ranting....

And now this embassy comes from Dar-Fur. What a sensation in the camp! This is no everyday happening—some Bedouin sheikh or Arab slave-dealer coming to join the Mahdi. The royal house of Dar-Fur, although recently overthrown, still enjoys great esteem. If a lady of this house is brought into the Mahdi's camp, it signifies more than just an affair of the harem; it is a great act of Oriental diplomacy. No doubt Dar-Fur is going to revolt with the Mahdi against the Egyptians; Slatin, the Khedive's governor, will have to look out....

I can see the scene in the hut: the eternally smiling Mahdi squatting on the *angareb,* and the ambassadors from Dar-Fur being presented to him—big, dark men in the garb of the nobles of the eastern Sahara, that is, in blue and white silk shirts, and with turbans made of Kashmir shawls loosely wrapped round their heads; they enter carrying many gifts, and a black eunuch, enormous in his oozing fat, stands beside a completely veiled young woman who smells of sandal-wood and of the liquid butter with which most certainly her deeply hidden hair has been anointed.

I see the scene: these men, very grave and dignified, all kiss the Mahdi's hand (while the Sultan's daughter stands quietly there, trembling a little beneath her veils, though, for sure, she likes the lord whom she is going to serve). Now pious locutions are interchanged, the quotations from the Koran, the invocations to Allah and His Prophet. Now the gifts are delivered up; the old sword of the kings of Dar-Fur is reverently taken out of its wrappings. A splendour of gold fills the whole hut.

Does the Mahdi perhaps kiss the sword? Must he not recognise in it an omen of coming victory?

One of the men of Dar-Fur, no doubt, tells the Mahdi about this sword. He does not know about the German knight who owned it, but he will praise the Frankish origin of the blade; all good weapons come from the lands of the Franks. But this sword, which from now on the Mahdi is to wield against the

FROM THE TRAVELLER'S NOTES

infidels, has been for centuries the weapon of Mussulman princes; as long as the kingdom of the Fur has existed, it has been among the most carefully guarded, almost sacred weapons of the King, each one of which was always looked after by a special dignitary of the realm: the shield of Sultan Suleiman Solon (this much venerated shield was adorned with tiny bells), then the seven ancient spears, then the curious throwing-iron and the first firelock ever introduced into the country.

The old man who now brings the royal sword of Dar-Fur to the Mahdi as a dowry of the royal princess must have been the hereditary guardian of the sword. Whenever the Sultan had to show himself in public, this guardian brought the sword to him. Once a year, on the feast of the kettledrum, the black King used to ride, clothed all in silk, with a conical silver helmet on his head, his face veiled with a silk *litham*, on his charger overloaded with golden ornaments, through the ranks of the army, amidst the wild din of the sacred drums. Beneath his scarlet saddle-cloth the long, straight sword protruded, fixed at a peculiar angle, and the King's left foot was propped against it.

.   .   .   .   .

I look at the Mahdi's son, trying to picture to myself how his father might have looked when the ambassadors from Dar-Fur brought him the Crusader's sword as an earnest of approaching victory; and then again I seek in the face of Abderrahman for the features of his mother. It vexes me strongly that I know so very little about the Mahdi's wives. Well, I have got their names—nearly seventy names of wives and concubines. (There were a hundred women in the Mahdi's house when he died.) Of his five legal wives (one died in Gadir, four were left as widows when the Mahdi died) three were called Fatima and two Aisha; Fatima, Aisha, Amina, Zainab —these are again and again the names of the concubines, daughters of Arab sheikhs who wished to ally themselves more closely to the Mahdi, and daughters of slain pashas, spoils of victory; women from Khartoum, from the Gesireh, from

Dongola, from Abyssinia. How did they look? What were they like? Did they love the Mahdi? It is impossible to know anything of a Mussulman's wives! It is impossible to ask questions about them, I know; I may not talk about Sir Abderrahman's mother, I can never see her, although she is alive and perhaps listening at this moment in the next room. . . .

And yet I am aware that I could only understand the real inner life of the Mahdi if I knew more about this huge harem, in which he was so entirely different, in which, from the lean revolutionary, he was metamorphosed into the fat and pampered potentate.

. . . . .

My notebook is full; and the master of the house has offered me that cup of coffee which, according to Arab custom, signifies the polite dismissal of the guest.

As, in taking my leave, I shake his hand, a strong black hand with manicured finger-nails, I feel real sympathy with the son of the Mahdi. It is not, certainly, an easy job to be the son of a disavowed prophet. Although the English conquerors, in their wisdom, have treated the Mahdi's son with much kindness, although he is called Sir Abderrahman and owns cotton plantations—do I not feel that his heart is entirely attached to the memory of his father, whom he never saw, but in whom, certainly, he still believes to this day?

And so I leave the English knight, Sir Abderrahman el Mahdi, holding in his hands the great golden sparkling sword of his father, the Teutonic Crusader's sword with which the Expected Mahdi tried to conquer the Universe.

# THE MAHDI OF ALLAH

## THE STORY OF THE DERVISH MOHAMMED AHMED

## THE MESSENGER

A RACING camel of the noblest breed was striding through the endless desert. It carried a messenger. Mohammed el Mahdi, the great Sheikh of the Senussi, was sending a message to Mohammed el Mahdi in the Sudan.

. . . . .

The founder of the mighty sect which has countless followers, from Mecca to the farthest west of African Islam, Sidi Mohammed ben Ali es-Senussi, had died about the same time as the Dervish Mohammed Ahmed on Abba Island had begun to dream strange dreams. The great Sheikh of the Senussi Order had in dying proclaimed his son as his successor and spoken certain prophetic words. The time, he said, was accomplished and the hour was near; in the year 1300 of the Flight the Expected Mahdi would perhaps appear to the world. The signs, the dying man intimated, pointed to his beloved son.

"Then he is the Expected Mahdi?" the wise ones of the Fourth Degree, the exalted "mujteheds," asked their dying master.

"The knowledge is with God!" he sighed, and expired.

. . . . .

His son Mohammed, the second Sheikh of the Senussiya, was now called by his followers Sidi Mohammed el Mahdi. He did not object to this added surname, but himself never claimed to be the Expected Mahdi. According to the teachings of the first Senussi, the Expected One was not to recognise himself; he would be recognised by a grateful world, perhaps late, perhaps not till after his death. The man who by his good works had changed the world—*he* was the Mahdi, by that he would be recognised. The man who was so saintly that all others learned to live God-fearing lives, who spread precious gifts around him, industry, prosperity, the joy of verdant gardens, the dignity of honest labour—that one would be recognised as the Mahdi. No prophets and no angels were to be expected to descend from heaven to tell the Chosen of Allah: *Thou* art the Mahdi! A world made happier would proclaim it of itself.

But least of all, the Senussi taught, was the Mahdi going to carry a bloody sword. He would be recognised by the fact that his empire came without violence or bloodshed.

Perhaps, as the Senussi brethren hoped, the time was now near. In the year 1300 of Mohammed's Flight, the founder of the sect had prophesied. . . . Now this year was already approaching (in the European calendar it would be 1883), when suddenly there came to the Senussi at Jerhbub a messenger from a man in the Sudan, declaring that the Mahdi had already appeared, that he was beginning the Holy War to conquer the world, and that the Senussi Sheikh himself should carry a banner, not as the Mahdi, but as a lieutenant of the Mahdi, as his third khalifa, in the war of extermination against three-quarters of mankind.

The second Sheikh of the Senussi, whom his people

## THE MESSENGER

had hopefully called the Mahdi and who had never yet dared to say that he was really the Expected One —decided, loyal to his own doctrine, that the pretensions of this Dongolese Dervish would have to be examined. Perhaps his works showed him to be the Mahdi? Perhaps around him the world was beginning to be made happier?

So the Senussi Sheikh sent the wisest old man of the council of his order to carry out the endless journey across the great Desert as a delegate of the Senussiya to the Expected Mahdi—if he was the Mahdi. The wise delegate was to recognise him by his works.

.　　.　　.　　.　　.

The monastic community of Jerhbub, where the Senussi Sheikh lived, was established in the land of Benghazi, west of that oasis of Siwa in which Alexander the Great listened to the voice of Jupiter Ammon. In Jerhbub, near the sacred tomb of the first Senussi, was the pious settlement, the Sheikh's palace, the cells of the brethren of the order, the house for the many pilgrims, the hut of the learned theologians and of the travelling scholars who had come from the whole world of Islam to learn the Senussi doctrine. Here the sect had its brilliant centre, its principal mosque, the beloved Sepulchre, the far-famed Academy of the Faith. But the envoy, riding towards the south, found in almost every oasis of the Great Desert a branch of the order. In the Oasis of Kufara he saw the brethren pray and, after the fashion of the Senussi, tend their groves of date-palms. In the solitary wilds east of Tibesti wild robbers assaulted him—and became, by a secret sign, his most zealous servants and friends. A horde of wandering Tuaregs made him welcome in their red leather tents; he was the most honoured guest of these ferocious masters of the Sea of Sand. He travelled on; the difficult paths of the desert opened as if by magic to him and to his *mehari* camel. For the messenger of the Senussi Sheikh the Sahara had no dangers. Without once unveiling his face, the old man, touching the Borku territory, came on to Wadai. Sultan Ali, the black-brown King of Wadai, the most powerful ruler on the Sahara border, was affiliated to the Senussiya, and one of the Fathers of the Fourth Degree was welcome in his kingdom. But the messenger of the Senussi Sheikh scarcely rested at the king's court and rode out again into the wilderness, ever onwards.

. . . . .

This traveller on the beautiful light-coloured she-camel wore, beneath the white burnous, the civilized dress of the Tunisian coast-dwellers; beneath the *litham*, the black face-veil of the Tuareg that veiled his mouth and nose, there was the face of a white man. This was no barbarian: a Mediterranean, grandson of Carthaginians, of Romans, of the Spanish Moors. Certainly he must have learned French in Tunis or Algiers. The Senussi knew enough of Europe—to reject it. Long ago they had understood the danger of subjugation that was threatening North Africa and all the countries of Islam. To save Islam and to convert to it all the negro world, was their aim.

But the old man, who was now riding across Africa alone, as the ambassador of a great idea, represented an Islam as the Western world once knew it, the Islam of the Spanish Moors. He was—perhaps he ignored it himself—the ambassador of the Islam which built

THE MESSENGER

the Alhambra, to the other which burnt the library of Alexandria; an ambassador from holy peace to holy war, from the light to the flame.

Did the messenger himself know what his message meant? And that it came too late? He rode on.

. . . .

This wise old man—for only the highest wisdom secures the highest rank in the Senussiya—forgot the length of the way and of the time in thinking and praying. Again and again he recited the sequence of prayers that the Senussi Sheikh had drawn up for his people: "The Great Rose" and "The Little Rose."

He prayed:

"God pardon me" one hundred times in succession.

Then: "There is no god but God and Mohammed is His Prophet, every glance and every breath is known to Him . . ." three hundred times in succession.

Then again the rider on the camel recited to himself the elegant Arabic verses which he had composed on the way in praise of his holy master, the Senussi Sheikh, and also of the beauty of his steed, the white she-camel. These verses he planned, if God granted him a safe return, to recite in the Jerhbub cloister, after having kissed the Sheikh's hand and prayed the Fatt'hah with him.

Trotting over the bleached sands of a desert valley, one morning after a rest near a brackish well—the she-camel had drunk, thanks to the Compassionate, and was fresh again—the envoy of the Senussi spoke the whole poem to himself.

. . . .

"In obeying the chosen Saint of God I desired to win pardon for my sins.

"Therefore I crossed the vales and the sand-hills of the desert; hardship I did not fear.

"I was riding a young she-camel, whose steps left tracks in the sands like the furrows of a plough. Quickly she runs over the highest hills.

"I mounted her at the hour when the sky was becoming grey like my own temples; and thanks to my swift steed the farthest lands became quite near.

"She was generated by two noble animals from the Hedjaz who used to race through the desert plains, where the ostriches run and the stars mirror themselves in the glittering salt."

. . . . .

"Whenever the poet sings his song, his camel presses her pace.

"The sultry breath of the noontide did not paralyse my zeal; I rode always more swiftly. Light-heartedly I climbed the sand-hills and the tread of my animal enlivened the desert valleys.

"O friends, do not lament that I am so far, for I am in safety.

"Why should he fear who serves the Holy One, whose prayers are the safest protection?

"Am I not like the diver who leaps into the floods to fetch the pearl? He also is risking his life for the sake of the desired treasure;

"Just as I am seeking hardship, in order to gain the reward . . ."

. . . .

The veiled man on the camel, the lonely poet in the desert, involuntarily stimulated his animal to a still swifter pace, as if he were intent on showing his sacred zeal very clearly to his distant master. "Yes," he felt, while reciting to himself the next verses of his poem, "great is the reward of my hardships! I shall come back"—he felt—"I shall live out my evening in the community of friends of whom I may be proud; we shall propagate the work of the Senussi, which is beautifying the earth of Islam . . ."

"O God——," he recited.

"O God, grant me the triumph of the return to Jerhbub!

"I implore Thee, grant my prayers, direct my steps back to the company of my friends!

"They have made Syria verdant once more; the palms of Egypt do not wither, because the Senussi tend them.

"The monasteries of the Senussi community are shining stars in a black night.

"Restless caravans press on towards them from the farthest lands.

"The wisdom of the Senussi Sheikh wells up like cool water with which a man quenches his thirst.

"His hand refreshes like blessed rain.

"Oh, to press my hot forehead against that blessing hand!"

The old man on the swift camel was travelling all the time farther and farther from the place he was yearning for. But he would return home, he felt it, he was going to kiss his master's hand, to say to him: "It is not true, nobody is like thee . . ."

. . . . .

Riding along the great caravan road from Lake Chad to the White Nile, the envoy passed the borders of Wadai, entered Dar-Fur and at last Kordofan. Here, in the western provinces of the Egyptian Sudan (but were they still Egyptian?) he found everywhere war and rebellion, fire and devastation. In Dar-Fur the Governor Slatin Bey was waging a desperate war against the Dervish hordes and the rebellious Arab tribes; he was still holding his own. In Kordofan the Mahdi's army had been beleaguering El Obeid for many months. As the envoy of the Senussi drew nearer he heard that the city had capitulated; the Dongolawi had conquered. Who could doubt now that he was the Expected Mahdi?

Through a burning country, dying and reeking of death, the white she-camel walked. In deserted, plundered villages hyenas were gnawing at human skeletons. One day the veiled rider saw a swarm of black vultures in flight. They were flying above a whitewashed mosque, above houses and huts: a cloud of carrion vultures between the blue sky and El Obeid.

· · · ·

The capital of Kordofan—an almost endless zigzag of peaked huts round the fortified citadel, containing the house of the Egyptian Mudir. Here, too, were situated the houses of the Greek traders who, from El Obeid, supplied gum arabic to the whole civilised world. Besides that, there was a Roman Catholic Mission with numerous nuns and priests.

The siege of El Obeid lasted a very long time; Mohammed Pasha Said (the same old colonel who had once let the Mahdi escape) had held the fortress until the hunger was too much to endure. Unclean things had been eaten: cats, rats, ants, and finally gum and the leather straps of the Sudanese bedsteads. In the last weeks little children had disappeared from many houses.

## THE MESSENGER

Now the red Turkish crescent flag waved no longer from the citadel. One day the people of El Obeid had seen their high and mighty Pasha riding through the streets, dressed in a Dervish shirt; in this fashion he had gone into the Mahdi's camp to surrender, followed by his beys and effendis, all the traders, every light-coloured face, every Turk, shivering and trembling, in new Dervish shirts.

The smiling Mahdi had received them graciously in his camp and had promised his pardon to all of them. But in the meantime the Baggara horsemen of Abdullahi were already busy plundering their houses.

The gold in the Pasha's house was too well hidden. For a long time the place where it had been hidden in the wall was not discovered. The Pasha, the poor old Turkish fogy, denied that he ever possessed a treasure. When, through a betrayal, it was finally found, the Pasha died by the axe. The Mahdi pardoned him once; but ought not a man converted to the Mahdi to renounce worldly goods and vain gold?

But the blood of this old man was just a tiny red wavelet in the bloody ocean that was flooding the Sudan.

. . . .

The city of El Obeid in the hands of the wild Bedouins and of the black slave soldiers of the Mahdi's army meant babies sucking in vain at the breasts of mothers who had died of starvation—so cold, so cold! It meant human spectres grubbing in the dirt to see if they could not find a remnant of the gums which the traders had buried; it meant hyenas feeding by daylight in the deserted lanes, and cries of tortured people who refused to yield up the hidden dollars to the Khalifa's treasure house; and the dead body of Father Losi, dragged from its grave because a Dervish had thought there was treasure in the graves of the Christian missionaries; and mutilated men, soldiers of the Mahdi, who had lost a hand or a leg as punishment for some crime; and people being flogged, receiving eighty lashes for drinking a pot of merissa or a hundred because they had been caught smoking.

El Obeid in the hands of the Mahdi's army: it meant a God-seeker with a kindly, loving, salvation-bringing smile, wrapped in purity and goodly perfumes, who did good deeds and spoke good words, now pardoning a trembling wretch of a Turk, now saving Roman Catholic nuns from violation, who distributed bounteous alms, who fed the starving; and it meant also Abdullahi, the Khalifa, the Baggara, whose dark soldier's figure loomed up more and more bluffly behind the kindly Mahdi's back; it meant the Remington rifles, the excellent guns, which Abdullahi had looted in such large quantities; it meant the banners, the drums of Holy War; war against Khartoum, war against Cairo, against England, against the whole world. Instead of the red flag of Egypt, the red flag of a world-wide conflagration had been hoisted over El Obeid. A benevolent, smiling friend of God and of mankind, with the light of exalted vision in his eyes shining with unearthly brilliance, was marching forward; behind him followed hunger, plague, processions of yoked slaves and swarms of bloated vultures.

· · · · ·

A messenger with a veiled face rode on a white camel through the stinking streets of El Obeid. At a well his camel knelt and drank. He drank himself. He spoke a long prayer: "Guide us to the path of those," his prayer ended, "with whom Thou art not angry, and who go not astray. Amen."

After the camel had drunk its fill, the envoy of the Senussi Sheikh climbed once more into the saddle; for he had decided to start off at once on the return journey back to his master. He had seen everything and had found out everything. He decided not even to spend the night in El Obeid; if he started at once he could already put behind him a part of the long homeward journey. He knew of a water-hole some way out of the town where he would be able to rest without smelling the revolting stench of corpses, and without hearing the howling of tortured human beings. There he would camp that night; the next day he would begin the journey back to Jerhbub. He had seen enough of the Mahdieh of the Dervish Mohammed Ahmed . . .

Over the sandhills of the desert the white she-camel would carry him; across the desert valleys her nimble hoofs would draw long furrows.

The veiled man, the envoy of the Senussi Sheikh, carried this message back to Jerhbub:

"No, this is not the Expected Mahdi!"

## THE BATTLE

Gustav came from Berlin; Gustav was a bright lad. He'd smelt a rat long ago. The show was going all queer. Rotten from beginning to end. Not for him, thanks—he wasn't having any. No fear!

Before it came to a battle, under *these* conditions, Gustav Klootz would rather go over to the blessed Mahdi. The devil probably wouldn't be as black as he was painted. He wouldn't eat him alive, anyhow. You just got there and spouted something about Allah and all that——

.   .   .   .   .

Klootz—Gustav Adolph Klootz—was, to be sure, in the so-called army of General Hicks, which was advancing from Khartoum against the Dervishes with the object of recapturing El Obeid from them, if it could.

Klootz had actually once been a Prussian sergeant in the Uhlan Guards—not the particular pride of that famous regiment, it is to be feared. Since then—what had been the subsequent course of his career? History, in which Gustav Adolph Klootz, too, has his little place, is silent about the exact why and wherefore of his journey to Africa. Probably Seckendorff had simply taken him with him—Major Freiherr von Seckendorff, the fair-haired giant with the beard *à la* Crown Prince Frederick, who was now marching with Hicks Pasha's

A WARRIOR OF THE MAHDI
From the painting by Leo Diet

## THE BATTLE

unlucky crew on this excursion across the desolate Sudan. When history first looked upon the freckled countenance of Gustav Klootz (it was a young countenance, framed in flaxen hair, and his nose was peeling in that infernal heat)—Gustav Klootz was serving in the capacity of batman to the Major. But then they had a row; Klootz gave notice—or else he caught Herr von Seckendorff's boot against some portion of his anatomy. At any rate, one thing is certain: he now became the servant of some kind of newspaper man—Mr. O'Donovan, Correspondent of the *Daily News*. You see, whatever might have been wanting in Hicks Pasha's army, it had its War Correspondents. There was another one—Mr. Power. He represented *The Times* (but then he got ill and stayed out of the expedition; lucky for him!). And Vizetelly, the draughtsman—he had to make pictures for the *Graphic*. The London public wanted to read war reports about the destruction of that wicked Mahdi.

So Gustav was serving under O'Donovan. But he was not liking the look of things at all.

. . . .

Gustav Klootz was an old soldier and knew what an army was. As for these people——

All very well—these war correspondents to describe victories. . . . But then, who was going to get the victory? This General Hicks, with the fiery moustache gone white, a pensioned Sepoy officer from India, might be a fine fellow—only what did he know about Africa? Since the year before, when the British Army of Occupation had settled accounts with Arabi Pasha so amazingly quickly and squashed the rebels, together with the entire Egyptian national army—people in

Cairo probably believed that all Englishmen could practise magic. If you made a pensioned English colonel into a general and raked up another half-dozen gentlemen who were willing to lend a hand—what could the Mahdi do? Colonel Farquhar as Chief of the Staff; Majors von Seckendorff, Massey, Warner, and Herlth. Herlth was an Austrian; Captain Matyuga was apparently a Croat. Moritz Brody, however, was a former non-commissioned officer in the British Royal Horse Artillery; now his title was lieutenant, and he was supposed to understand all about the guns. Four small mountain-guns, four real Krupps, six Nordenfelt machine-guns. All right. Besides that, the two doctors—one Greek, and Rosenberg, staff surgeon. All right. A few miscellaneous Europeans who knew something about the soldiering business had been found unofficially, for officially Old England wasn't sending any soldiers to the Sudan—Gladstone had had enough of the Egyptian mess. The Khedive would have to see about smashing the Mahdi himself. The British Army of Occupation wasn't there for that purpose, so the Prime Minister of England had declared.

So General Hicks's army was organized in Egyptian style: of the troops of the rebel Arabi, who at Tel El-Kebir had bolted in every direction before Wolseley's British, after barely forty minutes' fighting, a thousand had been rounded up again and fastened up with chains—poor yellow fellaheen—and had been dispatched up the Nile; they'd do, probably, only they *would* keep weeping the whole way up. Not till they got to the Sudan were the chains taken off the legs of these heroes. Poor Hicks, when he had to try and turn this blubbering herd into soldiers, received a pretty shock. Not one of them could shoot properly; they'd have been more effective armed with sticks than with real rifles. And the Egyptian officers! The scum of a routed soldiery; full of hatred against that Khedive in whose name they were supposed to fight, and against the Europeans who commanded them. The black Sudanese troops which Hicks levied in Khartoum were at least sturdy men. Only they had a superstitious idea about the Mahdi; you couldn't know whether these mercenaries would remain loyal—even if they were really paid; but General Hicks had received no money from Cairo and he couldn't pay them.

Order of battle of the 8th September, eighteen hundred and eighty-three, at Khartoum before marching: General Hicks, nine European officers, the rest worthless; seven thousand infantrymen, four hundred Anatolian bashi-bazouks, mounted (phew! what a rabble!). A hundred other horsemen in chain-armour; in addition, five hundred irregulars, Arabs on camels, strongly suspected of Mahdist sympathies; two thousand slaves, negro women and Greek merchants by way of extra baggage; six thousand camels.

"Gustav, my boy," Klootz had thought to himself at the very start, "you bet your life—there's going to be the devil of a nasty mess!"

. . . . . .

History throws its searchlight on the freckled face of Gustav Klootz, but leaves his mate, the other young German, in total darkness. It is only known that there *was* another German, a Saxon German, in Hicks Pasha's camp—a batman like Klootz, possibly in the service of the Austrian bimbashi Herlth. One day—to be exact, on the 20th October—six weeks after the army marched out from Khartoum, these two Germans were occupied in putting up the tents for their masters at a new encampment which had just been established in the neighbourhood of Rahad. For once there was some water available, too much even—a huge, swampy pond full of mosquitoes. A *zariba* had been built— a high hedge of thorns, which enclosed the camp. That meant that one would rest here several days before the advance on El Obeid was undertaken. They weren't very far from there now. "Too damn near," Klootz said to himself.

Six weeks they had been on the march. Little to eat, nothing to drink. Thirst and nothing but thirst. The Arab guides they had with them were a scoundrelly lot. ("If they haven't been bought by the Mahdi, then I'll be damned," said Gustav to the Saxon.) Even if a good way existed, they were sure to lead you by a bad one. Through thorny woods, through tall grass, just nicely missing the water-holes: those worthy guides never knew where there was any water. You marched and marched and died of thirst. No fighting—and yet the place was crawling with Dervishes. You hardly left a camp before they were all over it. At the rare water-holes lay filth and refuse left there by men who must have only just disappeared. The Dervishes infested the woods, dodging in and out of the bushes. You knew they were there, yet you rarely caught sight of one: they were like invisible mocking demons hovering on your flanks while you were being decoyed into God knows what inferno. Sometimes you heard a shot, sometimes you found a sentry with his throat cut; and in the vanguard there was at times a kind of highly suspicious moving to and fro of irregulars. So-called allies, brown sheikhs, followed by

## THE BATTLE

savage horsemen, would suddenly come dashing up; there they were—bosom friends of the guides—hurrah! They were going to help . . . Then suddenly they were off again—yes, but where to? At that very moment the generals were waiting for five hundred Baggara tribesmen who had faithfully promised to join them at that place; it was on their account that the camp was being pitched there.

Gustav Klootz said to his pal, the Saxon: "If they come, then I'll be——"

"If *anybody* comes," he said, "it'll be the Dervishes."

Everywhere you noticed them, smelt them. Thousands and thousands of them! The whole place was lousy with Dervishes, that was the truth! Ten Dervishes for one of Hicks's men; and it was not true that they had no arms—they had good rifles, guns, and everything! There were lots of men who had already served in the army, old soldiers, who were on their side now—much better men that Hicks's swinish riff-raff. Gustav's O'Donovan wasn't such a fool; he was always writing in his articles "the Gyppies are no earthly good, the Egyptian will never make a soldier; but the blacks are splendid!" If a single spotted Dervish shirt came in sight, the Gyppies ran, especially their worthy officers!

Gustav Klootz spat on the ground, so much did he despise those cowards. But wasn't he actually pale himself? Now and again he drew his hand across his throat. That's how the Dervishes would put an end to you, *like that*! No escape. One hadn't a dog's chance!

. . . . .

History shows Gustav Klootz (and a vague outline of his pal, the Saxony man), still on that same day, in the wood outside the *zariba*. The two had passed the chain of sentries, had shouted something to a stupid Fellah soldier: they had got to go and get wood. . . . Perhaps they did really only intend to collect wood for the camp-fires; they had their axes with them, and their rifles. Klootz was wearing (it is recorded on the Tablets of History) an extremely dirty cotton uniform, and there was a red fez on top of his bright young head.

Then—what happened? Did they both intend to do it? Or not? Had they planned together to try and get away—not exactly to the Dervishes, but only away, away from that camp of death? To hide in the forest perhaps, then see if they could struggle through to the Nile; there were ships there, at any rate, and, if they had a bit of luck, they might be in Cairo by Christmas, or, who knew, even back at home with dear old mother . . .

Then, perhaps, while both were still wavering, there was a shot. Had the sentry fired? Who else could it have been? The monkeys chased in terror through the branches overhead. Then the two men suddenly started running—but not in the same direction. The Saxon was suddenly seized with the fear of the Unknown. Or else he had not been serious about that plan . . . could not, after all, leave his chief in the lurch, and all the others. . . . Good Saxon, vague Saxon! He ran for all he was worth back to the camp. But Klootz ran forwards, into the deep forest; he was going to hide, they weren't going to get him; he was clearing out of that mess, he was not going to be done in with the others, oh no, not Gustav, thanks—he wasn't having any!

After he had drifted about a little, he fell into the greedy hands of the Baggara tribesmen, who were

## THE BATTLE

swarming in large numbers round the Egyptian camp. And just as one of these fellows lifted up his tremendous Crusader's sword, Klootz was saved by his three words of broken Arabic:

"Me Dervish! Where Dervish! Me Dervish! To Dervish!"

And:

"Mohammed, Mohammed. Me Mohammed!"

.     .     .     .     .

Fourteen days later Gustav Klootz of Berlin was standing——

No, Gustav Klootz existed no more. And where was Berlin? *Mustafa* was standing—

The Baggaras had brought the prisoner to El Obeid, to the Mahdi. They would not have taken the trouble to do that if Gustav had spoken Arabic a little better and told them who he was. So (how could they know?) they had taken this batman in his dirty jacket for something big; anyhow, he was an Englishman, and in that case——?

At the city gate an excited crowd had shouted:

"Hicks Pasha! No, Gordon! No, Queen Victoria's husband!"

(He was all bloodstained from the blows he had received; his feet were completely swollen and the cord round his neck had choked him horribly; he had thought, "It's all up with you now, my boy!")

In a tent, before a man who kept smiling, he had fallen on the ground like a sack. He had just been able to groan "Me Dervish!" The Mahdi—for it was, of course, the Mahdi—had said something long. Then they had gone to fetch somebody—a Greek, who had spoken French to Gustav. He could not understand a word. Then another one had come; he had looked at Gustav, and said a few words in English. Then suddenly it dawned upon Gustav: the fellow spoke German.

Yes, it was Ohrwalder, the Tyrolese missionary—also a prisoner of the Mahdi, also in the shirt with the coloured patches.

The priest had interpreted the question: whether Hicks had a strong army, how many guns he had, and who was stronger—the Mahdi or Hicks?

Gustav had told everything, everything. And, in the pauses, had kept muttering in abject terror:

"Me Dervish!"

The poor priest had had to ask whether Gustav would become a Mohammedan. Instantly he had said "yes"—and how willingly!

"Gustav is the name of this Englishman from Germany?" the smiling Mahdi had said to the priest. "Gustav—Mustafa! Tell him that his name is now Mustafa. But first he must say, 'There is no god but Allah——'"

. . . . .

Well, and now Mustafa was standing, a fortnight later, under an enormous forest tree—and how miserable the poor man felt! He was, of course, now wearing a Dervish shirt; and the little cap made of palm straw looked very odd planted on that blond Nordic skull. He was Mustafa, and a slave of Abdullahi, the Khalifa; and his master had taken him into the battle with him. Even now the bullets from the machine-guns were rattling amongst the branches of the trees; but of course those Gyppies were shooting too high!

Gustav did not know whether he wouldn't rather they shot better. Pah! Mustafa—a Dervish!

## THE BATTLE

Running by the side of his master's white horse, Gustav the Dervish (or was he Mustafa the Prussian?) had entered this wood of parched thorny trees, into which they had successfully enticed Hicks, like a fly into a spider's web. One thing Klootz had found out for certain during those fourteen days; although it had been very silly of him to go over to the savages—it was better to peg out (he knew that now)—there was no doubt that he had been right: there was no hope for Hicks! The priest might still go on hoping and praying —he was no soldier and knew nothing about it. The former Prussian Uhlan understood only too well what the Dervish spies had reported on that day: the ill-fated army was marching into an appalling trap! Those villainous guides—Klootz had known it all along —had all been spies of the Mahdi! The irregulars were sending messages daily to El Obeid! Many of the Egyptian beys were traitors—oh well, it was only because they were in such a funk. (All the same, Mustafa was morally revolted, and said so to the priest, from whom he got the evil news.) Every guide a traitor, part of the troops long since won over to the Mahdi— in this way the so-called army advanced from Rahad towards El Obeid; now they would soon be there, there was only this beastly thorny wood to get through. "Then," old Hicks probably thought to himself, "then we shall be near enough to capture El Obeid, and everything will be all right . . ."

There were seventy thousand Dervishes hiding in that wood.

.   .   .   .

A fact is a fact! When a non-commissioned officer of the Uhlan Guards sees a good soldier he knows him. This Khalifa was a good soldier.

A black monster, cruel and malicious, so they all said; always quick to order executions and have people whipped and mutilated the whole day long—but a fighter!

Once, when the Khalifa was again questioning him through Father Ohrwalder, Gustav had tried to frighten him; General Hicks, he had said, was not to be despised; and his cannon—four real Krupps! And the Nordenfelt machine-guns! They could mow down whole ranks of men!

"Death is the reward that the Ansari desires!" was all Abdullahi had said. And he had looked as if he meant it.

. . . . .

In the clearing in the great forest, as the bullets began to fly, Gustav Klootz saw the Mahdi pray, and then draw a great sword from its golden sheath.

But Gustav Klootz did not know that it was the sword of a German Crusader.

With the flashing sword in his hand, the Mahdi remained standing in the middle of the clearing. His Ansar all saw him there, as they rushed howling against the enemy.

The banners of the three khalifas, the great copper kettledrums, the frightful bellowing of the hollow elephant tusk that was blown near Abdullahi, the wild emirs—Wad en-Nejumi, Yakub——

"*Allahu akbar! Allahu akbar!*"

. . . . .

On the day after the battle Gustav Klootz was quite alone in that terrible wood. Although belief in the Mahdi rendered the Ansar invulnerable in battle, many had fallen, and there were a lot of wounded men in the camp. They were the ones—it was declared—who did not yet know how to speak properly the prayers of the new Mahdi Prayer Book (the Ratib). As a European, Mustafa was reputed, as a matter of course, to be a doctor. Perhaps he had himself professed to be one. The Khalifa had sent him back to the battlefield to collect bandages and medicines. The corpses of the beaten Egyptians had been plundered over and over again, the boxes and cases broken open; but immense booty still lay strewn among the bushes in the wood.

Poor Klootz, Gustav, Mustafa! A deserter, a bit of a traitor, a coward—well, yes. But now, so utterly alone in that dreadful wood, in which the bodies lay about, unburied. He found bandages enough—but what other things besides! There was the spot where the last square had been battered down by the Dervish masses. Not the whole army had run into the bushes at the first cry of "Allah"! . . . Round the European leaders there had been something of a tough kernel, which had put up a fight. Well, there they lay, in three huge mounds of dead bodies, spread over a distance of two miles. Klootz, the soldier, read the ghastly story out of the battlefield: the first attack; resistance, orderly retreat. The Dervishes once more make way for the well-formed square of the disciplined troops; these march on through the forest—into a second trap. Now the last remaining order is shattered; but the leader's flag is still flying; round it a remnant of wounded fugitives manage to make their way towards the huts of Kashgeil village. Probably they are seeking water. . . .

At a place not far from Kashgeil, where giant trees had provided a little cover, Mustafa found most of the bodies. Almost all the Europeans he had known in the army had got as far as this alive, and had been struck down in the final assault of the overwhelming enemy. And there they all lay now, in one heap. He could not mistake the gigantic Seckendorff, although the head with the beard *à la* Crown Prince was missing from the long corpse which lay there naked in the brushwood. There lay Hicks, also headless, and Herlth, completely ripped open, so that the bowels were oozing out. And Matyuga, Farquhar, Dr. Rosenberg!

They must all have fought like wild beasts. For a long time Mustafa could not find his master, the Correspondent of the *Daily News*. Then he saw a leather case in a bush—an object which was perfectly familiar to him; the case in which O'Donovan's manuscripts used to be—but, hullo! they were still there!

Mustafa drew the sheets of paper out; they were spattered with blood; and then, still deeper in the thorny undergrowth, he found something unspeakable; little pieces of Mr. O'Donovan. . . . Torn to pieces, chewed to bits by hyenas. . . .

Gustav Klootz rushed away, shouting, with the leather case. After a while, in the midst of his running and groaning and panting, an idea passed through this poor devil's head; he stood still, recovered his breath and began to read eagerly in the sheets of paper which were O'Donovan's diary. Surely *his* name must be mentioned there. . . .

Quite right—there it was, on October 20th; Klootz. "Klootz has run away," was written in the correspondent's war diary. Klootz understood that much English, at any rate. He deciphered some more:

"What must be the condition of our army when even

## THE BATTLE

a European servant finds it necessary to desert to these savages?"

And right at the end:

"Here I am, making my notes and writing my reports—but who is going to take them home?"

. . . . .

Klootz did not take them home—the notes, the case, and O'Donovan's bloodstained mackintosh—but brought them, sure enough, to Father Ohrwalder. For the story, which was preserved in a few lines of the dead reporter's war reports, the priest's good memory must be thanked.

. . . . .

Poor Mustafa! Deserving of pity, although no particular hero. He had found small pieces of Mr. O'Donovan, whom he had certainly been very fond of, and that paper on which the dead man had bequeathed him a brand of infamy.

And last of all, after he had been staggering for a long time from horror to horror, Mustafa—yes, Mustafa now, until the end—was destined to find his dear pal the Saxon. He was lying quite dead and stark naked, in the topmost branches of a tree. How in the name of God had he got up there?

. . . . .

All dead, all dead; they had fought like lions, now they were dead, dead. Poor living dog, Mustafa! Still alive, yes. But for how long? A day would come in the end, Mustafa, Mustafa——

A day would come when a miserable runaway slave

of the Dervish khalifa would die like a dog in the thorny Sudanese bush.

. . . . .

The heads of Hicks and von Seckendorff were in El Obeid, fixed on the points of Dervish spears. They were lowered to the ground, and they kissed the dust as the victorious Mahdi marched in.

Tom-tom-tom! tom-tom-tom! All the drums had gone mad. The Mahdi's army came back to the town; in front were the flags—the many-coloured banners on which holy texts were written.

"In the name of the Merciful, the Compassionate. There is no god but Allah. Mohammed el Mahdi, Successor of the Prophet of Allah. O Living One! O Eternal One! O Ruler and Venerable One!"

Behind the flags came the people on foot, the Mahdi's followers in their patched Dervish *jubbas*—a dancing, reeling, drum-beating multitude of people drunk with victory, with a murmur like the thunder of the sea:

"*La ilaha illa'llah! La ilaha illa'llah!*"

Then the three great copper drums of the three khalifas, and the ombaya, the ivory war-horn, the bellowing elephant tusk, which was only blown in front of Abdullahi's warriors. And the armoured horsemen from Kordofan in their chain-mail shirts and pointed steel helmets, like the Saracens of a thousand years ago. They levelled their lances, charged forward with the cry: "For God and His Prophet!" Before the wall of spectators they halted abruptly, turned and charged back.

And then a throng of bloodstained and almost naked prisoners was driven forwards, right in front of the Mahdi himself, who, smiling kindly, was sitting on a beautiful white camel, in a Dervish *jubba*, which was sewn with scarlet patches in a new and magnificent style; the patches were pieces of captured British uniform coats and pieces of brocade from the Mass garments taken out of the destroyed Catholic Missions.

As he rode along with his radiant smile, the crowd round him threw its last restraint to the winds. They danced round him, beating their drums and shouting: "*La ilaha illa'llah!*"—and weeping women threw themselves shrieking in the whirling dust: "*Mahdi Allah! The Mahdi of God! The Mahdi of God!*"

And Abdullahi, the Taaishi, big and grim on his splendid horse, looked round at the many guns which were rolling by, and at all the captured weapons . . . Woe to the Turk in Khartoum! The whole of the Sudan now lay open!

# THE TREE

At rahad, two days' journey from El Obeid, the Mahdi established a great camp, in order to assemble and prepare his army for the march on Khartoum. An enormous tree a baobab, which spread out to fantastic proportions, stood in an open place in the middle of the camp.

Beneath this tree the Mahdi appeared, in order to say the five daily prayers in the presence of all the people; here he preached, held his court, received the sheikhs and ambassadors who came to him to swear allegiance, and also the high officers and governors of the Khedive, who, in Dervish shirts, came before him to crave his mercy.

.   .   .   .   .

From every part of the almost endless encampment, above all the pointed *tukuls*, the huts of *durrha* straw, one could see the Mahdi's tree. Towards it all eyes were directed; in this camp everybody was always thinking about the Mahdi, always talking about him. The naked slave women, as they ground corn between two stones, steadily hummed the song of the Mahdi: "O Mahdi, thou light of our eyes!"—or "At Kana the Mahdi gave the Toork what he deserved!" And whoever, in trading and bargaining, wished to convince someone else, never swore otherwise than "By the Mahdi's God!" Or else he swore: "By our Lord,

## THE TREE

the Imam," or "By the Victorious Mahdi!" The many beggars in the camp had long since learned to beg for alms not in the name of Mohammed the Prophet, but of Mohammed the Mahdi. And in the evening, when the men were squatting in a ring to listen to the singing of those lyric odes which the common Arab people love, the clever singers substituted of themselves, for the name of the Prophet, that of the Mahdi; *he* was now called the Beloved, the Friend; *his* beauty was likened to the moon, to the gazelle. In the end the passionate adoration would pass altogether into frenzy; the two singers who, each leading a half of the chorus divided into two parts, had so far beaten time with staffs on the ground, leaped up, brandished the sticks as though they were swords, shouted the battle-cry *"Fi shan Allah!"* For God's cause!—the cause of God, of the Prophet, of the Mahdi: it was the same thing.

. . . . .

And the Kadi, the religious judge of the camp town, had a man put in chains because, in an argument with a friend, he had placed the Prophet above the Mahdi; for, he had said, God was higher than the Mahdi. This, the judge decided, was naturally the truth; but the tone of voice in which it was said suggested a belittlement of the Mahdi, and was to be punished.

. . . . .

Not far from the great tree was the market of the camp town; here, in a great motley throng, the new law of the Mahdi was ruthlessly upheld. The whole day long the market judge sat on his sheepskin waiting for the criminals who were publicly brought before him. Should the spies discover a secret drinker, then the *merissa* pot was at once broken over his head and a yelling mob dragged the sinner, dripping with beer and blood and bombarded with dust and filth by the children, along to the judge. The latter immediately ordered the stipulated punishment to be carried out: eighty lashes with the whip. But whoever was caught smoking tobacco received not eighty, but one hundred lashes. Young women who were seen with unveiled faces (the body might be naked, but not the face), or wearing golden or silver trinkets, were just as vigorously chastised. Until that time a certain coiffure had been in vogue among the Sudanese women: a kind of matting made of goat's hair, which was stuck with gum over the woman's own tresses. That also was forbidden, and women who ignored the interdiction had their own hair, together with the coiffure, torn from their skulls.

All the more lenient traditions of the Sheriat, the Moslem religious law, were thrust aside. A savage justice punished murderers and adulterers with death by the axe. Adulteresses were killed by stoning. For a small theft the criminal lost one hand and one foot.

Just as the laws were harsh, so also were all the judges under the Mahdi corrupt. The people were no freer, no less oppressed than under the Turkish rule. The Mahdi had proclaimed the new law of equality among men: "The least among the Ansar is in all things equal to the emirs, except when orders are given, that have to be obeyed." But in spite of that things went the way they always do. The powerful ones enriched themselves. The law that the Ansar must renounce worldly goods and that a common treasure-house, the "Beit el-Mal," the property of the pious community,

AN ADANSONIA TREE

Drawing by W. H. Fischer from a photograph

should be established for the use of everybody—this law hardly counted for sheikhs, emirs, and khalifas.

. . . .

But still the light which radiated from the Mahdi was reflected in all eyes. Like the great tree above the tents of the camp, a high purpose towered over all daily troubles. This place was not yet God's City, which was to be built; it was only a hastily established camp. They were on the victorious march forward. Everything would be wonderful and different and new when once Khartoum was conquered, and then Cairo.

. . . . .

The half-naked Arab shepherds who until then had been so terribly oppressed by the Turkish bashibazouk, the black soldiers whose backs were still sore from the pasha's whip, were the witnesses one morning, in the camp of Rahad, in the shadow of the Mahdi's tree, of an extraordinary scene.

The war-drums suddenly sounded in the camp; at the signal given by the Khalifa Abdullahi, the *ombaya*, his great ivory war-horn, was blown. The horsemen rode out before the camp; the armoured horsemen from Dar-Fur in their chain armour, and the others, who were covered with an armour of wadding. All this excitement, and the waving of the great banner, the glittering of the points of the lances, the wild volleys, the loudly shouted songs of praise were caused merely by the approach of a small blue-eyed man who looked, in his patched Dervish *jubba*, like a tragic harlequin.

## THE MAHDI OF ALLAH

The young European who was coming to kiss the Mahdi's hand was Rudolf Slatin, yesterday still Slatin Bey, Governor-General of Dar-Fur. With incredible tenacity and ability he had so far defended himself in his province, cut off from Khartoum and Egypt, whilst hoping against hope that Hicks Pasha's army might succeed in relieving El Obeid and thus enable him to save Dar-Fur. But now all was lost, and he had to give himself up. A Governor-General of the Khedive, a European! People declared that he was a nephew of Gordon!

He was now called "Abd el-Kader Saladin." Slatin, though not a man of deeply religious bent, was and remained at heart as good a Christian as any. During his desperate struggle in rebellious Dar-Fur, however, he had thought it expedient to adopt nominally, in the presence of his troops, the Mahommedan faith; this he did only because he thought it would restore confidence among his officers and men, and would help him to make a stronger defence, in this fanatically religious country, against the enemies of the Government.

That had not helped at all, either. And now Slatin came, deserted by his army, alone and without a sword, to the Mahdi at Rahad. (That they had taken from him his lieutenant's sword which he had worn in the Bosnian campaign was perhaps his greatest sorrow at that hour!) But he had been given a Dervish shirt, a horse and a spear like those carried by the bodyguard of the Khalifa; and as he now approached the spot outside the camp where Abdullahi was awaiting his coming, wild horsemen galloped up to him, shook their spears right in front of his sunburnt face and shouted at him tumultuously: "For God and His

Prophet!" They called this out and galloped back again to the man who was waiting under the banner. As they repeated the manœuvre, Slatin understood what he was to do; he brandished his spear and cried out in the same manner: "For God and His Prophet!" and rode up with the other horsemen to the man in the shadow of the banner. The *ombaya* sounded: Rudolf Slatin jumped down from his horse and kissed for the first time the dark hand of the man whose slave, confidant, and deadly enemy he was to be from then onwards—the Khalifa Abdullahi.

At noon, after the prayer in the open space under the great tree, the European, the former governor of the Khedive, took the "beia," or oath of allegiance, holding the hands of the Mahdi himself—the oath which bound him as a Dervish novice bound himself to a Dervish sheikh. "I vow loyalty to thee, and to renounce this world, to take pleasure in that which is pleasing to God, out of desire for the favours of God and for the world to come; further, that I shall not waver from the path of the Jehad . . ."

Slatin had placed his thumb upon the thumb of the Mahdi, who, slowly and smilingly, was speaking the formula; Rudolf Slatin, now Abd el-Kader, repeated it clearly after him. Thousands heard it and knew that the Mahdi was in truth victorious. . . .

.   .   .   .

In a tent in the camp—a few bundles of long *durrha* straw piled up into a hollow cone, a hole in it for a door—was sitting another white man, with a Christ-like beard and long hair, in a long, shabby Dervish shirt over his lean body: Joseph Ohrwalder. The Tyrolese father, the missionary of Delen, had suffered not a little since he had fallen into the hands of these Mahdists. Two years had passed since he had supervised, with so much satisfaction, the baking of bricks while the mission building was being enlarged. The mission building! The father had seen with his own eyes how it had been plundered by the negroes of the mission village before the Mahdists—the Bedouins from the lowlands—had yet arrived. Since then, poor Father Ohrwalder had been driven away from his mountains, of which he was so fond, had been driven as a prisoner, a barefooted slave, from place to place.

Now, if he walked out in front of the hut, he could see far on the horizon the shadowy profile of the mountains of Nuba, those Jebel Delen, which had always reminded him of his Southern Tyrol. Often he saw there a great smoke ascending, and at night flames. Then the young priest became a prey to sinful wrath, for he knew that one more peaceful village of those poor blacks whom he had grown to love was now burning. The Nubas had not submitted to the Dervishes, but were in the midst of a bloody war with them. Here, in the Rahad camp, there was a special pen for captured Nubas, a fence of thorns with death and misery behind it; sometimes the priest succeeded in going near it; then he often saw emaciated corpses being thrown out; but he had not been allowed into the interior of the fenced-in enclosure.

He himself was now the slave of a sheikh called Idris Wad el-Hashmi; he had come with him to Rahad as his camel-driver, running by the side of the loaded animal. Idris was by no means the worst master that Joseph Ohrwalder was fated to encounter; but, even as it was, the young priest had to get his food in the

## THE TREE

sheikh's stables, where he ate of the grain meant for the animals. If he left his hut, he was jeered at, beaten, spied on in the lanes of the camp—because he was an unbelieving dog. Sheikh Idris, however, never ill-treated him; he knew that the Koran ordered that captive Christian priests and monks should be treated with indulgence.

.    .    .    .    .

The poor young priest might almost have been forgiven his sin, even if he did swear a little to himself, from time to time, in his Tyrolese dialect. It was so dreadful to have to live there, in the field camp of that army which he hated, the victory of which meant despair for him. The whole day those abominable drums were going: tom-tom-tom! The *ombaya*, the Khalifa's elephant tusk, blew, and you knew that Abdullahi was having somebody punished again, the ever-mistrustful Abdullahi who, beside the ever-smiling Mahdi, ruled the army with such savage strictness. Whose turn was it now? Who was being flogged, tortured, beheaded? Ohrwalder trembled all over when he heard the *ombaya*, which was always sounded at executions. He had many friends in the camp, although he scarcely ever caught sight of a friendly face. His friend and superior, Father Bonomi, was also in Rahad; Ohrwalder did not see him for months at a time. Then the nuns: what the poor women had had to go through was cruel. They had been distributed to the harems of the emirs; they had been starved, beaten, tortured. Finally, one of the sisters in her despair had rushed into the Mahdi's hut and had shown him her feet bleeding from the lashes. Mohammed Ahmed, surprised, had said that he had not wished that and would not tolerate it any longer; and the next day he had caused the nuns to move into the walled-in quarter of the camp in which he himself lived with his wives and children. From that time onwards the lot of the nuns had become bearable.

Every time Father Joseph Ohrwalder thought of it, of that compassion which the Mahdi had shown towards the nuns, he became quite troubled and indignant; the thing did not fit into his philosophy. He hated that person, the Mahdi, held him to be a swindler, an impostor, a secret debauchee, and was firmly convinced of his wickedness and his devilish cruelty.

Only one single hope did Ohrwalder still cherish: the Austrial consul in Khartoum had succeeded in sending, by secret ways, a message to the missionaries in the camp at Rahad; they should be reassured—the message said—all was not lost, England was going to send an expedition into the Sudan; already General Gordon was back in Khartoum; a man like that could, and would, save them all. . . .

. . . . .

One day, shortly before the hour of the Mohammedan noonday prayer, some Arabs burst into Ohrwalder's hut and drove him before them with rough blows; the unbelieving dog must run, for our lord, the Imam himself had asked for him, the Mahdi wished to speak to him.

Running in front of these men (they belonged to the Mahdi's body-guard), the miserable prisoner went panting through the narrow, crooked streets of huts, which were swarming with men and beasts. The camp was fuller than usual; the Khalifa Abdullahi

THE TREE

had brought in all the people from El Obeid; whole Arab tribes with their herds were coming in daily, Homr, Bederieh, Ghodiat, the Miserieh, the Dar-Nauli. Now, at the hour of prayer, the men were sitting in thousands and thousands, in orderly rows on the ground round the great tree, and were waiting for the Mahdi, who was to come out of the hut, to lead the prayer of the faithful, as the Imam.

Father Ohrwalder was driven with spears to the trunk of the tree, and then left in peace. Groaning breathlessly, he leant against the tremendous roots.

. . . .

The Adansonia tree, or baobab, a monster, an elephant among trees, has at certain seasons of the year a dark green cupola of foliage and huge white flowers. At present, as at most times, it was bare, with a gigantic entanglement of boughs, from which here and there a single slender leaf hung down, or one of the fruits, a foot long and covered with a felt-like skin. The trunk was hollow and cleft, the bark damaged, for the eunuchs of the Mahdi's harem sold it as an infallible instrument against all troubles. The fact that the Mahdi prayed beneath it gave it an unspeakable holiness.

Under the tree, at a spot which was shaded by a thick branch, a sheepskin was spread out as a prayer-carpet for the Mahdi. All at once a dull acclamation went forth from the crowd. The Mahdi appeared, surrounded by his three khalifas and by the emirs of the army of the faithful. A look full of serene peace he allowed to flit over the ranks of his congregation. Then he gave a sign to those who had come with him to go to their places. With his gentle voice, which was barely raised, but was nevertheless heard everywhere in the broad space, he now spoke the noonday prayer. Murmurs and sobs shook the crowd. All repeated the holy words, all the turbans sank simultaneously, as the imam fell to the ground upon his sheepskin with his head in the dust before Allah.

.   .   .   .   .

After the worship the orderly rows broke up. Part of the crowd dispersed, but many pushed forward in order to come quite close to the Mahdi, who remained sitting on the sheepskin under the tree. The men of the Mahdi's body-guard, stately in their belted Dervish coats covered with regular coloured patches, pushed the people back with their great spears, though they could not prevent this or that one from reaching the tree and speaking a few words to the Mahdi, or delivering a petition to him. A soldier with a broad, leaf-shaped blade at the end of his spear stood behind the priest, who was still leaning against the roots of the tree. The spear was held out over the priest's head, the poor, unkempt head on which the tonsure had long since disappeared. There he stood, with death hanging over his head, like John the Baptist, whom he might then have resembled in his ragged desert garb and with his uncut beard. The Mahdi, who now nodded to him smilingly, seemed as though enveloped in a splendour, so well cared for and pure was everything about him. His dress was still of the coarsest material and garnished with big patches, the belt woven of palm straw; but the turban was of fine snow-white material; a corner of it flowed over cheek and shoulder down to the beard, the silky blackness of which was thereby enhanced. The dark face was carefully washed, a breath of freshness and sweet perfumes streamed out from it. The eyebrows were painted over, the nails of the beautiful hands dyed with henna; the perpetual smile revealed the pearly teeth.

.     .     .     .

The priest had already seen the Mahdi more than once; the last time was when he had been obliged to act as interpreter for the captured Klootz. With a kind of gratifying rage he noticed that the Mahdi had since grown much fatter, was actually corpulent. And yet he had always been so lean—like a monk who chastised himself very much, like a Trappist. So now (thought the prisoner, and felt glad) he was getting stout, the false ascetic, the impostor, the secret guzzler and harem saint!

He hated that man with all his soul—perhaps in a way that a priest should not hate—and yet, when those wonderfully big eyes were looking full at him, when that stirring voice spoke, he had difficulty in not succumbing to the charm of the man. Over and over again, whether he wished it or not, it seemed to him as if the voice of holy authority were speaking to him, a reverend bishop of his own Church. He checked himself, repented of the sin of even thinking of such a thing. But the impression persisted.

The Mahdi of Islam spoke to the Roman Catholic missionary as if they were equals, as if one of them were not an ill-treated slave, as if there were no negro soldier standing behind him with the menacingly uplifted blade. The priest did not forget that, but he was quite composed; he had sat down on the root of the tree and was looking the Mahdi in the eyes.

The Mahdi said that he had called the Christian that he might be present at the prayer of the Moslems, and tell him if the Christians also really had the same thing—that is, regular prayers, taught by the Divinity?

And when the priest answered emphatically that it was so, the Mahdi appeared to be astonished. Did he really know so little about the Christian faith? He desired to hear a Christian prayer. So Father Ohrwalder joined his hands and spoke loudly and clearly the Lord's Prayer in Arabic. The people crowding behind the Mahdi murmured half aloud and approvingly; perhaps they had not expected that—such simple, fervent words to God; they had thought this Christian person must pray blasphemingly!

The Mahdi nodded, pensively. He said that that was a very good prayer. All at once he looked at Ohrwalder and asked him whether it was not prophesied in the Psalms of David that

"The righteous shall inherit the earth and dwell therein for ever."

· · · · ·

Now it was the turn of the Catholic priest to be astonished. How did the Mahdi know the thirty-seventh Psalm? (The father did not know that this text, and this alone out of the whole Bible, is quoted in the Koran.)

"You see," said the Mahdi, "your book says it itself—that the earth is an inheritance of the righteous; why then do you Christians strive against my power, ordained by God?"

He began to lament about Victoria, Queen of England, who he had heard was completely impenitent; although her minion, General Hicks, had been laid low with the Queen's great army, yet she still thought, in her earthly and godless wisdom, that she could offer resistance to the power of God and of the Mahdi. Instead of being converted to Islam, she had now sent her Gordon to Khartoum.

The Mahdi became suddenly very vehement; for a moment the conversation left the strictly spiritual channel. (Why did the father breathe more freely?) The Mahdi wanted to know what that might mean, what Gordon Pasha was now contriving in Khartoum? The spies had reported that he was having a network of wire spread out on the flat ground round Khartoum.

To this Father Ohrwalde· said: "I know nothing of the art of war, but others say that this is telegraph wire which Gordon has put down so that in case of attack the horses would stumble over it."

The Mahdi's smile broadened. "See," he said, so loud that all heard him, "see how cunning is this unbeliever! But God is more mighty than all the tricks and artifices of men!"

.   .   .   .   .

Father Ohrwalder did not dare make any answer; he only bowed his head, above which the steel of the executioner was so threateningly raised. If he turned round only slightly he could see the great negro who stood behind him, in a new *jubba*, with a lance that seemed gigantic; the father felt the reeking breath of the black man on his neck. And the Mahdi saw it, thought Ohrwalder, and smiled as kindly as if there was nothing at all; he talked to him from time to time like a good friend—nay, like a father. He spoke of God in such a self-understood tone, as though he were referring to Him as a Catholic priest. "And yet," said Ohrwalder to himself, with fury, "of course he does not mean God, he means the devil, a false deity who is to destroy God's work on the earth. He has caused our church in Delen to be ruined. . . ."

The whole inner man in Ohrwalder was struggling against a great fascination, against the kindness and the priestliness in that smiling face opposite him.

Now the Mahdi was saying that God would soon assist him to conquer Khartoum, like El Obeid. Hatred and anger raged inside the young priest; he could have started shouting, raving—but he dared not. Perhaps a weakness, which suddenly overtook him, saved his life. With both hands he clung to the root of the tree. A thought had knocked him over almost bodily. Was it really possible, could it really be possible, would God suffer it—that this man, this Antichrist, with his hordes, would devastate the fine mission in Khartoum as well, the beautiful gardens, the church, everything?

. . . . .

Curious—at the very moment when the father (with horror in his heart) had thought: the Antichrist!—Mohammed Ahmed said the same word. He asked, without any preparation and with greater force than before, whether the father, then, did not believe in the holy book of the Christians? Would Isa, son of Maryam, return again or not? Would he carry through the great fight against the Antichrist or not?

The father was quite pale; he could hardly speak. At last he recovered himself and said that he believed in the return of Jesus.

"If you see Him return," said the Mahdi, quite simply, "you will also have to believe in my Mahdieh, for it is I who announce His return to the world and

## THE TREE

His Last Judgment, which He is to hold. As soon as He appears at Jerusalem on the Rock of Abraham your doubts, too, will vanish, and then you will have to embrace the faith of Islam."

The Mahdi was silent for a while; he looked up at the bare twigs of the great tree, as if there were something to be read up there. Then he spoke on slowly, more to the crowd of the Ansar pressing round him than to Father Ohrwalder.

"All this will happen in forty years," said the Mahdi. "The Compassionate One has announced it to me in my visions. It was made known that I would first conquer Egypt and the holy places in Hejaz. Cairo will yield without resistance to the army of the faith. But before Mecca bloody fights await God's army.

"Forty years more," said the Mahdi; his smile laid bare the gap in the teeth. "Forty years more am I to remain on this earth. Our lord the Prophet, on whom be blessing and peace, has announced that to me on Abba. In forty years from now the army of the Faith will stand before Jerusalem, and there it will see Jesus descending upon Abraham's rock. And then the Christians will all have to recognise Islam."

・　　・　　・　　・　　・

The Mahdi looked at the priest, as if he were waiting for an answer. The priest, however, remained obstinately silent. The negro behind him had lowered the spear still farther, as if for the blow; perhaps he was waiting for a sign from the Mahdi—the very slightest sign. The priest himself was very likely waiting for this sign. What would come next? he thought. Would the Mahdi demand from him the renunciation of his religion, an immediate and open profession of the Mohammedan faith?

Then, the priest knew that, it would mean obedience—or martyrdom.

A man is a man, and no one is a martyr before he is dead. But this time Father Joseph was spared the ordeal. Inscrutable, the Mahdi did not put the fatal question, did not signal to his executioner. Instead of that he even began to praise the Christians: "I know that you are good people; I have always been told that. You feed the hungry and earn merit by almsgiving. Nevertheless, he who only believes in kind deeds and not also in the Mahdi of God—how can he be saved? You are merely like bundles of dry wood which will be cast into the fire."

Then, for a short space, anger flared up in that smiling face. He stopped; he was seen to be thinking. He was murmuring something. A name was just audible: it was "Gordon."

. . . . .

"Gordon, too, is a good man," said the Mahdi at last, quite loud. He had become peaceful and benign once more. "Gordon, too, is good, but he ought to turn to Allah and be converted to Islam: for there is no escape except through God and except through obedience to His command, to His Prophet and to His Mahdi."

He closed his eyes for a little while: then he recited from the Koran:

"And do not slay yourselves by your own hand! In truth, God is compassionate towards you."

. . . . .

## THE TREE

The priest in Joseph Ohrwalder heard the unctuous tones with a keen ear, and it enraged him more than anything, so strongly that he could almost have hit that preacher in his smiling face.

"How fat he is getting!" he thought with fury, and that observation fortunately gave him a satisfying feeling of superiority, so that he could sneer inwardly, instead of raging. "He guzzles; his many wives are pampering him."

Because he was able to think that, the priest felt himself appeased; he said nothing—only lowered his threatened head. The Mahdi, with a kind gesture, signalled his dismissal. Father Ohrwalder, quite dazed, returned to his master's stable. But on the way numbers of excited people stopped him, coming out from every hut. Many of them mocked at him; but really he appeared to the people to be worthy of some respect. Had not the Mahdi spoken to him for such a long time under the big tree?

Father Ohrwalder took a little millet from the manger of the sheikh's horses; and so he lived on.

## THE COSTUME

Charles Gordon, now again Governor-General of the Sudan, or of that part of it which did not as yet belong to the Mahdi, was sitting one morning in March 1884 in his study in the palace at Khartoum. By him on the table, next to the cigar box and the Bible, lay an unpacked parcel and a letter, both from the Mahdi. They had been brought to him by two delegates from the enemy's camp, who had arrived in the town the previous night.

The Governor-General had read Mohammed Ahmed's letter already during the night. Gordon never slept much, and he had at once given orders to summon all the notables to the Palace in the morning for an important meeting; he wanted to read out to them the letter from El Obeid, and to make known his answer.

For this reason Gordon, in spite of the early hour, was fully clothed; indeed he was dressed up in the full uniform of a Turkish marshal. The slim and gracefully built man was all covered with scarlet and gold embroidery; the breast of his military coat was plastered with diamond orders; the star of the Mejidieh was hanging from his neck; another Turkish star-and-crescent gleamed over his heart; the satin band of a Grand Cordon stretched slantingly from the golden epaulette across his body. Besides this General Gordon —he was a general now in the British Army also—

## THE COSTUME

wore a few modest campaign medals; more than that England had never given him. The great heavy medal which the Emperor of China had once had struck specially for him, as the saviour of the Celestial Empire, Gordon had sold one fine day, when he needed money for some act of beneficence.

Above the chest covered with orders and gold and scarlet was Gordon's manly head. The hair under the somewhat too small fez was already quite grey, the side-whiskers also. The eyes were blue and as bright as ever, the face a little wrinkled; the moustache fell limply over the fine mouth.

. . . . .

Gordon had only been back in the Sudan for a few weeks. He had been away five years. What years, those five! Where had he not been! In India. In China. In Ireland. On the island of Mauritius. In South Africa. Home again. Then, an unforgettable year, in Palestine, where he had searched for the true scenes of the Bible and discovered them with the aid of the Holy Scriptures. Then, on the way back, in Brussels, with King Leopold.

What years! Missions and garrisons and journeys through half the world. The whole thing did not make up a particularly brilliant career; the times when "Chinese Gordon" had been a kind of British national hero were long past. A good officer of engineers, a bit unruly; many people said "mad." Between adventures, quite good enough to command the sappers of a colonial garrison here and there, or to build second-class forts.

In Brussels, on the way home from Palestine, this perpetually restless man had had some conversations with the King of the Belgians. The King wished to secure for his Congo State the man who had roamed so widely in Africa. Gordon was quite prepared, had already accepted, perhaps with a sigh, for in reality he was still yearning as ever for the Sudan, from which such wild news was now coming.

And then suddenly all the newspapers in London were full of his name. Gordon! Gordon! The news of the Mahdi's victory over General Hicks had touched the national pride; somebody asserted that what had happened would never have happened if Gordon, instead of Hicks Pasha—— All at once everybody was repeating it: only General Gordon! He alone could still avert a catastrophe! He alone could yet save Khartoum! Gordon! Gordon!

The London Press demanded Gordon, clamoured for Gordon, whom it had forgotten for so long.

The Prime Minister, Mr. Gladstone, alone hesitated. The adventure of the Egyptian occupation, on which he had so reluctantly embarked two years before, was causing him sleepless nights. Nothing was further from his wishes than to try to conquer that useless Sudan. What had to happen now was that the Egyptians should decently evacuate the rest of the Sudan; Khartoum had to be abandoned, of course, without allowing the Europeans and the Egyptian officials who were there to fall into the hands of the Mahdi. A difficult task. A particularly capable man would have to be sent out to Khartoum to manage it properly. On Gordon being named, Gladstone first sought the opinion of Sir Evelyn Baring, England's consul-general, England's proconsul, rather, in Cairo. Baring, who did not like Gordon, promptly cabled "No." The "No" decided the matter for several days.

## THE COSTUME

Then the pressure of public opinion became very strong. Mr. Stead, of the *Pall Mall Gazette*, spoke up violently for Gordon. A real Gordon fever had broken out. Thereupon Gladstone cabled once more to Baring, who finally submitted.

· · · · ·

Time and again during the past five years Gordon had vehemently assured people that he was no longer thinking about the Sudan, that he never wanted to set foot there again. Now, at the first request, he said "yes," and informed the King of the Belgians that he could not go to the Congo State. What demon was driving that lonely man? What mysticism, which of the Biblical sayings, in which he believed? The position which they were offering him was more than doubtful. He would be, as before, Governor-General of the Sudan, but with orders to dissolve this Government as soon as possible. From Khartoum and the other provinces not as yet occupied by the Mahdi, he was gradually to withdraw troops and officials, then to leave the Sudan himself. Perhaps in the retreat it might be possible to leave behind some kind of order, some Sultanate, a native state which would, for the time being, have to remain independent of Cairo: perhaps he would somehow manage to ward off that troublesome Mahdi.

Gordon had agreed to everything, had accomplished the journey in furious haste. On the 18th February he had already made his entry into Khartoum.

· · · · ·

A month ago. The man in the glittering uniform remembered, with wrinkled forehead. What a wonderful day! Although he had come alone, without troops, without artillery, the whole town had welcomed him as a protector, as a saviour.

"Long live Gordon, Sultan of the Sudan!" they had shouted in the streets. Yes, he would not only protect them from the Mahdi, he would protect them from the Turks as well; he would be their Sultan, gracious and mighty. The women had attempted to kiss his feet. He himself, completely happy and radiant with a new confidence, had announced great things: a new, a happier time was beginning. No more bashi-bazouks, no flogging, no violence; only justice. And he had immediately ordered the heavy chains to be removed from the feet of all the prisoners in the gaols. In the square in front of the palace they had broken to pieces, before the eyes of the people, the whips, the flogging benches, the branding irons. They had even burnt the taxing acts before the eyes of all: no one owed taxes to the State any longer.

More than that: soon after his arrival the Governor-General had expressly revoked the laws which had prohibited the owning of slaves in the Sudan. Yes, Gordon himself! The too hasty fight against slavery was one of the reasons of the Mahdist rebellion. And Gordon had a plan: Zubeir Rahamet was to create that settlement in the Sudan, that independent sultanate which would throw back the Mahdi—Zubeir Rahamet, that same powerful slave-hunter and slave-dealer who was now imprisoned in Cairo. Gordon himself had had Zubeir's son executed, through Gessi; none the less, he hoped to be able to win Zubeir over; his influence among the tribes was great. On the very day of his arrival the Governor-General had telegraphed to Cairo asking that Zubeir might be

## THE COSTUME

allowed to travel up to him. But Sir Evelyn Baring had refused.

. . . . .

When he thought of Baring, that obstruction in his path, Gordon made a wry face. The Zubeir plan was the only way out, and it would be necessary to proceed with it soon. Who knew how long communications with the Egyptian frontier would still remain open? Between Khartoum and Berber rebel tribes were already roaming about. Who, indeed, was still loyal? Where, indeed, was there a ray of light? To the east of Khartoum, Osman Digna, the Mahdi's emir, was conquering the land as far as the sea coast. To the south, only nine miles distant, stood the outposts of a great Dervish army, which was advancing to the siege. From the roof of the palace one could already hear the drums at night. The tribes on the Blue Nile were all going over to the enemy. In El Obeid the Mahdi was assembling a mighty host. That letter there was the formal summons to surrender which precedes a siege; an old soldier could not make a mistake about that. Yes, siege. How long, then, could Khartoum hold out? Two months? Or six?

Gordon no longer believed in evacuation. True, he frequently dreamed of it, of embarking on the steamers (he still had a whole flotilla) with his soldiers, with the Europeans who were still round him, and sailing away, not downstream, towards Egypt, but upstream to the Equator, to Emin Pasha—of pushing through somehow into the very interior of Africa, then to the coast.

Even now, as he sat there at the table, in his too gorgeous uniform, he was thinking of it, of some new and unheard-of anabasis. . . .

He braced himself up. He had to read that long letter from the Mahdi once more, because he intended afterwards to receive the two delegates in solemn divan. They were then going to deliver this letter once more to him formally, before the notables of Khartoum, and also that present which the Mahdi had sent.

That parcel containing the Mahdi's present attracted Gordon in a curious way. Often he approached it; several times already he had taken it out. Now he did so again, with a hand that trembled slightly. There appeared a *jubba*, a shirt garnished with patches, such as the Dervishes wear; trousers of rough material, a turban cloth, a skull cap, a belt of palm straw, and a wooden rosary. That was the present which the Mahdi had sent.

Gordon read a slip of paper, which was lying among the humble things: "From the servant of the LORD, Mohammed el Mahdi Ibn Abdullah, to Gordon. In the name of God, the Merciful, the Compassionate. On reading my answer to your letter you will understand me. Herewith a suit of clothes, consisting of a *jubba*, a *ridaa* (overcoat), a turban, a cap, a girdle, and beads. This is the clothing of those who have given up this world and its vanities and who look for the world to come, for everlasting happiness in Paradise. If you truly desire to come to God and seek to live a godly life, you must at once wear this suit and come out to accept your everlasting good fortune."

.   .   .   .   .

Gordon dropped the piece of paper as though it were scorching hot. What frightened him so? What was he so terrified of? An attraction? An allurement?

## THE COSTUME

And at once he took up the book which lay near by on the table, the Bible. It opened itself with no trouble at the place which during the last days—yes, and nights too—he had been turning up again and again:

Ezekiel xxix. 10:

"Therefore behold, I am against thy rivers and I will make the land of Egypt an utter waste and desolation from the tower of Seyench even unto the border of Ethiopia.

"No foot of man shall pass through it, nor foot of beast shall pass through it, neither shall it be inhabited forty years."

Gordon nodded to himself: Egypt from Seyeneh as far as the border of Ethiopia—that was the Egyptian Sudan. It was all predicted and predestined; so the land was now changing itself into a desert; for forty years.

The Mahdi, Gordon suddenly remembered, had actually announced that he would reign forty years more.

. . . . .

The religious mystic, the fatalist who turned over the leaves of the Bible in search of prophecies, when he was quite alone with himself, might have looked with a secret yearning at the ascetic's dress, at the rosary. That would have been a fulfilment, a kind of peace. . . . For the most secret and inner Charles Gordon, who did not know confessional barriers, Islam was only a kind of Christianity.

Such passages as this are to be found in his diary:

"I find the Mussulman quite as good a Christian as many a Christian, and do not believe he is in any peril. All of us are more or less pagans. Have you read

*Modern Christianity, a Civilised Heathenism?* I had those views long before I read the book. I like the Mussulman; he is not ashamed of his God; his life is a fairly pure one; certainly, he gives himself a good margin in the wife-line."

.  .  .  .  .

But (no misunderstanding!)—the mystic dreamer was also a soldier and a gentleman, and had his duties. It was this other Gordon who now closed the Bible and took the long letter from the Mahdi in his hand, like a diplomatic document that must be carefully studied. There might have been religious sentences contained in it which disturbed the private Gordon; but the British general found among them the invitation to go over to the enemy. That demanded an immediate reply. Gordon read with attention.

The Mahdi's letter was the response to a proposal of peace which Gordon had made. He had proposed to the Mahdi to recognise him as Sultan of Kordofan.

The Mahdi declined.

"Be it known to you that I am without pride, the promised Mahdi and the successor of the Prophet. There is no need for me to be sultan or king of Kordofan, or any other country, nor have I any desire for the benefits or adornments of this world. I am a servant, and my duty is to show the way to God and to His kingdom. He who wishes to be happy should hear and follow me, but he who wishes to be miserable should turn away from my guidance; him shall God remove from his position, destroy, and torment perpetually."

(Gordon looked up grimly. That strengthened him again; that gave him the anger against the Mahdi which he needed. The teachings of his own church, which preached the tortures of Hell, this religious man had never believed. They seemed to him to be a denial of the "Good Tidings," of the Gospel.)

So the Mahdi did not want any peace that would concede Kordofan to him. He also sent back a rich gift which Gordon had sent him. Of this he said:

"We have abundance of goods of the same description as your present, but in our desire to seek after God we have laid them all aside. Let me say to you as our Lord Salomon said to Belkissa (Queen of Sheba), 'You bring me money, but what God has bestowed upon me is preferable to your gifts. You are a people who delight in presents—I shall come upon you with an invincible army and drive you out of the city, despised and miserable.'"

Gordon's eyes now flitted impatiently over the sheets of the long letter. All that Gordon had proposed, conceded, the Mahdi contemptuously declined. He had offered to set free for the Mecca pilgrims the road to the holy places. "No," wrote the Mahdi, "how is it possible for one who is not a follower of the Prophet of God to wish to open the road to his tomb for pilgrims?" Gordon had spoken of the bloodshed that ought to be avoided. The Mahdi answered:

"If you pity the Moslems you should pity your own soul first, and save it from the anger of its Creator, and make it a follower of the true religion."

. . . . .

Gordon struck the paper with his fist. There followed now a passage of religious dogmatising that he could not bear. He had always said that a good Mohammedan was a good Christian; but here was set forth the why and the wherefore which was to prove that salvation lay only in certain prayers and formulae of the Mahdist Islam. Even Jesus Christ was quoted as a witness:

"Jesus has said:

" 'Ye disciples, ye build up your worldly abode on the waves of the sea, and do not therefore take it as your permanent abode.' "

Gordon, the connoisseur of the Bible, started, then he smiled. No such passage exists in the New Testament. Farther on came a quotation from the Koran. There the Dervish knew his ground much better.

"Those who believe in God and His Prophet, and the true followers, they are the people of God, and shall be victorious."

Gordon should therefore be converted to Islam, wrote the Mahdi. In the event of his doing that, he promised him safety—more, indeed, even honour and the lieutenancy of a province; should he, however, remain obstinate, it would go ill with him, as it had done with Hicks and that Turkish pasha of El Obeid, Said, who had been slain on account of his stubbornness.

General Gordon stood up from the table, stiffened himself, pulled his uniform straight. It was time for the assembly of the notables.

·   ·   ·   ·   ·

In the great hall of the palace waited Colonel Stewart, Gordon's able assistant, the British consul, Mr. Power, who was also the correspondent of *The Times*, the French consul, Herbin, and Martin Hansal, the Austrian consul. Besides these there were the leading merchants, Greeks, Levantines, and Arabs, and

## THE COSTUME

the Mohammedan clergy. The Catholic missionaries had, together with most of the other Europeans, already left the town.

Gordon Pasha, gleaming with scarlet and gold, stepped before the assembly. A band struck up the Khedivial Anthem. Then the two delegates, the envoys of the Mahdi, were brought in. They came armed with lances and swords; they had refused to lay aside their weapons, and Gordon had allowed them to come like that, as they wished.

He had had the letter and the gift handed back to them; it was necessary that they should present them to him once more before all the people.

Then the Governor-General read out the Mahdi's epistle to the whole gathering. When he had finished, he rose from his seat.

"And now my answer!" he said.

He threw on the floor the costume which the Mahdi had sent, the Dervish shirt, the turban, and the belt— and trampled upon it with his feet.

. . . . .

The notables of the town of Khartoum broke into joyful applause. The Mufti Musa Mohammed and Sheikh el Emir, the first *ulema*, and also the Kadi Mohammed Khovajli came forward and offered their services: in a learned *fethwa* they would prove once more exactly how and why the Dervish Mohammed Ahmed, according to the holy books and according to the best authorities, could not be the Expected Mahdi.

The general rejoicing was great. Even the men of commerce gained a little more confidence. The Governor-General must have been sure of his ground, else he would never have dared——

After the Mahdi's envoys had departed, Gordon spoke boldly and energetically to the gathering of notables. Everything would be all right. The Khedive would send help. England was now in alliance with Egypt. . . .

.   .   .   .   .

But that evening, when all was quiet in Khartoum, one could hear quite distinctly the war-drums of the Dervish army, which must again have approached considerably nearer to the town.

# THE PILGRIM

This is the story of the Frenchman, Olivier Pain.

While the Mahdi's army, with waving banners and beating drums, was marching, or rather rolling, against Khartoum, a shapeless, broad, burning stream of devastation, there dismounted in El Obeid, in front of the *mudirieh*, the administrative building in which a Dervish emir was now installed as a lieutenant of the Mahdi—there dismounted from a camel a young, cheerful-looking man, slim, tall, and with a fair, elegantly curled beard, such as no Arab has; he was browned by the sun and dressed like a Bedouin, but a European at the first glance. Two desert Arabs, who had accompanied him as guides, unloaded from a pack-horse a quantity of neatly tied-up baggage. He himself sprang down confidently on to the main square of the teeming Dervish fortress-town from the saddle of the kneeling camel, said something like *"Me voilà,"* and then announced, in a language which he alone took to be Arabic, that "So there he was, Monsieur Pain, Olivier Pain, Journalist, from Paris. . . ."

And, as an outcry around the stranger at once arose, as fanatical voices began to shout "A spy! A Turk! An infidel dog!" the man with the fair beard hurriedly added:

*"Allah est Allah et Mahomet son Prophète!"*

He smiled rather coquettishly. Well, now everything was in order, what? He looked round him, saw dark faces; everything was not yet quite all right, it seemed, so he shouted out quickly and heartily: "*Vive le Prophète! Vivent les derviches! Je suis un derviche, moi!*"—and tore open his desert burnous so that they could see underneath it a real Dervish shirt, an elegant black and white one with attractive patches. As still nobody seemed inclined to embrace him, he tried with Arabic again: "By Mahomet, he was a good Moslem, always had been one at heart, and the best friend of the Mahdists; and he had now come secretly through the Anglo-Egyptian sentry lines; they had set a price on his head, of course, but he and his *guides arabes* had evaded the English, and so there he was now, with an important secret mission to our holy father, the Mahdi. . . ."

The wild Baggara warriors, who were keeping guard with sword and lance in the courtyard of the *mudirieh*, understood not one single word of the gabbling of this Christian dog. The emir who commanded these men (he was called Ali Balkhit and was usually known as "The Buffalo," because he looked so like one) came along, looked this unbeliever up and down for a second or two, and then had him seized; he regarded him as distinctly suspicious. While they were still hunting for an interpreter, the rumours were already careering through the whole of El Obeid: the Emperor of France had surrendered himself to the Mahdi. No, he was a spy; he wanted to murder the Mahdi. Gordon had sent him. He was the Khedive's favourite, and the husband of Queen Victoria, and so on.

The hastily summoned interpreter appeared at the *mudirieh*; it was one of the captured priests, not Ohrwalder, but Bonomi, his superior. The Italian Bonomi did not speak French particularly well, and it was most difficult to make anything understood. The buffalo-emir, with his black hand on his sword, asked impatiently and mistrustfully what those two dogs were such a long time palavering with each other about. In the end the priest managed to understand about half and was able to translate it, though it was something that did not give him much joy.

The gentleman there, Olivier Pain, had come, so he asserted, in the name of the great French nation, indeed really in the name of the whole of Europe, on a very secret mission—for the purpose of bringing the sympathy, in fact the actual help of those peoples who hated England, which meant, practically, all peoples. . . .

"Translate, *mon père: La perfide Albion.*"

Father Bonomi had to explain that the great French nation would never leave their Moslem brothers in the lurch. The English had occupied Egypt in a brutal manner through treachery. *Eh bien*, the Mahdi would drive them out of Egypt. He, Olivier Pain, had come in order to discuss certain secret plans with the Mahdi in person. Also he had had letters on him from Zubeir Rahamet and others, secret letters to the Mahdi from the adherents of the sacred cause; but these he had been obliged to destroy so that the English should not find them on him. He had been tracked; in fact, he had been betrayed; there was a price on his head; but, thank God, with these three faithful guides, he had finally got away, and there he was, *le voilà.* . . .

"Translate, please, *mon père: Vive la France! Et vive le Mahdisme! Vive Mahomet!*"

Father Bonomi, with lowered eyes, had to translate that. The Emir Ali Balkhit, black and bulky as a buffalo, listened attentively. Probably he had never heard the name of that country—France. This unbeliever who suddenly appeared on the scene declaring that he loved the Prophet and the Mahdi, was most certainly mad, or worse still, a spy.

Ali Balkhit suddenly stretched out his black arm: "Seize him! Search him!"

Greedy dusky hands rummaged in the Frenchman's baggage; they found a Koran in French and an Arabic-French dictionary. The most suspicious thing was a map of Kordofan. What, El Obeid was clearly marked there? And Rahad and the sea? The Nuba mountains? How could these unbelievers, unless it was by black magic, know all that? Had that cursed Gordon also such a magic paper?

Olivier Pain did not get his baggage back, and was strictly guarded in a hut. Still, he kept smiling; the Mahdi, *sans doute*, would receive the French pilgrim better, as soon as he heard about him. If only, in the meantime, there were some proper food to be had! No good bread and no meat, nothing but millet and maize and suspicious sauces. Olivier Pain suffered through this, for he was rather fastidious.

. . . . .

A few weeks after that the buffalo emir sent him with a strong escort after the Mahdi who, meanwhile—it was the end of August—had left the Rahad camp and was advancing on Khartoum.

In the train of the Dervish army were to be found several Europeans, though none of them was there quite by choice, not even the Berlin Dervish, Mustafa Klootz. The former Governor-General of Dar-Fur, Rudolf Slatin, walked or ran beside the horse of the

## THE PILGRIM

Khalifa Abdullahi, who had now made this important captive a member of his body-guard. There were also numerous Greek merchants in the Mahdi's camp, renegades, who, as semi-orientals, had won the Dervishes' confidence and played an important rôle in the army. Slatin, Klootz, and the Greeks did not see each other often on the march; they were too jealously guarded. Each of them, however, had heard the rumour of a Frenchman who had come of his own accord, it was said (of his own accord!) to the Mahdi. Straight into Hell!

(The rumour of this Frenchman—the Sudan is the land of rumours—filtering through all the front-lines and outposts, reached even Khartoum and General Gordon. Charles Gordon wrote down his fantastic hypothesis in his war diary: this mysterious Frenchman, in his opinion, could be none other than the writer, Ernest Renan, the author of the *Life of Jesus*!)

. . . . .

One evening, while the army was camping near Sherkela, the Khalifa Abdullahi, sitting outside his tent, turned suddenly to Abd el-Kader. This was Slatin, who was humbly standing behind the Khalifa's seat, as an orderly or servant—the man who not long before had victoriously commanded an army of the Khedive in great battles. The Khalifa, with the somewhat ferocious indulgence which he lavished upon his favoured prisoner, turned to him and asked him whether in that Europe of the unbelievers there also existed different tribes, as the Baggara, the Danagla, or the Hadendoa in the Sudan? What were, for instance, "Frenchmen"? Did not all the tribes of the land of Europe obey the English queen, then?

"Ali Balkhit is sending us a Frank from El Obeid, who says he is a 'Frenchman' and hates England. How is that? You, Abd el-Kader, who belong to us, who are one of us" (the Khalifa said this with the false smile of distrust), "you speak the unbelievers' language and therefore you will have to be there when this stranger comes to me."

"But take care," said the Khalifa suddenly, with a black look, "I will know it if you do not translate properly, and then you will be put in chains!"

. . . . .

In the camp of Sherkela, the Mahdi spoke the midday prayer as usual with the assembled army; after the religious ceremony he sat on a sheepskin, in a *jubba* shining with cleanliness. It seemed that the turban to-day was wound with more care than usual; the eyes were skilfully painted under with antimony; that gave him a fiery aspect.

The Khalifa's servant, Abd el-Kader, that is, Slatin, now appeared and led the stranger forward, the pilgrim from Europe, the Frenchman. He had become rather pale and thin, yet his fair beard was carefully curled and he was beaming.

The Mahdi asked the Frenchman, through Slatin, whether it was true that he was a Mohammedan.

"At heart I have been for a long time," Olivier Pain asserted loudly. "And in El Obeid I actually acknowledged it publicly before the emir. But now, once more: There is no god but God, and Mohammed is His Prophet!"

The Mahdi nodded. He looked round him to see if his warriors had all heard what this stranger, who had come in pilgrimage from so far, was saying. Then he graciously gave the new convert his hand to kiss. Olivier Pain kissed the dark brown hand of the Mahdi with a kind of gallantry. Then he began to explain, using Slatin as interpreter, that he had come to help the Mahdi. England, he declared, the great enemy of the Mahdi, was also the hereditary enemy of the French nation. That England had occupied Egypt, France would and could never tolerate. Therefore France, Olivier Pain affirmed seriously, was willing and decided to negotiate with the Mahdi and in the most active way to lend him assistance in his just war.

"Under certain conditions," he admitted lightly.

Slatin translated with a frigid face. It was repulsive to him to have to repeat that; but he felt the look of the Khalifa, who was watching him, and he did not dare interpret wrongly.

Then the Mahdi turned his smiling face again to the Frenchman:

"We have understood," he said very clearly, so that as many as possible of his men could hear. "We have understood your message; but know that I, the Mahdi, do not count on human power and support. We will conquer England and all other Turks and unbelievers with the help of the Merciful One alone; with Him is the might and the strength. Your nation, of which you speak, is it not itself a tribe of the unbelievers? How should I ally myself with it? My trusty Ansar is sufficient to conquer the world, from here to Jerusalem. And if its strength is too small, does not the Compassionate One send into each of the battles of the Mahdi legions of angels, who fight for us, and Azrael, with a banner made of light?"

A great shout of acclamation from the ranks of the

army surged round the Mahdi. His look was quite clear and firm. Certainly he was going to triumph over the whole world. . . .

. . . . .

"For God's sake, Monsieur, haven't you got a cigarette?" asked Olivier Pain afterwards, in Slatin's tent, when the two were at last alone with each other.

Slatin shrugged his shoulders. A cigarette! You got a hundred lashes if you were caught smoking. Yes, yes . . . that was what things were like in the paradise which Monsieur Pain had taken so much trouble to enter voluntarily.

Olivier Pain still smiled, perhaps no longer quite so perkily, but still cheerfully: "*Que voulez-vous? La politique, monsieur!*"

Now, alone with the Austrian, he let himself go; he no longer played the Mussulman, and as for his secret diplomatic mission—— He was simply a journalist, he confessed, a radical journalist, on the staff of Henri de Rochefort's famous *Intransigeant*. A secret mission, of course, but—more than anything else—a journalistic reconnaissance. When he had first (as indeed it seemed to be actually happening) established the best personal relations with the Mahdi, then the political value of the mission would become clearer. . . .

He hinted mysteriously that a royal fee was promised him for his visit to the Mahdi, a highly important sum. Not for nothing had he left his charming wife for so long, and his ravishing children. But now he would very soon complete his mission, and be able to return to his dear ones.

Slatin looked at him in amazement. To him, who hated the Mahdists (he did not show it to them, he kept up a good pretence; he felt himself in the position of an officer living in the enemy's camp as a spy)—to him this European was incomprehensible, this fellow who came along to offer these barbarians and black devils an alliance! But the man must be crazy! Really, he was to be pitied.

"Go home? End your mission? How?" said Slatin, with despair in his voice. "You really mean that they're going to let you go? Never! No more than me! Like me they'll keep you here, like the priests, like all the Europeans who have fallen into the Mahdi's clutches!"

The Frenchman continued to smile, but he was pale; his eyes were full of horror. He said nothing for a while; then he spoke up lightly and confidently.

"Come, come! Not at all! *Quoi donc, mon ami!* They are good people, *au fond*, the Mahdists. One must only know how to deal with Mohammedans. We French, *mon cher*, we comprehend the Mussulman soul. Napoleon, already, on his march through Egypt and Syria——"

. . . . .

Then, all at once, a little childishly, Olivier Pain began to complain. He did not doubt about the success of his mission—but these hardships were intolerable. These endless marches. And this food. The food was frightful! If only one could soon——

But Rudolf Slatin had already had the kind idea of entertaining in European fashion his guest and companion in suffering, and he had invited Klootz also, that poor devil, to eat a respectable soup, a piece of roast meat, and who knows what else besides. The Austrian in Slatin knew all about food, and his Arab servants were willing. The three of them, Slatin, Klootz, and

Olivier Pain, sat down there in the tent, very pleased, and waited for the famous soup. Ah well, everything would be all right, after all; things would not be so bad. . . .

At that moment there appeared, black and ominous, two enormous spearmen at the entrance of the tent. They belonged, like Rudolf Slatin, to the *mulazemin*, the body-guard of the Khalifa. They remained standing, and only said a few words:

"The Khalifa's orders. Yussef the Frank is not to remain with Abd el-Kader."

Yussef the Frank—that was what Olivier Pain was now called. The Khalifa, suspicious as he was, had ordered that he should stay in the tent of a certain Zeki, who would have to keep a strict watch on him.

Abd el-Kader sought an excuse, desperately:

"But Yussef the Frank does not yet speak our Arabic language; how can he talk with Zeki?"

The two said nothing more, but only repeated: "The Khalifa's orders."

And as one of them happened to glance at Gustav Klootz, he added, with a look full of meaning:

"Mustafa, our lord the Khalifa has inquired about you also. . . ."

. . . . .

The good rice soup remained uneaten, and all the other things as well. Slatin screwed up courage and went himself to negotiate with the Khalifa. Abdullahi was friendly, as always, towards his favourite Abd el-Kader Saladin. But he repeated his command. The Frenchman was to go at once to Zeki. Had not Abd el-Kader servants enough in his tent? Mustafa, too, was not to remain with him.

## THE PILGRIM

"This Mustafa," said the Khalifa, suddenly frowning, "this Mustafa hardly shows himself any more. He will be put in chains; he must be taught once and for all who is his master here."

"Oh, only for a few days," said the Khalifa, smiling once more, and looking the while at Slatin, who felt a shiver run through his bones.

Mustafa was promptly fetched and they fastened chains round his legs, so that he could neither stand nor sit. Slatin had become mute. The Khalifa smiled at him grimly.

. . . . .

The Mahdi's army pressed onward as far as Shatt. Here the Mahdi knew perhaps his greatest triumph, his greatest satisfaction. Once more there came a man who wished to kiss his hand, who wished to take the oath of allegiance. And this was not merely some Turkish pasha, a harassed Governor-General, a pilgrim from France—but Mohammed Sherif, the Sheikh of the Sammaniyya Tarika.

"*El-hamdu li-llah!*" "Praise be to the God!" It was Mohammed Sherif himself, the master who had kicked the young Mohammed Ahmed from his hearth, and who only a short time before had denounced him in a skilfully rhymed poem—as a heretic, an impostor, possessed by the devil. This same holy man had now secretly absconded from Khartoum, for he no longer believed in the cause of the Turks, he no longer believed in Gordon Pasha. The "miserable Dongolawi" had been victorious. The old sheikh recognised in this the finger of God, and submitted—very dignified.

Now he came before him without any trembling; he still had much to offer him, together with his oath; his influence was still considerable, and in Khartoum there were many who still obeyed him.

What was the Mahdi feeling? His mask remained smiling and immovable as he received his former teacher in the view of the entire army. They were all to see how that old man publicly wept, begged forgiveness, how he touched the earth before the Mahdi with his green turban, repeated the oath of a disciple, promised obedience and fidelity, covered that hand with kisses. . . .

He did all this quietly and with dignity, as one who knew what he was about.

Then Mohammed Ahmed, the holy Mahdi, not only forgave him for the old sins, but heaped up presents in a magnificent tent that stood ready for the guest. The finest horses were to be led to him, two beautiful Abyssinian slave wives. . . .

And the Mahdi, who had once quarrelled with Mohammed Sherif on account of a small festival, now ordered the arrival of the same man to be celebrated in the camp by joyous festivities. . . .

During the festivities, Rudolf Slatin took the risk of visiting Olivier Pain. He found Pain ill, neglected, in Zeki's miserable tent. He could bear the food and the water no longer; he was feverish. His jaunty confidence was gone; he knew now, he said quite softly, that he would never see his wife again, his two children. . . .

What had he done? What a mad thing to come over to these barbarians of his own accord! "Slatin, *mon cher camarade*, if you should ever get out of this and come across my wife, then tell her. . . ."

GENERAL RUDOLF SLATIN PASHA (1927)
From the portrait by Philip de László

## THE PILGRIM

Near Duem on the White Nile, the Mahdi held the last great review before the attack on Khartoum. Before the assembled armies he pointed towards the flowing Nile. That was the river which was running through his life, ever since his father had bathed him in it. "O ye Ansar," he said, "God has created this river. He will also give you its waters to drink, and ye shall possess all the lands along its banks."

Here Rudolf Slatin ventured to tell the Khalifa that the Frenchman was dying. Perhaps, if he was not taken along any farther, he could be saved. Could he not be left behind in a village? And if (by the grace of our lord) he received his belongings back, and the money which Ali Balkhit had caused to be taken from him, so that he might be able to buy some better food——

But the Khalifa Abdullahi looked sternly at his servant Abd el-Kader, who had formerly been Slatin. They stood side by side, the Taaishi big and dark, Slatin frail and fair.

"If he dies now, he is a happy man," said the Khalifa, and his eyes darted suspiciously. "Can one who has just been converted to the faith meet with a greater happiness? He is dying on the pilgrimage, dying after he has kissed the Mahdi's hand. Is it not better to die in such a blessed manner than perhaps to fall back again into error?"

The Khalifa fixed Slatin with a piercing gaze. Slatin realised the hidden threat and lowered his eyes. He thought to himself: "When shall I too die just as miserably?"

As the two stood thus side by side, vanquished and victor, slave and master, who could have guessed the future, foreseen Rudolf Slatin's triumph at the end?

. . . . .

Slatin had provided poor Olivier Pain with a slave boy, who was to look after him. The little black fellow had the quaint name of Atron, which means "natron."

One day, as the army was marching, little Atron came up to the Khalifa's escort and tugged at Abd el-Kader's shirt. Slatin shuddered; something surely must have happened to Olivier Pain.

"Yes," the negro said tearfully, "Yussef is dead. This morning early he was very ill; he could not ride any more." Then little Atron had bound the sick man, together with his Sudanese bedstead, on the camel—but unfortunately not securely enough. Yussef the Frank had suddenly screamed, had hit out round him; the cords had come loose; suddenly the sick man had fallen to the ground, very heavily, and then he was dead.

"This Yussef is truly happy," said the Khalifa once more, when his servant had informed him of the case. But when the Mahdi heard of it, he appeared much affected. He spoke personally the Islamic prayer for the dead over the grave on the bank of the White Nile, in which Monsieur Pain of the *Intransigeant* in Paris was carefully buried—the pilgrim who had come to express to the Mahdi the sympathies of Europe. . . .

The Mahdi marched ever onwards against Khartoum, against Gordon. From the White Nile to the Blue Nile tumultuous drum signals went forth, and the fires blazed at night. From the roof of his lofty palace, Gordon saw the fires and heard the drums of the Dervish army.

## THE ROOF

The flat roof of the palace in Khartoum is the highest point above the steppe in which the capital lies, and from here one can see the two Niles and the desert horizon. Through the powerful telescope a man would descry the smoke of every steamer that might be coming up the Nile, or the dust around troops on the march, if they were approaching from the north.

· · · · ·

In the night of 17th January, 1885, General Gordon had not been able to sleep. In the middle of the night he had jumped up, because he thought he had heard something. No, not a distant thunder of guns, but a high, shrill sound like—yes, like bagpipes. Folly! But Charles Gordon, in his wildly over-fatigued head had nevertheless pondered whether they had really brought their Scottish bagpipes with them across the desert, these Gordon Highlanders who were now coming to his aid. Certainly to-morrow—at the latest next week!

In the journals and letters which he was still able to send home until the last, General Gordon had more than once impatiently complained about the intelligence service of the British army of the Nile. (A Major Herbert Kitchener was at the head of it.) But the service was not as bad as all that; through the Dervish army the news had long since arrived in Khartoum that the English were coming—a very small army, but real British Tommies, picked from the Guards and from the most trusty regiments. In the mounted infantry—mounted on camels—there were Scottish Highlanders, the Gordon Highlanders. It was wonderful: the Clan Gordon was pressing forward to save its clansman. It was almost as though one already heard the pipes shrilling, as though one saw the Tartan colours: green and yellow lines, with blue checks. . . .

.   .   .   .   .

For a moment—only for a moment—it had really appeared so to the sleepless man. Everything was simple and straightforward; the Gordons were coming to the rescue. He had sat down to write a sanguinely optimistic letter to his sister Augusta. Then he had suddenly remembered that he could not send that letter off to her now. The last time he had written was a month before, on the 14th December, when it had been found possible to smuggle two letters through the enemy lines. One official one, the military diary, and one private one to Augusta.

Gordon recalled every word. To Augusta he had only written this:

This may be the last letter you will receive from me, for we are on our last legs, owing to the delay of the expedition. Well, God rules all, and as He will rule to His glory and our welfare, His will be done. I fear, owing to circumstances, that my affairs pecuniarily are not over-bright.

Your affectionate brother,
C. G. GORDON.

And a P.S.:

I am quite happy, thank God, and, like Lawrence, I have *tried* to do my duty.

## THE ROOF

Those were the last words.

. . . . .

Now Gordon could have written something else, something more consoling. He believed again, now, that—— Why, actually, did he believe? There was no obvious reason. A few days earlier his most important exterior fort, Omdurman, on the other side of the Nile, had capitulated. Now the town was for the first time completely cut off. There was only left the waterway. Gordon still had two steamboats, which lay ready for the worst eventuality.

The rest of the flotilla the general had already sent up the Nile months before, as far as the cataracts, so that the relieving army might have them at its disposal.

Yes, and then there had been yet another steamboat there, the *Abbas*. . . .

. . . . .

When, so late in the sleepless night, his thoughts had turned upon the steamer *Abbas*, Charles Gordon had been able to stand the confinement of the room no longer. He had taken his old soldier's overcoat and had hurried out into the frosty night air, up the stairs to the flat roof, and, despairingly, had put the telescope to his eye, long before the light and the day. But he could see nothing; and the night was perfectly quiet. He had heard a hyena howling.

So lonely! So lonely!

Already at the beginning of September, General Gordon had sent away on the Nile steamer *Abbas* the two Englishmen whom he still had with him—one staff officer, Colonel Stewart, and Mr. Power, the correspondent of *The Times* and British consul. The French consul, Herbin, was also on board, and numerous Greeks.

Colonel Stewart had not wished to leave Gordon. But the General had explained to the able man why he was sending him. A British officer from Khartoum had to go to meet the expeditionary force; it was absolutely necessary.

("Evasions," thought Gordon now. "I wanted to save the man. Or I wanted to be without him, without his efficient severity. Do I know which of the two? Does one ever know such things?")

A few weeks after the departure of the *Abbas* a Greek renegade had then come to Gordon's outposts, with a letter from the Mahdi. Not merely a letter full of quotations from the Koran and efforts at conversion, but with this news in it:

The steamer *Abbas*—it was learned from the letter —had arrived as far as the vicinity of Abu Hamed, almost as far as the foremost British positions. There the ship had struck upon a rock; the Arab tribes on the bank had massacred the stranded passengers and crew.

Colonel Stewart dead, Power dead, the consul Herbin——.

And the Mahdi's letter had, as full proof, quoted passages from Gordon's own letters, from his letters imploring quick help, which Stewart had taken with him.

. . . . .

The lonely man on the roof of the palace shuddered at the grey dawn. So lonely! He should never have sent Stewart away. Indeed, Stewart had not wanted to go. Nobody should be as lonely as that. Now, of

GENERAL GORDON

From the portrait by Leo Diet

European people, there was only Hansal there, the Austrian Consul, whom Gordon could not bear; the drunken tailor, Klein, and the Greeks. The Egyptian officers Gordon had sent northwards with the steamer flotilla, with the express request to the British high command not to bring them on any account up the Nile again.

Nobody ought to be so lonely. . . . Every person who was still in the town was either already a traitor, or would be one to-morrow. The few so-called Christians as well! Christians, like that Italian Cuzzi, who stood in such favour with the Dervishes, and who was now trying to come out of their camp to Khartoum, as an agent of the Mahdi. But Gordon did not allow him in the town, resolutely kept him off. Certain things he never forgave. Nor could he forgive that other one, Slatin, who had turned Mohammedan in order to save himself. . . .

Yet Gordon had released the Mohammedan priests from prison, where he had at first put them on account of their secret intercourse with the enemy. Yes, they had written letters to the Mahdi, whom they had first denounced as a heretic and a swindler. But these *ulema* of the chief mosque, the Sheikh ul-Islam, the Kadi, they were, after all, Mohammedans. They actually believed, in reality, what the Mahdi believed. Could one keep them locked up when one heard that, in the Dervish camp, the Italian ex-consul Cuzzi, and Rudolf Slatin from Vienna, and, indeed, the Englishman Lupton Bey had renounced their faith and had declared themselves Mussulmans? Yes, so it was affirmed, even the missionaries, the priests. The nuns were probably all married by now. . . .

## THE MAHDI OF ALLAH

In the earliest grey of dawn Gordon saw the outline of the landscape. There, beyond the Nile, lay the suburb of Omdurman. There the Mahdi was now established. The fortress could no longer be held now. The military engineer, the builder of forts, knew that—since that one side of the fortified triangle had been lost. It was only a question of time. Why didn't those Dervishes attack? If they did, who was going to put up a resistance? The garrison was half starved. *It wasn't going to do anything. Or else without hope.* Yes, if just one little steamer came, early to-morrow, with fifty, with ten bright red British uniforms on board. For so long the leader had been promising his faithful black soldiers the sight of red coats; they would never believe him. . . .

. . . . .

The first ray of sunshine found Gordon at his telescope. This was a different Gordon from the scarlet-and-gold marshal who, two months before, had trampled on the Dervish outfit, amidst the applause of the assembled notables. The Gordon of that moment was thin and unshaven; his hair was grey no longer, but white. He was wearing a uniform coat of drill, still spruce and military, even after the sleepless night. But the face was ravaged by anxiety and fatigue.

He gazed through the telescope northwards. Nothing to be seen. Even in the camp of the Dervishes beyond the Blue Nile nothing stirred. The eye, scanning the horizon through the swinging telescope, saw nothing and found nothing. No little pillar of smoke in the hazy distance, from a steamer flotilla. No moving dust, away to the north, in which a marching army could have been hidden.

## THE ROOF

The man at the telescope suddenly shrank; he had seen something, after all: a flight of storks in the grey-blue morning sky.

.   .   .   .   .

On that very morning of 17th January, 1885, the bugles were sounded in the camp of the British vanguard in the neighbourhood of Abu Klea, as soon as Venus, the morning star, had appeared in the desert sky.

The camel corps, which had hurried forward in advance of Lord Wolseley's main expedition, had almost reached the Nile again here, about a hundred miles downstream from Khartoum. To guard against the enemy, the men had slept behind a hastily erected stone wall, or had not slept at all, for they had heard continuously, through the interminable night, that hellish drum-beating of the natives, and astonishingly near. Now, in the grey morning, the commander of the column, General Sir Herbert Stewart, gave the order for the march forward. It was necessary to drive off the Dervish army which had so audaciously occupied the ridges on the previous evening, in order to secure the approach to the next water, the well of Abu Klea, and the way farther on, to the Nile.

The troops left the camp in good order. The cavalry covered the flanks; the other fighting forces formed a strong square, in the interior of which remained the camels, the doctors, and the wounded. In the forefront, ahead of a row of guns, marched the mounted infantry, among which was also the detachment of the regiments of Gordon Highlanders, the Coldstream Guards, and the Scots Guards. On the other side of the strong square were the Grenadiers, the Marines, the Fifth Lancers, the "Blues"—from all the most renowned regiments one little sample, a fighting deputation. But still it was a very small army, and already tired out by endless desert marches.

And then suddenly the Arabs were upon them, as if conjured up out of the desert ground. They had mostly only spears and swords. What did these half-armed savages want to do against the Martini-Henry rifles? Against the British artillery? But they came nearer, in good formation, in a kind of threefold phalanx with three thrust-out peaks; at the head of each, as leader, a bearded emir with an enormous banner. What did they want to do? Demolish a square of British guards with spears?

And all at once—nobody knew how it could have happened—these niggers, these savages, these Dervishes had broken through, were in the middle of the closely knitted square. They hacked and struck to right and to left, and one of the flag-bearers, an old white-bearded sheikh, planted his great banner right in the centre of the square, where the camels were standing. The sheikh held a book in his hand; it was the book of prayers which the Mahdi had compiled, the new Koran of that sect, and he began chanting prayers, beneath the waving Dervish banner. A shot rang out; the old emir—he was the prince of a tribe from Kordofan—toppled forward on his grey-bearded face. The banner fell also, slowly, and covered him over. Now the Arabs crept in hundreds between the camels. A wild scuffle began; revolver shots cracked, not too carefully aimed; General Herbert Stewart had his horse shot; there was confusion.

But only for a few minutes. The square closed again; it stood firm again, could strike forward, over the Dervish corpses. But what losses had that short panic cost! A great many officers and men fallen. The camels simply decimated, and ammunition become really scarce. How was one going to march on farther? As far as Khartoum?

Sir Herbert Stewart, the victor (but at what a price!), occupied the desert well of Abu Klea. Now, perhaps, one would yet get as far as the Nile. But then? A hundred miles more to Khartoum, as the crow flies.

Slowly, tired and lame, the little army crept up the Nile, the army for which the man on the roof in Khartoum was waiting so longingly. Somewhere in the desert sand lay a dead soldier of the Highlanders, in a kilt in the colours of the Gordon clan, and his rigid eye was staring southwards. . . .

．　　　．　　　．　　　．　　　．

The lonely man at the telescope had turned pale when he had seen the storks. Nothing is more common on the Nile in winter than a flight of storks. But there was a memory bound up with the sight of storks. . . .

Charles Gordon had long known that that island he had passed then must have been Abba; and when the storks had laughed like that, the man who later became the Mahdi had certainly been standing somewhere in the night; certainly he had seen Gordon's ship on the moonlit river. Since then they had never met one another, the Mahdi and Gordon. But Gordon felt, he knew that it would yet come to pass, that he would once again meet the Mahdi, this time face to face, quite soon. It would come. In his tortured nights he understood that it would indeed have to come.

When he saw the storks in the sky he again remembered the Bible passage, the mystic prophecy about him and the Mahdi.

JEREMIAH viii. 7:
"Yea, the stork in the heavens knows her appointed time. . . ."

. . . . .

Gordon's telescope searched the horizon for the pale yellow clay walls of Omdurman. Over there, life and animation already prevailed. One could hear the Dervish war-drums quite distinctly, calling for a muster, perhaps for the attack. White-clothed figures were visible between the houses. Somewhere there was HE, the enemy, to whom Gordon knew himself to be bound by such deep and secret bonds.

"We are going to meet," thought Gordon. "Quite soon."

The clear blue eyes of the lonely dreamer swept round; his face was tired and sad. Then all at once, waking up to the day's work, he drew himself up more stiffly; in his eyes will overpowered reverie, the British general won the mastery over the fantastic highland mist of that Celtic soul.

General Gordon, as if he had come on to that roof for no other purpose, began to reconnoitre to find out at which places one could arrange sandbagged look-outs for snipers. A few good snipers could be most effective against those Dervishes over there; unfortunately, they were quite near enough.

"And this evening," thought General Gordon, "I will attempt another sortie. It keeps the troops busy. . . .

"And, who knows," he thought, suddenly cheering up, "who knows, perhaps the relieving army is quite near after all, and we don't know it!"

# THE HEAD

In the Mahdists' camp outside Khartoum, Rudolf Slatin, formerly Governor-General of Dar-Fur, lay in a tattered Bedouin tent. He lay because it was not possible for him to sit or stand, so heavily was he fettered and loaded with chains. Round his naked feet ran stout iron rings, hammered firmly round the flesh and fastened from leg to leg by short, thick rods. Another thick iron ring lay round the neck; from it hung a long chain of many links. Only a short time before, at the command of the Khalifa, they had doubled the weight of the iron, for Slatin had refused to assist in firing a siege-gun.

(Another Egyptian governor, Frank Lupton, until then Governor-General on the Gazelle River, had been standing for a long time, also with chains on his legs, behind a gun and was obliged—he, an Englishman—to bombard Gordon's fortress. But he shot very high!)

Rudolf Slatin, or rather the Mosem Abd el-Kader, had at first been fairly well treated. But then he had begun to send letters to Gordon. Gordon had not replied; he had written his reply in his military diary —cutting sentences against Slatin: Gordon did not forgive him his change of faith. Slatin, deeply distressed by Gordon's silence, for he liked Gordon very much and admired him and had reasons to be grateful to him, had written again, secretly. And then—but this time by order of the Mahdi and with the Khalifa's knowledge—he had written a letter addressed to the consul Hansal and supposed by Abdullahi to contain an invocation to surrender; but the letters smuggled through secretly were directed straight to Gordon—passionate appeals that Gordon should believe in his loyalty, in the honour of an officer of His Imperial Austrian Majesty; and there was information in them: about the strength, the armaments, and the plans of the Dervish army. How much of this correspondence the Khalifa had discovered Slatin himself did not know yet. It was enough that he was lying there and could not move. Why didn't they kill him, then? It was the habit in war to kill people who sent information to the enemy. . . .

There he lay, on a mat of palm straw in the ragged tent, seeing nothing, but hearing the cannon which were attacking Khartoum. Although no visitor was allowed to pass the thorn hedge which encircled the tent, Slatin knew very well what was going on in the camp. Among the black soldiers who were guarding him there were often some of those who had served under him in Dar-Fur. They spoke openly. Often they also brought him something to eat. But now Slatin had not received anything more for two days. Abu Anga, the emir of the black troops who by the Khalifa's orders had to watch over the imprisoned Slatin, was too busily occupied during the battle. His wives, it seemed, were letting Slatin starve on purpose. It was still asserted in the Dervish camp that Slatin was Gordon's nephew. The fat principal wife of Abu Anga was angry because Gordon's guns kept on shooting. Very well, let Gordon's nephew starve!

The chained man lay there with closed eyes and

pondered. Was this the end? Was Gordon lost? A few days before the Khalifa had come to the tent and had given Slatin a piece of paper to read, a letter written in French, which had been found on a spy from the besieged town. Gordon had written: "I still have ten thousand men. Khartoum can hold out until the end of January."

Slatin had told the Khalifa that he could not decipher it—that he did not understand the writing. . . .

Until the end of January! It *was* the end of January. In a few days. And Omdurman was in the hands of the Mahdi. The stronghold should be ripe for assault.

.        .        .        .        .

The chained-up slave of the Khalifa changed inwardly into the officer of the Austrian Army who had studied military tactics. For nine months these Mahdists had been encamped round Khartoum in such overwhelmingly superior forces, and the Khalifa had not yet ventured to undertake a serious attack. Meanwhile the floods had recently damaged the parapets on the banks of the White Nile; on that side the fortifications were practically of no further use. Why did not the Dervishes attack? They were shy of Gordon's artillery; just as they had only forced El Obeid to surrender through starvation, they would make Khartoum yield in the same way. Nobody in the Dervish camp had believed in the coming of the British expedition, because the Mahdi had not prophesied it.

The long chain on the prisoner's neck clinked; he had moved himself vigorously. A feeling of joy had welled up inside him and would not let him lie still. They had tried to hide it from him, but he knew very well what kind of news had arrived the day before. Abu

Anga's wives had first started weeping and wailing, until a eunuch had laid about them with a whip: the law of the Mahdi forbade the display of sorrow or grief for those who died, or were killed, because they had entered into the joys of Paradise. The English had been victorious at Abu Klea! The Barabra, the Jaalin, the Degheim, the Kenana, all the tribes under the Emir Musa were totally destroyed; thousands dead! And the English were said to be coming up the Nile in steamers! Rescue! Help! Even before the end of the month! Until the end of the month, Gordon had said, he could still hold out. . . .

. . . . .

Outside the tent in which Slatin was lying there suddenly arose a commotion. The prisoner jerked himself painfully into a squatting position, although then the chain round his throat half strangled him. It might be the Khalifa Abdullahi who was coming; he frequently sought out his prisoner to see whether he was already penitent, or to ask him some more suspicious questions.

But this time it was only the black principal wife of the Emir Abu Anga, who was standing outside the tent; Slatin could hear her scolding voice. This wretch Abd el-Kader, the son of an infidel dog—his father would be tortured in hell—ought, before he was fed, to induce his uncle Gordon not to shoot at Abu Anga. . . .

Rudolf Slatin listened awhile, then lay down again, with a noise like a dog straining at a chain.

. . . . .

Somewhere in the desert, not far from the Nile, but oh so far from Khartoum!

## THE HEAD

A British officer, still a young man, with the badges of a major of the Royal Engineers, had dismounted during a reconnoitring ride, climbed upon a stony hilltop and was now bending over a big map. In the distance a small escort was waiting.

The major (his name was Herbert Kitchener) wiped his moist forehead. When he took off his topee a sunburned, soldierly face appeared, a face with bushy eyebrows, bushy moustache—an iron face fit for an equestrian statue.

Major Kitchener examined his map: yes, he thought, that was how the thing would have to be done, that was how it would have to be prepared. Gordon's own mistake, in reality. He ought to have insisted himself upon the building of that railway, before it was too late. A railway line there, where the Nile is unnavigable because of the cataracts—that alone guaranteed the possession of the Sudan. A line from Wadi Halfa along the river, or, better still, if it could be ventured, here, straight across the empty desert to Abu Hamed. In that way you cut off the great bend of the Nile, avoided the third and fourth cataracts, reached the river where it was again navigable. That was absolutely the only way the Sudan could be held, that was the only way to reconquer it. This present expedition of theirs with the picturesque camel corps—quite laughable. There was no sense in Wolseley's reinforcements; how could one get to Khartoum in time? Unless a miracle happened and the steamers found Gordon still alive. . . . But the Dervishes would have to be crazy indeed. . . .

Herbert Kitchener drew a vigorous line across the map with his thumb at the place where the great bend of the river was marked, and said to himself, audibly:

"So long as the railway is not there, the Sudan belongs to the Dervishes. If the railway is built one day, then we have the whole Sudan. I should like to see the man who can prevent me. If I can get reinforcements straight across the Nubian Desert, then the so-called Dervish army no longer interests me, or what the Khalifa thinks he is or what the Mahdi preaches. But for the incompetence of this Government things would never have gone so far; the Gladstone Cabinet has lost the Sudan and upset everything for many years.

"If they would only leave it to me——

"I build the railway and then Khartoum is mine!" thought Kitchener.

.    .    .    .    .

Two paddle-boats were steaming full speed up the Nile towards Khartoum. The *Bordein* and the *Telahawieh* belonged to the little flotilla which Gordon had sent out of the besieged city to the cataracts to meet the British expedition. After the sanguinary battle near the well of Abu Klea the camel corps commanded by Sir Herbert Stewart had at last reached the Nile near Gubat, and there had found the steamers. They were still attempting to proceed farther on land and to take the next fortified village, Metemmeh; but it was beyond their power. The troops had been through terrible fighting; their General Stewart lay mortally wounded. The expedition remained hopelessly stranded; but one could still try, with the help of the steamers, to reach Khartoum quickly and save Gordon.

In the place of Sir Herbert Stewart, Colonel Sir Charles Wilson had taken over the command. He decided to travel himself on the *Bordein* to Khartoum

## THE HEAD

and to take the *Telahawieh* also; these were the best of the four old paddle steamers at his disposal. Space was very restricted, and Colonel Wilson had only been able to take with him twenty English infantrymen from the Sussex Regiment, apart from the two hundred negroes of Gordon's who were on the steamer. Even if Wilson had dared to weaken his land troops still further, there would not have been any room on the boats for Europeans. They were both very small, and Gordon had used the space on deck for a breastwork of boiler-plating, which could partly protect the vessel from rifle-fire from the river-banks. They were fitted with bullet-proof turrets in the bows and amidships, and armed with small brass howitzers. Cast-iron sheets on the deck served as protecting shields for the infantrymen.

The boats were by no means ill secured against attack; but they were thick with dirt. For five months the negro soldiers had been leading here the life of Nile pirates. Now people were still stuffing into every corner that was still empty sacks full of *durrha* for Gordon's starving garrison. The deck was clogged with *durrha* and iron bulwarks. In the little reeking cabins were piles of *durrha*. Wherever you looked—*durrha* and armaments.

It was not very comfortable on board those boats: nothing but *durrha* and sweating people and rats which had been allured by all that *durrha*. Besides the combatants there was also the bevy of black women, without which one could not imagine Sudanese troops.

Slave women who pounded up the *durrha* and baked breadcakes made of *durrha* at dangerous open fires. Even black babies crawled among the sacks of *durrha*.

All that was not very pleasant for the twenty British

Tommies of the Sussex Regiment, and they swore a bit and grumbled, as soldiers will. But really this adventure was more welcome to every one of them than the endless desert marches of the previous weeks and those many fights in which you got such a frightful thirst....

Now the twenty redcoats at least had water! Yes, one could now call them redcoats again. It had been a difficult thing to raise the twenty red parade uniforms in the little expedition, but it had been managed. Each of the twenty soldiers had his British scarlet coat; this was expected to produce a great effect. General Gordon had written pressingly that there should be red uniforms to be seen when the steamers appeared before the besieged fortress.

.   .   .   .   .

More than show the red coats of live Tommies—more than that Colonel Wilson would hardly be able to achieve if he reached Khartoum. He had received from the Commander-in-Chief, Lord Wolseley, only orders to convey an important letter to Gordon, a supply of *durrha*, a big case full of silver dollars as pay for his troops—then to parade his British uniforms through the whole of Khartoum, and then to re-embark with his small detachment and return back to the column. For the time being, one could not hope to do more than support Gordon morally. A proper assistance, a relief of the besieged town, would be possible in four weeks' time at the earliest. Then perhaps Lord Wolseley, with the bulk of his little army, would have arrived as far as the place where the flying column now found itself in such difficulties. The march forward through the pathless desert was

STEAMER CROSSING NILE RAPIDS

Contemporary photograph taken during Lord Wolseley's Nile Expedition

so terribly arduous. Perhaps in another month, if everything went well . . . So long at least Gordon would have to hold out.

The two boats which had to bring him that consolation and the dazzling sight of the twenty redcoats sailed on as fast as they possibly could. But the Nile was very low; they were constantly getting stranded, although the Arab captains were skilful. Also it was necessary to stop again and again in order to demolish houses and water-wheels in deserted villages: they used the wood to heat the boilers. And each time they had to do that there was a sudden hullabaloo, for the black soldiers, instead of hacking up wood, started to plunder. Colonel Wilson used his hippo-whip ruthlessly; but still the journey was constantly being delayed.

The river-banks on either side were enemy country. Many times everything seemed, from the boats, to be deserted and empty of human beings; then suddenly there came shots out of the fields of tall *durrha*; or else a gun was hidden somewhere and suddenly opened fire on the steamer. All that was of little use: those two tiny wooden boats, about as big as the "penny steamers" at home on the Thames and barricaded with sheets of iron, with their modern guns on board, were actually a redoubtable force in this half-savage land; and if the low water-level did not hold them up the Dervishes would not be able to do anything serious against them.

But on the 26th January, just before the gorge of Shabluka (not far from Khartoum), the sandbanks lay bare and the steamers had great difficulty in proceeding any farther. One of them ran aground twice. Colonel Wilson was consumed with impatience.

A whole day lost! And who knew what was happening in Khartoum meanwhile?

Who knew . . . ?

. . . .  .

On the 25th January, 1885 (it was a Sunday), Khartoum was full of rumours of victory. People did not know from where they came, but in the starving town they spoke of a great success which the English Expeditionary Force had achieved—at the well of Abu Klea, it was said. Yes, even that steamers with English red-coated soldiers were already on the way to Khartoum—some people professed to know. Such rumours, if they were rumours, reached Gordon's palace from the Dervish camp in the course of a few hours. Then, in the outposts and the barricades and the fortifications, there had been lately a suspicious movement hither and thither, to and fro. No one knew that better than General Gordon.

The good news hardly caused much joy now. This was the three hundred and sixtieth day of the siege, and people felt too miserable even for rejoicing. For a long time no one had eaten properly in Khartoum. There was a kind of bread which Gordon had invented, made of the bark of palm-trees and gum. . . .

That was the state of affairs in Khartoum then. The money which one had to accept by the Governor-General's orders consisted of some kind of pitifully printed pieces of paper on which could be read: "Worth one Egyptian pound."

That such bread still passed for bread and such money still for money was Gordon's triumph. It was a wonder what confidence this man was able to spread around him! Even now the Greek merchants refused

## THE HEAD

to flee on the last steamers. As long as Gordon was there all was well. And the black soldiers were still as loyal as ever. They wore, with great pride, the decorations that Gordon conferred. Gordon, Gordon, nobody but Gordon was still holding this doomed fortress. . . .

On that Sunday evening the Governor-General, who was always having new ideas, had ordered a kind of festival of victory to celebrate the rumours. The band had played the Egyptian anthem outside the palace, *Salaam Effendina: Greeting to our lord the Khedive*—and then *God save the Queen*, and some fireworks had been let off.

Gordon himself had not appeared. He was so tired. For three hundred days he, and he alone, had been holding the town against the Mahdi. If he only had one single British officer by him who could re-build the fortifications on the White Nile which had been destroyed by the flooding of the river!

It was no use brooding. General Gordon lay down to sleep, dressed as he was, of course, in his uniform of white drill. Sword and revolver lay beside him.

.   .   .   .   .

As he was falling asleep, Gordon was still thinking of that parapet on the bank of the White Nile, which was so much damaged, and of the canals choked with debris. Who was preventing the Mahdi from breaking in there? To-morrow already? Or this very night?

Gordon could not help thinking about it. At that point Faraj Pasha commanded the front, an officer whom he no longer trusted at all. But which of his officers did he still trust? Only the soldiers, those black children, were good.

## THE MAHDI OF ALLAH

Gordon sighed; he fell asleep.

.   .   .   .   .

He dreamt about Scottish pipers who came marching up in tartan kilts, with beribboned bonnets, playing *The Campbells are coming!*—no, not the Campbells! It was the Gordons who were coming. Clan Gordon, for thousands and thousands of years. All the ancestors were marching together—and Augusta was there, too, and she smiled and stretched out her arms....

But of a sudden the shrill tones of the bagpipes changed and turned into a frightful laugh. Gordon, in his sleep, knew that it was a stork that had laughed. A voice spoke: "The stork in the heavens knows her appointed time."

Then all was still and Gordon was alone in an infinity of space with an awe-inspiring presence—a man whom he had never seen but knew nevertheless. It was the Mahdi. He was smiling benevolently. Gordon tried to jump out of his bed, and could not. He knew quite well, in his sleep, that he was lying on the bed and could not move. And yet he wanted to ask the Mahdi something important, the decisive thing: whether the Mahdi was really a good or a bad man. Everything depended on that. For three hundred and sixty days Gordon had really been thinking about nothing else....

And then the Mahdi opened his lips at last and made an answer, at last, at last, to the unspoken question. The Mahdi spoke sonorous words out of the Bible, not out of the Koran, but Gordon knew now that it was the same. Those words from the Bible which Gordon had read only yesterday evening, but which he only now understood properly, contained—it was so clear

## THE HEAD

now—the real great mystery: the co-existence of good and bad, the unity of God with Evil.

The Mahdi, in the dream, said, smilingly and clearly:

"Isaiah, forty-five, seven:

"I am the Lord, and there is none else. I form the light, and create darkness; I make peace, and create evil; I am the Lord, that doeth all these things."

The voice swelled; Gordon did not know whether it was still the Mahdi who was speaking to him. But he was going to meet the Mahdi yet, who knew. . . .

The stentorian voice said:

"Amos, three, seven:

"Shall the trumpet be blown in a city, and the people not be afraid? Shall evil befall a city and the Lord hath not done it?"

No, not the Scotch bagpipes. Not the Dervish drums. The trumpet, the trumpet!

And suddenly Gordon knew, still in his deep sleep that it was not the trumpet either, but the ombaya, the hollow elephant tusk, the war-horn of the Khalifa Abdullahi. . . .

Quite near. A tumult. Outside people were running. Gordon knew instantly: the weak spot by the White Nile! Somebody yelled "Help! They're in the town already!"

General Gordon, fully awake, grabbed his revolver and plunged headlong out of the room.

. . . . .

In the camp of the Dervish army near Omdurman, Slatin was still lying in his dire chains. He was crouching on all fours outside the tent, trying to see as far as possible what was going on; but he saw nothing but a blood-red morning sun which was rising in the east.

Before daybreak the terrific din of rifle fire had awakened him. The firing had only lasted a few minutes; after that there were only single shots. Rudolf Slatin knew what the shooting must mean. The afternoon of the day before he had learned that there were really two steamers quite near to the town, with red-coated soldiers on board. Also it was being said in the camp that the Khalifa now wanted to attempt an assault at any price. The shooting in the night was an attack on Khartoum—but how had it turned out?

Slatin still cherished hopes. The fight had not lasted long, anyhow. . . .

But now there suddenly arose a great clamour, quite near. The prisoner raised himself painfully, trying to see something. He perceived a knot of people who were coming straight towards his tent. Their cries could be heard already.

Slatin turned pale. Yes! those were triumphant cries!

In front of that crowd, which was moving nearer, in disorder, marched three black giants, slave soldiers. Slatin recognised one of them: he was a negro, called Shatta, the slave of a certain Dafalla who had once been a guest of Slatin in Kordofan. This negro, Shatta, was now carrying something in his paws, a dripping bundle, a bloody cloth. . . .

Somebody shouted exultantly; somebody was weeping aloud; somebody jeered. Slatin no longer distinguished anything; his heart stood still. The negro, Shatta, removed the cloth, and a bloody head appeared, with snow-white hair and side-whiskers—Gordon's head!

## THE HEAD

The blue eyes were open, the mouth was smiling peacefully.

"Is that the head of your uncle, the unbeliever?" asked the negro, Shatta.

Slatin answered at once: "He was a brave soldier, and he is happy now that he has fallen!"

He said this firmly and defiantly, from the depths of a great despair. He was indifferent now as to what happened to him. Gordon was dead and had not forgiven him!

The prisoner's hands tightened convulsively over the chains. He made an oath within himself.

. . . . .

Gordon's head, fixed to a tall spear, was set up outside the Mahdi's tent. The Arab warriors who had slain the Governor-General of the Sudan on the steps of his palace, had gone before the Mahdi with the greatest fear, because he had ordered that Gordon should be left alive. But he had pardoned the disobedience and the trophy of victory stood before his tent.

The camp of the Dervishes was now almost deserted, for over there on the other side of the river there was the town to be plundered, women to be carried off, men to be tortured, hidden treasure to be extorted. The savagery of Africa was let loose, robbery and murder and the whip ran riot in Khartoum, and a ghastly tumult of animal-like cries sounded across the peacefully flowing Nile. . . .

In the deserted camp all was lonely and quiet. Mohammed the Mahdi was alone with Gordon's head, outside his tent. Now, at last, they had met each other. However much their two lives had touched each other, they had still never been so close together. Unless it was one night years before, when a steamer was passing by a certain island in the Nile....

.    .    .    .    .

The Mahdi sat with crossed legs on his sheepskin at the entrance of the great tent, opposite the spear with Gordon's head. The Mahdi was now extraordinarily fat; ponderously he sat there, the bulky thorax quite shapeless under the Dervish shirt. With his left hand he supported himself on his haunches, as though he could not sit otherwise; the free right hand fingered the rosary. Was the Mahdi praying? The full lips were not moving. The face was curiously bloated; the usual radiant smile was frozen into a mask....

No, that was no longer a smile. It was rather the dead man who was smiling. Of the two faces looking each other in the eyes there, that of the dead man was more alive, more open, more cheerful. The living head of the Mahdi, a mask of fat and unction and godliness, looked horrible. Only the eyes were as clear as ever and wonderfully beautiful beneath the long lashes; those eyes could never doubt.

The Mahdi's face gazed at Gordon's head. What was going on behind that mask, behind both those masks? The dead face also might have been able to see, with its clear blue eyes. Did those two there know at least in that hour that in reality they had always stood close to one another, the Christian mystic to the Mohammedan Sufi, the interpreter of the Bible to the interpreter of the Koran? Could there really be between them now, face to face with each other, a genuine hatred still?

For hours the Mahdi sat thus, opposite his enemy,

who, in a differently ordered world, would have been his closest brother. The open eyes of the dead man gradually veiled themselves, saw the other no more. ... The other, motionless, smiled always more serenely. Only his hand at the wooden rosary moved a little.

What formulas was he repeating inside himself, what intoxicating sequences of long prayers which bring about the uttermost ecstasies? Great are the mysteries of which a Sufi of the highest grade is master, boundless the raptures which the union with the consciousness of God can bring him. As he sat there, a mighty pile of flesh, swollen out of all shape, inhuman, the Mahdi was a mountain of superiority over earthly things. It was no common joy over victory, no mean exultation over the fallen foe that looked upon that bloody trophy, but rather self-assured knowledge, floating sublime above that head, which was European in spite of everything, and after all, had striven and doubted and despaired all the days of its existence....

A great, a permanent serenity was in the eyes of the squatting Sufi. Everything was as it had to be. This victory was only a proof, a self-evident one, in support of the Faith. The future was equally certain: that the Khedive, that Victoria would have to recognise the Mahdieh, soon, even before the day when Isa, the son of Maryam, would descend upon the dome of the Mosque of the Rock at Jerusalem, to begin the Judgment. A stern judgment for all; but not for the one who had already grown out of all worldly things, the virtues and the vices of ordinary people—for the one who had long since united with the Divinity, the Wise One, the Twelfth Imam, the Mahdi.

•   •   •   •   •

## THE MAHDI OF ALLAH

Two days afterwards two small steamers travelled along the river before the battery at Halfaya and passed the difficult spot safely, although under heavy fire. In the armoured turret on board the *Bordein* stood Sir Charles Wilson, sheltered by the iron bulwarks, and bit his lip. General Gordon must now have long since seen the steamers from his look-out on the roof of the palace. The sortie must have been effected by now.

Nothing!

Then could it, in Heaven's name, be true—what a Bedouin horseman only yesterday had called out to the steamers from the river bank?

The river banks were swarming with Dervishes. Everywhere shooting was going on; everywhere enemies lay under cover. On the island of Tuti, also, at the junction of the Blue Nile with the White Nile there were enemy trenches and the two steamers were shot at from there. But Gordon had a fort there, hadn't he?

And now it was seen quite clearly that they were firing from the peninsula between the two Niles also, they were firing at the steamers from the town itself. Now the boats were so near the town that the tallest building, the Government House, could be clearly seen. The big Egyptian flag which had always waved there was not to be seen. No, the flag was no longer floating above Gordon's palace. . . .

The enemy's fire grew hotter; it was becoming menacing since the bullets were coming from positions in Khartoum also. Colonel Wilson now knew all. There was no object in going any further, straight into the lion's jaws. Wilson gave the order to turn back. If they were lucky and the steamers did not get stranded, they would fight their way back again as far as the British advance guard and be able to bring the terrible news to Lord Wolseley.

## THE VICTORY

THE WHOLE world heard the news of the victory of the Mahdi, and was shocked and amazed.

In her castle at Osborne, Queen Victoria was sitting and writing a letter to Gordon's sister Augusta:

". . . and what I do so keenly feel, the *stain* left upon England for your dear Brother's cruel, though heroic fate. . . ."

The old lady clenched her small fleshy hand. Her feelings were the same as those of the entire British public. The idea was intolerable that a British General, the nation's favourite, had been overcome by this black Dervish.

All the enemies that Great Britain had in the world looked on hopefully.

Through occupied Egypt, slight, but noticeable, there went a tremor, a quiver of excitement. But not only here: the whole of Moslem Africa was filled with attention, expectation, hope. From Morocco envoys were on their way to Khartoum, to see the Mahdi. In distant Afghanistan the name of this Sudanese stiffened the resistance against the British power; in India young Moslems dreamed of the coming of the Mahdi. France, still irresolute whether the *revanche* for 1871 would not have to be achieved in a struggle with the British world empire, followed vigilantly the events in the Sudan. Would not the Mahdi now lead a powerful army against Egypt? Would not the Egypt-

## THE VICTORY

ians greet him as a saviour, as a liberator? Would he not triumph in Egypt as in the Sudan? Would not a mighty rebellion sweep the English army of occupation into the Mediterranean? Then, perhaps, the decisive hour would have arrived for France. . . .

The eyes of the whole world were turned towards Khartoum, towards this half-savage Dervish. For a moment it seemed as if from his next action hung the fate of the earth.

He, however, did nothing; he was savouring his victory.

.   .   .   .   .

It was victory, complete victory. When the crews of Colonel Wilson's steamers, after epic adventures on their way back, brought the news of Gordon's death to the British, Lord Wolseley's advance guard withdrew from its perilous positions; the British expeditionary force forthwith relinquished the town of Dongola and marched slowly back over the Upper Egyptian frontier. In Eastern Sudan, in Sennar and Kassala, the Egyptian garrisons were still holding out, were holding out obstinately; but how much longer? Otherwise the whole Sudan was more or less completely in the hands of the Mahdi. In the distant Equatorial Province on the upper Nile they were feeling the pressure of the victorious Dervishes more and more strongly; Emin Pasha, when he learnt of the fall of Khartoum, was forced to abandon Lado and withdraw to the south; his troops were beginning to mutiny.

It was victory, the complete victory of the Mahdi.

.   .   .   .   .

There lay Khartoum, Gordon's fortress, the citadel

of the Turkish tyranny, Khartoum, that magnificent centre of civilisation which Gessi had been so enthusiastic about—defenceless, open, shattered. All the hordes that ferried across the Nile from Omdurman, could murder and plunder all day long. The few Europeans who were still in Khartoum were cruelly massacred—the Greeks, the Copts, the Egyptian government officials. The Austrian consul, Hansal, once a schoolmaster in Vienna, was dragged into the yard of his house and there beheaded. On his corpse they threw the tobacco which was found in the house, a strangled parrot, and a dead dog, and then the whole was sprinkled with the consul's brandy and set alight. The Greek consul, Leontides, had his hands cut off, and only then his head. The tailor, Klein (strange that he should not have died of drink!), had his throat cut from ear to ear before the eyes of his family and was left to bleed to death. As he lay there, they speared his eldest son over his body. The unhappy mother, who was forced to witness all this, became as though raving mad, beat about her in the air, shrieking. That had an effect on those savage murderers; they spared the tailor's remaining children. But they carried off the eighteen-year-old daughter into a harem. Mohammed Pasha Hussein, Gordon's Finance Minister, found his daughter and her husband murdered. He himself could have fled, but instead of doing so he stayed and shouted imprecations against the Mahdi, until they came and cut him down.

Ten thousand people died in the fatal town. Slaves killed their masters; every revengeful lust could be appeased. It was enough if a man was from Egypt or of the tribe of the Shaigieh which had stood by Gordon. Such people, and the dogs, were killed in

every street. The doctrine of the Mahdi was hostile to impure dogs. A Dervish proverb prophesied:
"The Shaigieh, the Egyptian, and the dog will find neither rest nor peace in the Mahdieh."

Only boys were spared, for they could be sold as slaves, and women who were suitable for the harems of the conquerors. Older women were cruelly tortured to make them confess where money was buried. All over Khartoum were heard the cries of tortured people. They were hung up by their thumbs, or a hoop made of bamboos was tied round their temples.

All that happened on the 26th January, while Wilson's steamers were still on the way, and Gordon's unburied corpse was lying headless outside the palace, and the Mahdi was sitting over there in Omdurman, with his impenetrable smile.

.   .   .   .   .

On the following day mercy and indulgence were proclaimed. Even the merchants of Khartoum were to remain alive, as long as they renounced vain worldly riches. They were left free either to cast their wares into the water, or to send them to the Beit el-Mal, the communal treasure-house of the Dervishes. All of them understood the hint and chose the treasure-house.

On that day, Tuesday, the Mahdi and the Khalifa went on board the *Ismailia*, on which Gordon could, perhaps, still have fled, had he wished to—and travelled up from Omdurman to Khartoum, where the finest houses were held ready for them. The Mahdi had been in Khartoum when the two English steamers appeared before the town; while Colonel Wilson was so anxiously searching for the Egyptian flag on the roof of the palace, the Mahdi was there. But it was not his wish to make Khartoum—a city of the unbelievers, the sinful city which had been punished by God—the capital of the new empire. He inspected the enormous booty in Khartoum, prayed publicly in the mosque, and then returned to the other bank, to Omdurman. There a new city sprang up within a few weeks.

．　　．　　．　　．　　．

All the riches of Khartoum were conveyed to Omdurman. In Khartoum only the arsenal and wharfs for the steamers remained. Everything that was movable was heaped up together in Omdurman. The Arab warriors who had plundered so zealously now had to listen to a new preaching: whoever kept so much as a nail of the booty of the unbelievers would at some future time have to search for it in the bottom of the burning furnace of Hell! And there was no lack of equally diabolical earthly punishments for those who clung to their booty. None the less, the great ones, the sheikhs and emirs, became very suddenly rich.

But the Beit el-Mal, the communal treasure-house, was full to overflowing of the stolen treasures. In one courtyard the *durrha* lay stacked so high that one could see the pile, like a real mountain, from afar. There were whole rooms filled with gold jewellery and silver jewellery and English gold sovereigns and Maria-Theresa dollars. In separate rooms of the Beit el-Mal gold brocade and costly coloured silk stuffs were cut up into tiny pieces; these were made into decorative patches with which to adorn the beggars' costumes, the garments of humility—the Dervish shirts.

In the Beit el-Mal lay pell-mell the bric-à-brac of European civilisation, which had commenced so full

HANSAL, AUSTRIAN CONSUL IN KHARTOUM, KILLED
BY THE MAHDISTI

of promise in Khartoum: those jam-pots and oil-lamps, about which poor Gessi had been so enthusiastic in his letters to the *Esploratore*. There lay bath-tubs, printing-presses, the Governor's carriage—and a magic lantern. . . .

. . . . .

To the Beit el-Mal was also attached a big slave *zariba* with two divisions: one for the black slave-women and slave-children and one for the whites. The slaves, with iron rings round their necks and fastened to a long chain in groups of twenty and thirty, waited there until they were sold by auction for the benefit of the treasury; but first the youngest and prettiest women, the white ones above all, were distributed to the great men of the Dervish state. The first choice fell to the Mahdi himself, then came the three khalifas, then the great emirs and finally the ashraf, the relatives of the Mahdi.

The wives and daughters of the Turkish pashas, of the Oriental Christians, often entered the harems of the men who had murdered their husbands and fathers.

A certain Amina was brought, among many other women, to the quarters of the Mahdi's wives. Her father was Abu Bekr el-Jarkuk, a Khartoum notable who had also been murdered; Amina's husband, too, had been among the victims and her children had died of starvation. She was a woman of rare beauty; so she was chosen for the Mahdi. People said in Khartoum that she loved the Mahdi with passion.

. . . . .

After the news of the retreat of the British Nile

army had arrived from the frontier near Dongola, the Mahdi preached about it publicly in the mosque. There was no further doubt: this was victory, complete victory! The Mahdi had beheld in a vision how things were going with the fleeing English, Turks, and men who refuted the Mahdieh: he knew that in the middle of the desert their water gourds had suddenly begun to leak and all the water had run out; in a miraculous way holes had suddenly appeared in them, so that the enemy would all have to die of thirst....

Now, in the Sudan, only Sennar and Kassala still had to be forced to surrender, and then——

Already the Mahdi's scribes were preparing the letters through which, after the complete subjugation of the Sudan, Mehemed Tewfik, the Viceroy of Egypt, John, Negus of Abyssinia, and also Victoria, Queen of England, were to be enjoined to convert themselves: if they did not acknowledge the Mahdi's teaching they would certainly suffer Gordon's fate, for he, also, had been full of pride and arrogance!

In all the lands of Islam secret messengers travelled with letters in which the new doctrine was preached. The Mahdi was even looking already to far-off Morocco. In Egypt he had plenty of secret friends. His dream of a victorious march through the whole world had not yet faded away.

. . . . .

But the victory had made everything so different. Now, besides the dream, there was also an empire which had to be ruled—an everyday reality which had to be dominated every day.

The campaign against Egypt demanded arms and equipment. The steamers had been captured, but

## THE VICTORY

they were damaged. There were masses of arms, but not enough powder. There was gold and silver, but not sufficient minted gold. On the wharf at Khartoum, in the arsenal, and in the mint, work was beginning again. The workshops and tools had been captured, but the workmen had been killed—the skilled Egyptian dock workers and those who understood steam engines and knew what gunpowder can be made out of. The Mahdieh, which had taken up arms against the civilisation of Europe, looked round, as soon as its domination had been established, for European armourers, for engineers, for people who were capable of printing the Mahdi's Prayer Book. Here or there, in some prison or other, there lay in heavy chains a European or an Egyptian who perhaps knew how to do it. Ought one to flog him, ought one to kill him, or ought one to employ him in the arsenal, or on the wharf?

There was Frank Lupton, the Englishman, there was Slatin....

. . . .

The Expected Mahdi, who had set out to renounce earthly goods, had, in spite of everything, to pay his troops. Soon silver pieces were struck, Mejidieh coins, with the heraldic sultan's hand on one side, though not with the name of the Turkish sultan upon it, but with the inscription: "By order of the Mahdi."

And on the reverse: struck in the year of the Hejira 1302.

Above it was also a number: 5. That meant "In the fifth year of the Mahdieh."

Five years had gone by since the Dervish of Abba, in his dream, had stretched out his hand towards the sword of the Prophet, the sword that meant war against all worldly things. Now an image of that same hand was stamped on 20-piastre pieces.

.   .   .   .   .

Before the victory it had been different; one could dream of pure renunciation, of a wealthless community in God, of equality among the Ansar. . . .

Victory, booty, power—that changed everything. Just as the lean Dervish of Abba swelled bodily almost before the eyes of his people, so his band of inspired followers grew into an army, and then into a state: this Beit el-Mal into which men, renouncing the world, had to pour their earthly possessions, became a Finance Ministry, paid out wages and took in taxes—yes, taxes, just like those which the Turk extorted. In place of the beys and pashas, who had been killed, a host of scribes, administrators, and governors of provinces assembled round the Mahdi. It could not be otherwise, all this was now no longer a dream—it was a government.

The Mahdi had told his companions that they were to be equal and like brothers, except in war, in commanding and obeying. Now, so shortly after the war, they were already unequal in rank. Those who had formerly been disciples of the wandering Dervish, even before the vision of Abba, called themselves the "First-born" of the Mahdieh and looked down on the Ansar, who had only come to Abba to fight against the soldiers of the pasha. The Ansar of Gadir, who had come to the Mahdi on the mountain, were again lower in grade; the later a man adhered to the party the less he counted for now, after the victory and in the division of the booty.

## THE VICTORY

The ashraf also, the relatives of the Mahdi from Dongola, reckoned themselves much more important than the others, by reason of their Sherif blood. The cousins of the Mahdi behaved as if the fighting had been done solely on their own account; they were hated because of their overbearing attitude. Between them and the relatives and countrymen of Abdullahi, the Baggara, prevailed a deep-rooted enmity. Only the fact that the Mahdi and the Khalifa were so firmly united prevented open conflict between camel Arabs and cattle Arabs, between the Ashraf and the Baggara.

But in this hour of victory Mohammed Ahmed and Abdullahi were as close to one another as they had ever been. Success had changed everything, except only this alliance between these two men so unlike each other, between the dreamer and the soldier, the gentle one and the violent, the spirit of the new faith —and its mailed fist.

. . . . .

Soon after the fall of Khartoum the Mahdi issued a new proclamation:

Know ye, O my followers, that the representative of the righteous (Abu Bakr) and the emir of the Mahdi army, referred to in the Prophet's vision, is Es Sayid Abdullahi Ibn Es Sayid Hamadallah. He is of me and I am of him. Behave with all reverence to him as you do to me, submit to him as you submit to me, and believe in him as you believe in me, rely on all he says, and never question any of his proceedings. All that he does is by order of the Prophet or by my permission. He is my Agent in carrying out the will of the Prophet.

If he sentence any of you to death or confiscate your property, it is for your good, therefore do not disobey him.

All those who believe in God and in me must also believe

in him, and should anyone notice anything apparently wrong in him, they should attribute it to a mystery which they cannot understand, and that therefore it must be right.

The Khalifa Abdullahi is the commander of the faithful, and is my khalifa and agent in all religious matters. Therefore I leave off as I have begun—"believe in him, obey his orders, never doubt what he says, but give all your confidence to him and trust him in all your affairs." And may God be with you all. Amen.

That raised the Taaishi high above the two other khalifas of the Mahdi, placed him almost on a level with the Master, raised him above the Ashraf, although they were of Mohammed Ahmed's own blood, above the brothers, the young sons of the Mahdi.

That the Khalifa would one day be the successor of the Mahdi was not written in the proclamation. The Mahdi would die, of course, but only after distant decades, in Jerusalem!

.        .        .        .

Rabia et Tani, Jumad el Auwal, Jumad et Tani, Rejeb, Shaban—so the months of the Moslem year succeeded one another; in Europe—the end of January till the middle of June. Gordon had died at the end of January, and still the Mahdi's army had not set itself in motion to conquer the remaining parts of the world. Omdurman, first a camp, was now a big town. The Khalifa had built himself a house; Gordon's bath-tub could be found in it, and mirrors out of his palace. The Mahdi still lived in simple huts, but the dwellings of his wives covered a whole quarter which was carefully enclosed and hedged in. The number of the women in the harem grew and grew: it was quite a hundred already.

## THE VICTORY

Was it true what people were beginning to whisper—that the Mahdi had long ceased to be the ascetic of former times? That he was not only immoderate in his appetite for women, but also yielded to extravagant excess in eating? That is to say, that he liked simple dishes, the coarsest kinds of fish, *durrha* cakes with sour *mulakh* sauce, beans, nuts, sesame, and all such plain, common things—but that he consumed the food in prodigious quantities, entirely without moderation. He, the man who had preached on Abba:

"The way of Mahdieh is based on six virtues: Humility; Meekness; Patience in suffering; Praying at the tombs of holy men; Abstemiousness in eating; Abstemiousness in drinking."

.   .   .   .   .

After victory everything is different! The young Dervish Mohammed Ahmed had once fallen out with his teacher, Mohammed Sherif, because he had not forbidden a circumcision festival.

The victorious Mahdi caused the ceremony to be performed on his sons on the day of the Ascension of the Prophet, and there was a mighty banquet; cattle and sheep were slaughtered; the Ashraf, the emirs and the great ones regaled themselves with feasts of raw camels' livers and other luxurious dishes; rejoicing and pleasure reigned in Omdurman.

.   .   .   .   .

The Mahdi's star stood very high; now, after the crushing of Gordon, very few indeed still doubted in him, not even the people whose sufferings had not diminished. The hot summer, the influx of humanity in the alleys of huts in Omdurman, the poverty of the masses, had provoked diseases; hundreds died daily of smallpox. That disturbed the festive spirit. Some said that the English had poisoned the conserves which had been found after their retreat. "No," others said, "the smallpox is a punishment from God; only those die who do not recite the Ratib, the new prayer-book compiled by the Mahdi."

So great was the reverence for the Mahdi still, that people believed that and died without a murmur. But some few began, nevertheless, to whisper. A spy of the British Intelligence Service in Cairo, who was roaming about in the Sudan, noted down some satirical verses which he said he had heard:

> Speak to the disease: Thou and the Dongolese—
> Have a little sympathy for the poor people!
> One of you is quite enough affliction!

And Father Ohrwalder, who was still living very wretchedly in El Obeid, heard (not without pleasure, it is to be feared) such talk as this: What an impostor, what a glutton, a woman-chaser the Mahdi was, how he was gorging himself and getting fat—this sanctimonious hypocrite!

·   ·   ·   ·   ·

Was he not simply a Sufi who had been taught in his youth that for a higher grade of knowledge higher virtues were necessary? The common herd of humanity needed certain barriers which did not count for a urefa, for one united with God?

Six virtues of the common crowd the Dervish of Abba had once preached were the way of Mahdieh: Humility, Meekness, Patience, Prayer, Abstemiousness in eating and drinking.

## THE VICTORY

Later he had taught that Mahdism rested on quite other virtues: Fixity of Purpose, Trust in God, Prudence, Surrender of one's will to God, Unity of Faith, and Holy War.

That was before the victory. But what was going on now behind the smiling mask of the Mahdi? For what reason should he still keep himself tied down—he, who was united with the Divinity and so high, so high above every human sin?

## THE PULPIT

On the last day of the Month of Shaban (it was Friday, and therefore the day of the gathering for prayer), a large crowd of the faithful very early besieged the court of the mosque at Omdurman. Next day began the month of Ramadan, during which the Koran was sent down to earth: the fasting month of Islam. On this Friday before the beginning of the fasts the Mahdi was expected to pronounce an important sermon. Perhaps he would announce the great things for which people were waiting—the new campaign against Egypt and the end of the smallpox and of all the afflictions under which the faithful were suffering. One would see him, in any case, perhaps touch his garments!

. . . . .

The first to arrive pressed round the gate which led to the place of worship; there they had found a sheet of paper nailed up, and some man who was able to read, a *fikih*, read the Mahdi's proclamation to his followers.

In the name of God, the merciful.—The servant of the Lord Mohammed el Mahdi, says—The coming month is the month of Ramadan. This is the time to draw nearer to God and to contend with one another in living a God-fearing life. Consecrate the whole of this month to God, and accustom yourselves to abstinence and affliction. Troubles and afflictions come to us by the will of God to try our faith and patience. Therefore trust in God and commit yourselves to Him, and whatever happens believe that it is the best for your good and welfare, even if it seem not to be so. God is infinitely good and will not permit any evil to come upon us if we put all our trust in Him. Complain of nothing that happens to you; be patient in affliction, however severe it may be.

There is no God but God, and there is no power except it be from God. Be sure of this, my brethren. Commit yourself to Him, and speak to Him of your wants, as we are all His servants. Do not trouble me this month in any of your affairs. Let me consecrate it to God, to prayers, and to holy meditations. If any one of you lack patience and is not satisfied, then let him submit his case to my khalifas and agents and the judge; he need not trouble me.

.    .    .    .    .

While the first devout people were assembling outside the mosque and reverently listening to the proclamation, the Mahdi was lying only half awake in his house. The hut in which he spent most of his time was roomy; it was built of wooden boards and furnished with carpets.

The Mahdi—fat, swollen, enormous—lay on a fine couch which had been brought from Yemen; under his head he had a cushion of gold brocade. Here, inside the house, the Mahdi did not wear the Dervish *jubba*, but white fabrics of silky softness, and on his head an embroidered silk cap. So he lay, between sleeping and waking; perhaps the early meal had been too copious.

As he lay there—a colossus—everything about him was quite motionless, except the eyes alone, which were already awake and could see. The Mahdi's look followed his head wife, Aisha, or the black Amina, daughter of Abu Bekr el-Jarkuk. Aisha, who was called "the Mother of the Faithful," was his cousin, the daughter of Ahmed Sharfi; she had the highest rank among his wives, and perhaps really was the one nearest to the Mahdi's heart. The other was that concubine whose father and husband had perished in the massacre after Gordon's death, and who now lived in the Mahdi's harem—a gorgeous, dusky creature. At the moment she enjoyed the Mahdi's favour.

Besides the two who were always round the Mahdi there came, under the pretext of administering small services, still other wives, gliding softly into the room.

Some of them had the duty of standing behind the couch with ostrich-feather fly-brushes and fanning the flies away; others again were engaged in massaging, and were gently kneading the feet of the resting Mahdi.

These wives of the harem were white or brown or black, and of many tribes. There were copper-coloured Abyssinian Christian girls among them and Dinka negresses, as black as ebony. Their clothes indicated the degree of favour which these wives enjoyed; they were of wool with many-coloured edges, or worked through with silk, or of Egyptian shawl material. As the law of the Mahdieh forbade gold jewellery and silver ornaments, the women only wore mother-of-pearl buttons and rings and chains made of coral and onyx on their foreheads, arms, and ankles. Their hair was skilfully plaited and strangely perfumed.

Aisha, the "Mother of the Faithful," walked up to the Mahdi's resting-place. Aisha (she bore the same name as the favourite wife of Mohammed the Prophet) was no longer young and almost as fat as the Mahdi himself, whom she loved tenderly. She bent over the couch and kissed him on the forehead and neck.

## THE PULPIT

He smiled—and his eyes sought Amina.

. . . . .

While the Mahdi was still lying there and resting, the murmuring of the people outside could already be heard. The crowd on the square of the mosque had already grown thicker, and hundreds of the Ansar of superior rank, veterans of the first battles, companions of Abba and Gadir, surrounded the thorn hedge which encircled the Mahdi's collection of huts; it was their custom and a kind of privilege to receive a special blessing on such days. Several times black eunuchs came in from outside and whispered with Aisha: the crowd was growing impatient already.

But the fat "Mother of the Faithful" said, after a glance at the resting master:

"The Mahdi is still in deep contemplation and cannot come yet. But he sends the Ansar his holy blessing!"

The eunuchs went out with a deep salaam. Perhaps they grinned inwardly. When the crowd saw the Mahdi's messengers they became quite dumb with reverence, and the head eunuch solemnly spoke a formula of blessing and greeting. Those who had collected before the thorn hedge went back, filled with joy, to the court of the mosque. From the throng waiting there eager hands were stretched out towards them; it was good to touch one whom the Mahdi had blessed—holy strength went out from him.

. . . . .

It was soon time for the noonday prayer; but the Mahdi's strange sluggishness had not yet passed off. He had dropped off to sleep again; Aisha even had to wake him up. Then the women of the harem streamed in from all sides to help him in washing and dressing. Four wives brought the water bowls and then carried them away again; they took the greatest care that not a drop of the dirty water should be lost. This washing water was very holy and healing; it was sold out of the harem to sick people, who would be cured if they drank it.

In the same manner the eunuchs of the harem sold little bags full of earth; at the places on which the Mahdi had trodden, the ground was afterwards dug up. And when the Mahdi walked in the room—he had been walking with some difficulty during the last weeks—the women fell down and kissed the places which his feet had just touched.

The Mahdi's clothes were brought—the red shoes, the patched *jubba* of rough frieze, and the snow-white turban cloth. While the turban was being wound with great art, the Mahdi chatted with little Bashra, his son, and the one he was most fond of among his children. The boy, very lively and rather proud, had the large eyes of his father. He received a mild rebuke because of a gold ring which somebody had presented to him and which he was wearing on his finger.

"O my son," said the Mahdi, "only Turks wear gold ornaments, for they love worldly things."

But the Mahdi smiled as he said that. The boy—he might have been ten years old—ran off with the ring.

Outside the *zariba* the Mahdi's armed guard came up, in order to accompany him to the mosque and protect him from the rapture of the waiting people.

．　　．　　．　　．　　．

The Mahdieh scorned the magnificent edifices in

## THE PULPIT

which the Turks pray to Allah. The Mahdi's mosque in Omdurman was nothing but a huge open space; it was surrounded by a clay wall, and on rough wooden pillars rested a kind of roof-shelter of dried palm-leaves. The prayer-niche, in the direction of Mecca, was constructed of iron sheets, which had been found in the arsenal at Khartoum. In this niche the Mahdi spoke the prayers, as the imam of the assemblage of the faithful; here he could be seen from all sides. If he wished to preach, he left the prayer-niche (the *mihrab*) and mounted the *mimbar*, that is, the pulpit, exactly in the middle of the great square. The pulpit was only a simple wooden platform, to which one ascended by a few steps. But from here the Mahdi looked down upon the whole congregation and once more all could see him.

. . . . .

The Mahdi, surrounded by his armed guard, arrived at the west gate of the great square. He went in and entered the sacred niche. Outside the spearmen had had difficulty in keeping back the crowd that pushed forward. But when the Mahdi had entered the place of prayer, calm descended quite by itself—the strict order of the religious worship. Each one's place was settled beforehand, according to his rank. The khalifas, the emirs, the ashraf sat behind the Mahdi. The great crowd, numbering thousands, squatted in ten endless rows on the ground covered with mats; each one had his shoes and his weapons before him; in this way they marked their exact places, which it was very important to watch. At this spot the head of the praying man would touch the earth.

On that Friday the open-air mosque was even more

crowded than usual. The great square was quite gay with white garments. In a special place, so that one could count them, stood the *mussalamieh*, the newly-converted ones, who once had been Christians. Rudolf Slatin was not in this group; true, he now no longer lay in chains, but as a member of the Khalifa Abdullahi's body-guard, his place was next to his master.

It was quite quiet. Then something went through the silent, white-robed throng like the wind through a field of white poppies. Each one had performed the prescribed movement, had laid his hand against his ear in order symbolically to shut it against the world, and had murmured audibly:

"I will imitate this Imam and say what he is saying."

They sat stiffly erect, on their crossed legs, their faces turned towards the niche which pointed towards Mecca. Again there was quiet; and all at once the Mahdi's voice was heard, beginning to speak the prayers. It was an intoxicating voice, the flaming voice of old which, in the fattened body of this man, had not been dulled or extinguished.

. . . .

The Mahdi announced the chapter of the Koran, spoke the praises to Allah. At the customary places he threw himself down on the floor of the niche, and with a noise like a storm the thousands followed suit, each at his place. Where the toes first stood they must always remain. The position of the hands was previously determined, and also the moment when one had to stand up and bow deeply, and when one had to fall down again on one's face. The Mahdi accomplished the movements before the crowd; with one voice they repeated what he said:

## THE PULPIT

"Praise be to God, abundant praise, as He hath commanded; I testify that there is no deity but God alone; He hath no companion: affirming his supremacy, and condemning him who denieth and disbelieveth; and I testify that our Lord and our prophet Mohammed is His servant and His apostle, the lord of mankind, the intercessor, the accepted intercessor, on the day of assembling.

"O God, aid El-Islam, and strengthen its pillars, and make infidelity to tremble, and destroy its might.

"O God, assist the forces of the Muslims, and the armies of the Unitarians. O God, frustrate the infidels and polytheists, Thine enemies, the enemies of the religion. O God, invert their banners, and ruin their habitations, and give them and their wealth as booty to the Muslims."

. . . . .

There was a wave, a rushing sound; each one turned his head; the Mahdi had left the mihrab. He went straight across the place of worship as far as the steps of the pulpit. There he remained standing; all eyes rested upon him. A *murrakki* came forward—a servant of the House of God—and handed the Mahdi his sword.

In the lands which Islam had conquered, the wooden replica of the victorious sword was shown to the people during the Friday prayers in every mosque. But the sword which the Mahdi now held, with the point at the end, was not of wood. An enormous steel blade with a golden crossed hilt. It sparkled. The sword of the Mahdi, the wondrous sword surrounded by legends, which had conquered the Sudan and presently would conquer the world . . .

Involuntarily, the dark-skinned warriors of the

Dervish army laid their hands on their own weapons. Soon they would be fighting and conquering anew.

. . . . .

With the sword, which he held raised in both hands, the Mahdi climbed the steps up to the wooden platform. In the pulpit he sat down. Two crossed banners, sewn with religious texts, were lifted over the head of the preacher. He held out his sword in front of him. A pious formula was chanted. Then the Mahdi stood up. His glorious voice was heard through the deep silence of the listening thousands.

. . . . .

The sermon began with an exhortation to repentance, to contemplation during the coming Ramadan. He complained of the vices to which the Mussulman people still clung.

"Even my kin, the Ashraf," he said with severity, "are not free from them. They vie with one another in mischievousness; they believe that the Mahdieh is there for them alone."

The Mahdi took hold of his Dervish garments and shook them. He said with raised voice, as he made this gesture, symbolical of throwing something off:

"O ye Moslems! I am guiltless in their doings. Be ye as my witnesses before God the merciful!"

The Mahdi looked at the place where his relatives were sitting. They were hanging their heads, not daring to move. Possibly one of them cast an angry glance towards the Khalifa. Abdullahi was smiling coldly. The Baggara all around him began to murmur with pleasure. But the Mahdi's voice, swelling more strongly, again forced all to listen:

## THE PULPIT

"While in the world I practised two virtues. Those who love me love to follow these virtues, those who hate me also hate these virtues. Those who follow these virtues are happy in themselves, and the light of God is poured down upon them; their great aim is the practice of everything which brings them daily nearer to God. But those who do not follow these virtues are ever in trouble, in whatever station they may be they are never satisfied. It is said, 'If a man possesses two valleys of gold he will wish for a third.' Nothing satisfies him but dust. Cling therefore, my friends, to these virtues, preach them to the heathen. They are poverty and holy war."

.   .   .   .   .

The word swept over the assembly like a stormy gust of wind.

"War!" the Mahdi had said; and as he said it, he lifted up his sword with both his hands; and the gold of the sheath blazed with a fire no greater than the fire of his voice.

This was no longer the lazy, elderly man of an hour ago who had lain sleepily on his bed. There he was once more, the Dervish of Abba, there it was again, the flaming voice, the breath of which had fired a continent. Among the listeners at the Mahdi's feet were people who hated him sincerely: Rudolf Slatin, who only a short time since had been lying miserably in chains, and the half-starved Mustapha Klootz, who was dragging out a pitiable existence to its end; and the Greek and Coptic merchants—trembling renegades, they stood with downcast eyes in this hated mosque. Yet all of them felt strangely moved and impressed as they heard that voice, as those eyes rested upon them. Their rebelling hearts began to beat more strongly as the Mahdi spoke; such magic was not to be resisted.

. . . .

The Mahdi spoke of that sword, of the great deeds which it was still to accomplish in the four decades which were still allotted to him on earth. Great visions, often repeated, had announced it time and again. Angel messengers had spoken, only the previous night. . . .

In the great, devout silence of the breathless assembly the Mahdi's voice said:

"In the name of God, the merciful, the compassionate!

"I have beheld a great vision, O ye faithful. I have seen the Prophet and around him the Great Ones, the four first khalifas of Islam: Abu Bekr, Omar, Othman, the Imam Ali. And behold, they came close to the Expected Mahdi.

"And a radiant angel descended from the heavens bearing in his hands a green crown. And the angel saluted the Prophet and spoke to him thus:

" 'Your Lord salutes you and sends you His blessings, and He informs you that this is His crown of victory, His present to El Imam el Mahdi. It is a mark of victory, and He orders you to give it to him with your own hands.'

"Thereupon the Prophet presented it to the Mahdi, saying: 'There is no victory save from God.' When the Prophet had given the crown of victory to the Mahdi as a gift from God Almighty, he addressed him as follows: 'God has guarded you by His angels and prophets. No nation shall be able to face you in battle, whether of the human race or of the race of genii. These warriors who have gone forth for the religion of

## THE PULPIT

God shall be welcomed by God in the world to come. They shall be allowed into the paradise wherein are lofty palaces, chaste wives, and the greatest happiness and prosperity. These palaces are brilliant with illuminations, but some of them are left in darkness. These are given to those who have hidden or kept for their own use the booty taken in war without the permission of the Mahdi or his khalifa.' "

. . . . .

The Mahdi spoke on for a long time, now admonishing and stern, now kind and fervent. He spoke, with his sword in his hand, of the victories of the faith which God had accorded, and of those which He still would accord: after Khartoum, the Mahdi would conquer Cairo, and Mecca, and in the very end, Jerusalem.

He stood on the high pulpit and spoke with that heavenly voice; and, among the Ansar, the doubts of the latter days vanished. What mattered the diseases, or the iniquity of the Ashraf, or the severity with which the Khalifa ruled? Did not the crown of victory float visibly above the Mahdi's head? Did there not stand behind him a Shapeless One, a Prodigious One —Azrael, who held a flaming banner, as he had done in all the battles?

. . . . .

Almost everyone saw him. But, a few days later, this or that person would tell in whispers that the Azrael of that Friday in the mosque was not the same as the Azrael of the victorious battles of the Holy War. The Angel of Death, usually the Mahdi's invincible companion, in so many fights had, they said, suddenly bent forwards over him, shadowing his radiant face. . . .

## THE ANGEL

On Friday the Mahdi had preached of forty years of life and of victory. Four days went by; and then the usher at Abdullahi's gate noticed that his master, the Khalifa, did not return home from the Mahdi's house during the whole day.

That usher, who was waiting there barefooted and in the harlequin shirt of a Dervish, was Rudolf Slatin. Since they had released him from those terrible chains, he was once more the servant of that Khalifa whom he hated so candidly; he walked by the side of his horse and watched outside his doors.

Rudolf Slatin knew, before the other people in Omdurman, that the Mahdi lay dying.

. . . .

On the fourth day of Ramadan—it was Wednesday, —a heavy fever had overtaken the Mahdi. Yet on Friday he had seemed so full of strength—a mountain of flesh and muscle! What sudden illness could this have been?

The first murmurs in the narrow streets of Omdurman, at first only whispered, were still hardly believed. How could the Mahdi have fallen ill?

But the whispering went on, grew louder and louder. Already people were talking of poison. If someone falls ill in the Sudan, people always talk of poison. A woman of his harem was said to have poisoned the Mahdi.

## THE ANGEL

It was Amina, they said, the daughter of Abu Bekr el-Jarkuk, who had been slain. She had poisoned the Mahdi in revenge!

On Thursday evening an enormous crowd pressed round the Mahdi's *zariba* and the open-air mosque. The people could no longer be pacified. They wanted to see their Mahdi.

And then the Khalifa Abdullahi came out, with a serious face. He spoke to the people and told them it was true: the Mahdi was very sick. The crowd slunk away, perplexed.

The next day, on Friday, the Khalifa preached in the mosque instead of the Mahdi, and spoke the prayer. He exhorted the faithful to pray for the Expected Mahdi, whose life, he said, was in grave danger.

. . . . .

How was that possible? Could the Mahdi die, then? Could he be already dying now?

A stupor overcame the people, a chilly astonishment which paralysed everybody; then hot excitement. While they were still struggling to recover from the shock, the already familiar proclamation of the Mahdi was read outside the mosque and in the public places—the proclamation that raised the Khalifa Abdullahi above the other khalifas of the Mahdi: "For he is of me and I am of him." Only now people understood that here it was a question of the succession, that the Taaishi would be the heir, if the Mahdi died . . .

"But after all he cannot die," people said.

And also: "The cow-Arab? The Baggara are to rule us?"

The people of Dongola at once rallied together; while the Mahdi was still living, the deep dissension between the Baggara and the Danagla was revealed, between the Mahdi clan and the Khalifa clan.

. . . . .

The sick man lay in a spacious hut not far from the bank of the Nile. The river remained close to him until the very last.

Round the bed the bustling activities of the agitated wives were going on. Each one knew of methods used in her own country which would surely help. All the healing arts, magic formulæ and medicines of the whole of Africa were tried on the sick Mahdi, who lay there indifferent and seemed insensible of everything.

The best thing—they all knew that—was liquid butter, poured in large quantities into the sick man; also a decoction of pomegranate skins was effective. They cupped the feverish man with cupping-glasses made out of the horns of young gazelles; they burnt him with scorching irons, they injected his own urine into his eyes, they filled the room with the aroma of smouldering essences: sandal-wood, camphor, jessamine, acacia-gum and asafœtida.

Then again they tried the power of the holy talismans, the formulæ out of the Koran, the magic sentences. Ancient women and holy, wild-eyed Dervishes muttered and screamed by the sick bed. They hung a piece of the curtain of the Kaaba round the Mahdi's neck, sprinkled him with the water of the well of Zemzem, pushed between his open lips a wafer made with dust from the tomb of the Prophet. They wrote prayers on the sick man's stomach and on his hands; they wrote Suras on a piece of paper and then washed them off again; the inky water they gave to the Mahdi when he desired to drink.

## THE ANGEL

As nothing had the slightest effect, a real physician was fetched. An Egyptian doctor, Hassan Zeki, who had worked in the Khartoum hospital under Gordon, by a miracle had not as yet been executed. Now they remembered that he was available. He was very unwilling to come, but they forced him to do so. At the Mahdi's bedside he murmured undecidedly the names of diseases: Fatty Degeneration of the Heart . . . Meningitis Cerebro-Spinalis . . . Typhus Abdominalis. Yes, typhus most likely; there was an epidemic of it just then.

It may be that the Egyptian doctor in reality did not understand much about it. But one thing is certain: he took good care not to give any definite instructions. If he prescribed something and the Mahdi died, whose fault would it be then? The *hakim* took refuge in vague phrases: he had been called in very late, and all the power was with God, and Allah would help, for He was merciful . . .

. . . . .

When the lunar month of Ramadan comes in summer the fasting is extremely trying. For during the daytime the Moslem is not only forbidden to eat, but he must not drink either. Not drink, during the Sudanese summer day! It is difficult, it is almost impossible to bear. The endless hours of the frightful heat, before the night comes and one may eat and drink!

In spite of this, the whole day long a silent crowd hung round the Mahdi's huts and paid no heed to the sun. The brown and black people of the Sudan could think of nothing else but the dying Mahdi.

They could not realise that he might die now very soon . . .

They could not realise the truth—that he simply could not go on living. This forty-two-year-old man in that hut was dying—not of typhus and not of his fattened heart, and not of poison; he was dying because he had achieved his aim and because his life was accomplished. Could that African dreamer go on living, and conquer Europe? He had understood his own torrid Sudan, because the Sudan had understood him. The whirling pillar of the desert storm sinks down again to the ground once it has reached the highest limit of its ascent; it is a law of the desert.

Why was the Mahdi dying so suddenly? Because he had so swiftly vanquished Gordon, so swiftly conquered the Sudan.

The people standing round the *zariba* did not know it. Dumb and bewildered, in the scorching sun, in the drifting dust, in the torture of the dreadful thirst of the Sudan, they thronged round the African hut in which this destiny was being accomplished. It was not like the death of a human being; it was like a natural catastrophe of tropical lands—sudden, terrific, and inevitable.

. . . . .

On the ninth day of Ramadan the fever seemed to be less persistently violent. The sick Mahdi appeared now and then to be awake and conscious. He recognised Aisha, the "Mother of the Faithful," and smiled at her. Then once more he sought somebody with his eyes. Was it his children? Was it his lovely slave-girl, Amina?

But Amina, of whom the rumour was going about among the people that she had poisoned the Mahdi for revenge, was not present. Aisha would not tolerate that.

## THE ANGEL

Later the Mahdi seemed to feel better; his look became clear; he saw the solemn gathering at his bedside. The harem had been sent away, and the great ones of the Mahdi's empire had been admitted. Only Aisha, deeply veiled, was lying in the corner, restraining her sobs.

The three khalifas stood in the dying man's room, the nearest relatives of the Mahdi, his scribes, the highest emirs. The sick man had recognised them all. Then he shut his eyes; he seemed exhausted. Abdullahi came lightly up to the bed and looked at the Mahdi for a very long time. Then the Mahdi opened his eyes again; he smiled and spoke a few sentences, with his wonderful voice, which did not sound very much changed. It was not the suffering human being that was talking, but the founder of a state, the leader.

"The Prophet——" said the Mahdi.

He was struggling, making an effort; but he added the customary formula:

"The Prophet, on whom be blessing and peace—the Prophet has appointed Abdullahi as my successor. He is of me and I am of him."

The big eyes of the dying man rested a moment upon his relative, the second khalifa, Mohammed esh-Sherif. The latter was pale and bit his lip.

The Mahdi was silent; he sank down, seemed no longer conscious. Then the voice was heard once more, as clear as ever.

. . . . .

Two young Egyptian Arabs, students of the High Theological School of El Azhar, had travelled into the Sudan after the fall of Khartoum in order to see the Mahdi. They had traversed the Nubian desert dressed as Bedouins (on account of the British), and were still wearing Bedouin costume. But their young faces were finer, more intelligent and delicate than the faces of Bedouins; those features bore the stamp of centuries of culture. They were not entirely free from the influence of Europe—which they imagined they hated.

The two Egyptians were adherents of Ahmed Arabi Pasha and of the National Party and consequently enemies of the British occupation. They had left the school of the mosque of El Azhar because they cherished the hope that the Mahdi would free Egypt from the foreigners. But hardly had they arrived at Omdurman, after an arduous journey and after many dangers, than they heard that the Mahdi was dying.

The two were sitting on the bank of the Nile, at a place where a ruined water-wheel provided a little shade. They were sad, but were facing their disappointment in a manly spirit.

"When the Prophet Mohammed died," one of them remembered to himself, "the multitude of the faithful would not believe it. The Ansar stormed Aisha's house, in which the body was lying. Omar threatened with uplifted sword to kill anyone who dared to say that the Prophet had died. But Abu Bekr said: 'O ye Mussulmans, if ye pray to Mohammed, then know: he is dead. But if ye pray to God, then know—God is great and He does not die.'"

The young Egyptian was silent for a moment; then he continued, in a choked voice to which he tried to give firmness:

"So Abu Bekr saved Islam. As the first Khalif of the Prophet of Allah he won great victories in Arabia and outside Arabia and helped to spread the Faith.

THE ANGEL

The Mahdi announced in his proclamation: 'After the Prophet, Abu Bekr was the greatest of men and the most just. The Khalifa Abdullahi stands by me in the place of Abu Bekr, and the Prophet commands that he be my Khalifa.'"

The young student of El Azhar looked at his friend, whom he would gladly have persuaded. Most certainly, even if the Mahdi died, the cause of Islam need not yet be lost. How many fervent dreams had these young sons of Egypt dreamt in the court of the mosque of El Azhar—of a re-birth of Islam in the Arab nation, of a last and successful resistance against the foreigners—against that Europe which was at once admired and hated? Then the Mahdi had come, a sudden flame, a great blazing hope....

The other *mugawir* of El Azhar said, following with his eyes the flowing water of the Nile:

"No. It is useless. If the Mahdi dies—if it can be that he dies,—then I shall go back to Cairo."

"Although the English are there?" asked his friend.

"Although the English are there. It is useless. As God wills!"

.　　.　　.　　.　　.

Round the dying man's bed no one dared breathe. The Mahdi seemed to fall asleep. The face became peaceful, the smile had returned, and the features were fine and manly as they had been once before.

Then the eyes opened again. What were they seeing? Did the old visions come back at that hour, bringing consolation? The visions that the young Dervish had beheld in his cave? Did radiant beings stretch forth magic swords and crowns of victory, sent from God?

Did Jesus and Mohammed bow down to greet this man who was joining them through death?

The Mahdi's mask was impenetrable as ever. What was happening within him, what had happened within him?

He sighed a little; the lips moved. Perhaps he was standing now in the water as a little boy, in the water of the Nile, with his father, the boat-builder. Now, perhaps, he was proudly reciting his ancestral family lineage. Now he was the devout youth, the disciple of the holy sheikh....

Then the smiling lips in the Mahdi's face were closed; the mask became colder and harder. Now it was the mystic rider on the desert storm. It was the Twelfth Imam, who suddenly came out of the Unknown—the Expected Mahdi, who rose up to conquer the world for God. That human countenance had beheld great wonders; those eyes had dared to gaze fearlessly at the splendour of the Divinity himself; and, stern and frigid, with the pride of the exalted, they had contemplated Gordon's severed head....

What were those eyes seeing then? What was going on inside the dying Mahdi? The mask did not fall away until the very last.

. . . . .

The friends and followers of Mohammed Ahmed who were gathered at the death-bed had believed fanatically in their Mahdi. The Mahdi's Ansar had seen the banner of light in a dozen bloody battles— the banner which a superhuman being, a shapeless, fabulous being carried before him.

Why did not the khalifas, the emirs, the Ansar of the new Islam, now see the Angel of Death, Azrael—

see him gaining shape and figure and human features? Beautiful, smiling features? The Mahdi saw him; he raised himself up; they could hear his heavy breathing. The angel let his banner drop down over him. The Mahdi fell back heavily. From the corner came the cry of the woman who had loved the Mahdi.

. . . . .

The great saints of Islam are always buried at the place where they have died. Just as the Prophet was entombed in Aisha's house, so the Mahdi was laid to rest in his hut, even before the tidings of his death had spread outside. The Mahdi's relatives washed the corpse; they pulled at the dead man's beard, for it was the general belief that the hair came out easily when anyone died from poison; but the suspicion was not confirmed.

Meanwhile the three khalifas had moved the Mahdi's bed to one side and with their own hands had dug a grave on the spot where it had stood. They laid the Mahdi in it, without a shroud, in his Dervish shirt. The grave was covered over with bricks; the Khalifa Abdullahi promised that he would erect a great monument over it.

He himself, as the new imam, led the Islamic prayer for the dead. Those who were gathered in the hut—they were only the nearest and truest who had been present at the Mahdi's death—repeated the solemn words:

"Whatever is in the Heavens and in the Earth is God's: and whether ye bring forth to light what is in your minds or conceal it, God will reckon with you for it; and whom He pleaseth will He forgive, and whom He pleaseth will He punish; for God is All-powerful.

"God will not burden any soul beyond its power. It shall enjoy the good which it hath acquired, and shall bear the evil for the acquirement of which it laboured. O our Lord! punish us not if we forget, or fall into sin; O our Lord! and lay not on us a load like that which thou hast laid on those who have been before us; O our Lord! and lay not on us that for which we have not strength: but blot out our sins and forgive us, and have pity on us. Thou art our protector: give us victory therefore over the infidel nations."

. . . . .

On that day—the ninth Ramadan of the year of the Hegira 1302 (Rudolf Slatin reckoned the 22nd June, 1885)—it was made known in Omdurman that the Mahdi had voluntarily exchanged this world for Heaven.

It was forbidden, on pain of severe punishment, to say that he had died. Even the wailing of the dead was prohibited. None the less the crowd wept in the mosque when the Khalifa Abdullahi appeared before them in order to receive the oath of loyalty of the Ansar. The Khalifa displayed great sorrow, but he spoke with confidence of the future. The work that the Mahdi had begun must be completed. The struggle of the Mahdieh for the conversion of the world would continue. When the world was conquered for Islam, then the Expected Mahdi would come back again. . . .

While the Khalifa was speaking to the assembled people from the platform of the court of the mosque, his guard, Slatin, was standing nearby and thinking:

"When will there be a vigorous English offensive

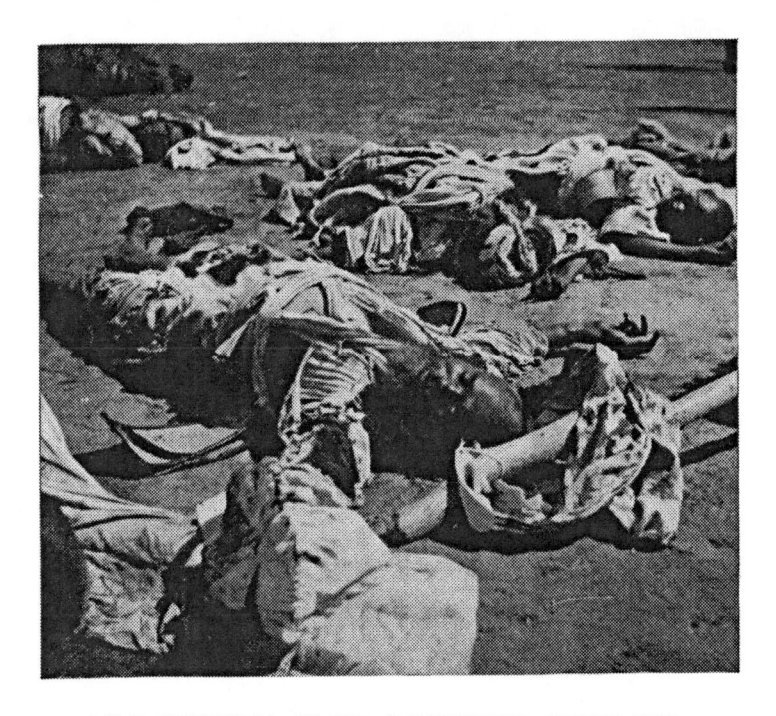

DEAD DERVISHES ON THE BATTLEFIELD WHERE THE
KHALIFA WAS KILLED

The man in the centre is Ahmed Fadil, the Khalifa's cousin

against Khartoum? It ought to come now, before this tyrannical impostor consolidates his power. The Ashraf are against him; even the Jaalin cannot bear him. . . . If I could only send a message to Kitchener! If the Khalifa is given time now it may be years before one is finished with these Dervishes. . . . Should I not attempt an escape?"

.     .     .     .     .

In the evening the two young Egyptians, the students of El Azhar, were walking along the bank of the Nile. The two young men were holding hands like affectionate boys. The stars in the tropical heavens mirrored themselves brightly in the swift-flowing river; the air was warm. From the villages on the island of Tuti came the sound of drums: probably a band of Dervishes were celebrating a night of prayer in honour of the dead Mahdi.

The two Egyptian youths were sad, because their hope had died and because they must now separate: Omar was going back to Cairo, while the younger one, Hassan, in defiant desperation, had resolved to remain in Khartoum and to enrol himself in the Khalifa's army if it should begin the campaign against Egypt now occupied by the British.

"Islam," said the more resigned Hassan, "Islam was once a stupendous flame in which the whole of God's world began to melt and combine into a unity. For centuries already it has burned more and more faintly, and the world does not attain its unity. But Islam can never renounce its dream. Islam is nothing but the flame that strives to melt everything into one: it must either consume the world or else be extinguished. . . . We, O my friend, have seen that ancient flame blaze up once more, once more we have seen it leap up mighty and awe-inspiring to heaven. And now that the Expected Mahdi has died, must the flame of Islam, which has burnt so brightly through thirteen centuries—must it now, its force spent, subside and grow dim?"

# FROM THE TRAVELLER'S NOTES

# FROM THE TRAVELLER'S NOTES

*SENNAR: 12th February,* 1929.

So civilised already, and yet so wild still, is the Sudan three decades after the collapse of the Mahdist empire that you can travel on and on in a saloon compartment of the admirably organised State railway until you can spread salt on the tail of the first wild monkey in the African forest, if you feel inclined.

The saloon compartment which I occupy—a first-rate compartment, with a good bed, a ventilator, a comforting refrigerator—is standing at this moment in the station of Sennar-Makwar and is waiting for me, while I visit the district by car, with my Nubian dragoman Sherkawi, and with Ibrahim. Ibrahim is the brown chauffeur, an Arab of the Jaalin tribe. The Jaalins have lived for so many thousands of years with camels that they have themselves acquired the profile of camels—soft, but capricious. Ibrahim (dressed in a kind of grey sack and with a dagger fastened to his left arm by a leather strap) looks like a very young camel; he is fourteen. The old Ford which he is driving might by and by develop humps and even learn to kneel down. But for all that—here is a motor-car. And there are perfectly good motoring roads, too, on the banks of the Blue Nile, up towards Abyssinia.

. . . . .

I am able to have a look at the monkeys—long-tailed, reddish-brown ones as big as four-year-old children. I see them in large numbers in the forest of Deim el-Amarna. They chase up and down in the branches of the gum-acacias, an agile troop, in a dry and thorny copse devoid of any tropical exuberance. It is frightfully hot here and frightfully dusty, although the Nile flows by so close at hand. The wood lies on the raised bank; beneath you can see the sandbanks and crocodiles sunning themselves, and a big golden eagle sitting on a rock in the midst of the foaming water.

Everything is very hot, very wild; and so are the people here. In the forest live charcoal burners—negroid descendants of the Fung tribe. I see their almost naked figures round a fire, which stinks to the heavens. My efficient dragoman, Sherkawi, palavers with one of them over some business with monkeys: they have got to catch a monkey alive for an English lady in Khartoum; Sherkawi will pay them well for it.

He explains the transaction to me and tries to make me believe the old nursery tale which says you can catch monkeys by putting gourds full of Merissa beer under a tree; the monkeys all come and get drunk on the beer, and then they are helpless to defend themselves!

. . . . .

On the way to this monkey wood I saw ruins in the middle of the wild country. They were the remains of the ancient town of Sennar, which after the death of the Mahdi the Khalifa entirely destroyed. A new Sennar with corrugated-iron roofs has arisen in the neighbourhood, inhabited by workmen and engineers of the great dam.

In order to see this Sennar dam (and not so much, actually, on account of the monkeys) I have undertaken this expedition here. "You can only get an idea about the possibilities of the Sudan in the Sudan itself!" the great English engineer who is supervising the waterworks of the country said to me in his office in Khartoum.

An extraordinary man, that engineer! A kind of poet, who creates a poet's dreams out of nothing but Nile water. In his room I saw the maps and the carefully worked-out plans. Not one drop of the precious water is forgotten there; every bit of it is saved, stored, and finally conducted to the fertile soil, till bread and cotton grow out of it. As soon as the new treaty between England and Egypt has been concluded and

FROM THE TRAVELLER'S NOTES

confidence and peace prevail in the Nile land, not only will the vast plan for the dam of Jebel Auliya on the White Nile near Khartoum be made a reality, but the still much bigger dam-building project, by which the Albert Nyanza will be converted into the biggest reservoir in the world, will be taken in hand. That is not all: the White Nile, after leaving the lake, makes those great bends and loses almost half of its precious water in an illimitable, desolate swamp-land. This wasted water also can probably be saved: the corner made by the bend of the Nile is cut off; the canal which will have to be built will, it is true, be bigger than the Suez Canal. But vast quantities of water will be spared for cultivation, the swampy region will be left dry and parched deserts will be irrigated both in the Sudan and in Egypt.

All that is not yet. And the waterworks on the Abyssinian Blue Nile, on Lake Tsana, are still promises for the future. Still, the Sennaar dam has been completed since 1925, and it has converted the Gesireh—the peninsula between the two Niles—into a rich agricultural land. It is to see this that I am here; for I would like to know what has grown up out of the Sudan of the Mahdi.

. . . . .

In my note-book, among mere dates connected with the life of Mohammed Ahmed, certain statistical figures are marked down: the dam is so many feet long, so high, so broad; it stores up so many million cubic feet of water. It can irrigate so many hundred thousand *feddans* of land, and does actually irrigate them. For that purpose so many thousands of miles of canals are employed. So many *feddans* are planted with cotton, and the *durrha* fields yield so many *ardebs* of *durrha* per year.

("I ought to look up in Baedeker what an *ardeb* is and what a *feddan* is," I think to myself in passing.)

This sandy, thirsty land of the blacks, the Sudan, needs nothing but a wise distribution of water, so that it may yield bread and wool, food and clothing for innumerable people.

. . . .

## THE MAHDI OF ALLAH

I am now near Meringan, the centre of the cotton plantations. I leave the motor-car and go on foot through the endless fields which are just now in bloom. I do not remember ever before, on all my travels, having seen cotton bushes in flower, and I am quite enchanted by the beauty of the sight. The individual flower is golden-yellow, with a gleam of purple in the interior. The peculiar green of the foliage makes a lovely contrast. Such a cotton-field in flower in the flat and (in itself) dreary landscape, is something so refreshing—it revives the tired eye. A negro fellow, a Fung or a Hamag, stands in the middle of the field and rakes an irrigation canal with a hoe. A brilliantly coloured butterfly flutters up. . . .

. . . . .

In the middle of this flowery sunlit plain something sullen and mechanical juts out: a stark and prosaic-looking factory with a huge smoking chimney-stack and a noise of machinery audible a long way off. A big shed covered with corrugated iron, which looks like a Zeppelin hangar, is really a ginnery, i.e. an establishment for the removal of the seed from the cotton harvest. I go into the factory halls and find a buzzing and whirling of wheels and transmission belts; great steel racks comb out the cotton, mechanical presses prepare mighty bundles of the white fleece.

And I see a terrific negro, almost entirely naked, his titanic limbs anointed with oil so that he shines like a great idol made of black bronze—I see him standing there, next to a polished machine; he performs (he is himself like a machine) the same movement over and over again, with a mechanical placidity. He is so incredibly big, his muscles are so powerful, that, beside the cylinders and rods and knobs of the machinery, he does not appear in the least diminished. His pock-marked face is rigid and grave; there is no trace in him of that comical negro quality which we so easily imagine we discover in black faces.

He must be about forty years old, I reckon. Consequently he has certainly once been a slave.

And so now he is free, I reflect.

## FROM THE TRAVELLER'S NOTES

I ask the yellowish Levantine foreman who is showing me round the works what daily wage this free negro might approximately receive? The Greek, or he might be a Copt, exclaims:

"Oh, that fellow! He's a very good man, and well paid. He gets one English shilling a day."

.　　.　　.　　.　　.

I stop, and stare at the big negro. He pays not the slightest attention to me; he performs always the same movement, doing something inside a big rack which claps down with a rattling noise on to a mountain of cotton fleece. The foreman is making a mistake about me: he supposes that my interest in ginning machines must be considerable; therefore he speaks at length about the difference between the old and the new systems. . . .

But I am thinking of one thing only—of how much I would like to know what Charles Gordon would have written to his sister Augusta, in one of those spirited, sincere letters of his, if he could have had any presentiment of this. Was it for this that he wanted to free the negro slaves? For, after all is said and done, that is what he lived for and died for.

What would he have written—this man who would never lie either to himself or to Augusta?

.　　.　　.　　.　　.

It was to this end, after all, that Gordon died—in order that a steel machine in Meringan, Sennar Province, in the Sudan, should be able to clean cotton which another clattering machine, in Manchester, would work up into cloth. This black workman tosses the bales to the white workman over there in England; the latter tosses a bale of cotton cloth back again to the Sudan, into the negro villages. And simultaneously there arrives in the negro village a teacher, civilised by Europe, and instructs the people to wear shirts—cotton shirts.

The hero (I reflect) who is dear to me, Charles Gordon, died for the one shilling which the negro now receives as his daily wage. He is no longer a slave; he gets a shilling—and, in consequence, can buy cotton cloth from Manchester. Why should he buy it? Because, of course, he is civilised now. He makes bundles of cotton because he has got to earn a shilling. When he has earned his shilling he buys a cotton shirt. . . .

Well, that is History's decision between the Mahdi and General Gordon. They resembled each other more than they knew; both were dreamers and idealists—only, in the end, Gordon stood for cotton shirts and the Mahdi for ascetic nakedness. Every bale of cotton from the Sudan is as a monument to General Gordon; and, nevertheless, nobody hated the incursions of civilisation more than he.

I am still looking at the negro who is standing behind the polished machine. It was over him that the battle was waged. *His* future was at stake when the Mahdi fought with Gordon. Between begging-bowl and ginning machine, between the call to prayer and the factory siren lay the fate of Africa. The game is decided; the Sudan of the Mahdi, indeed the whole of black Africa, is to-day already quite full of motor-cars and railways and waterworks and machines and trade and corrugated-iron sheds and wireless telegraphy. . . .

The Mahdi taught that man needs a begging-bowl, a staff, a patched shirt. . . .

Gordon was first vanquished, and then he conquered. Above his martyr's grave grow the cotton bushes. Manchester gets its raw material and its market. The negro, who was formerly a slave, gets his shilling a day. All that, Charles Gordon, an idealist without economic understanding, certainly did not want at all, but has created none the less.

.   .   .   .   .

Two others of Mohammed Ahmed's European antagonists helped later on to civilise the Sudan: Slatin and Ohrwalder.

Father Joseph Ohrwalder, after the reconquest, once more became a member of the Sudan Mission. He died one day in 1912 in Khartoum immediately after having said grace amongst his fellow missionaries before sitting down to dinner. Thousands of Mohammedans followed the bier of that excellent priest.

# FROM THE TRAVELLER'S NOTES

Slatin Pasha, knowing the state of things in the Dervish camp so well, was able, after his dramatic escape, to render the most precious services to Kitchener's army in 1895, and the speedy reconquest of the Sudan was partly due to him. Subsequently he took part, up to 1914, in the magnificent work of reconstruction in the Sudan, under the title of Inspector-General. Now the old gentleman with the epic biography is living in Meran, as the last of the important figures who played a part in the tragic history of the Mahdi. He has survived all the saints and prophets. After having held Gordon's gory head in his trembling hands, he has lived to see the new Sudan, those great dams, those rotating machines, those motoring roads.

.    .    .    .

In the evening, while the sun is sinking, my motor-car, on the way to the railway station and to the train, passes by the great Nile dam, over which the road leads. The road across the dam will be closed after dark; consequently the traffic at this moment is very thick. The motor is hardly able to proceed, is constantly being held up in a turmoil of men and beasts. The great road leads westwards over the dam to Kosti and El Obeid—the road which links up with the caravan routes coming from Lake Chad. To the East it continues to Kassala, to Italian Eritrea, to Northern Abyssinia, to the Red Sea. Here is a great highway of Africa, and all Africa moves past before my eyes: men belonging to hundreds of tribes, on their camels and horses and donkeys, with their herds and their goods.

In the covered-over baskets on the camels one divines thickly veiled women; but others, naked and grimy, drive the black sheep or carry burdens. The men are all armed; they carry spears with barbed hooks; or antelope horns in which several daggers are thrust, or great swords in blood-red sheaths. From the grotesque curly coiffures tallow drops on to the naked shoulders. Here flow white garments full of dignity, there flutter unspeakable rags. A young noble, some powerful sheikh or other, clothed in striped silk and gold embroidery and mounted on a horse, accompanies the beautifully adorned camels of the women of his harem. Negroes and Arabs stream past—all Africa.

Behind the dam the sun sinks down into the reservoir of the Blue Nile. The immeasurable flat sheet of water gleams in the colours of the wildest dream. Against a sky that is purple and green, or like ignited gold, or an amethystine diamond, the silhouettes of serried birds fly past—deep black. I could almost weep; it is all too beautiful and dream-like.

.    .    .    .    .

Sudan! Burning land, so boundless, so illimitable. Prodigious Africa! What unimaginable things can still happen here?

I stand on this dam and turn my eyes to the sinking sun. Behind me is the great confusion of African voices and noises. It seems to me as though I hear, far in the distance, the drums of future hosts. Where from? Where to? On this bridge, which Europe has built for you, whither are you marching, incomprehensible Africa?

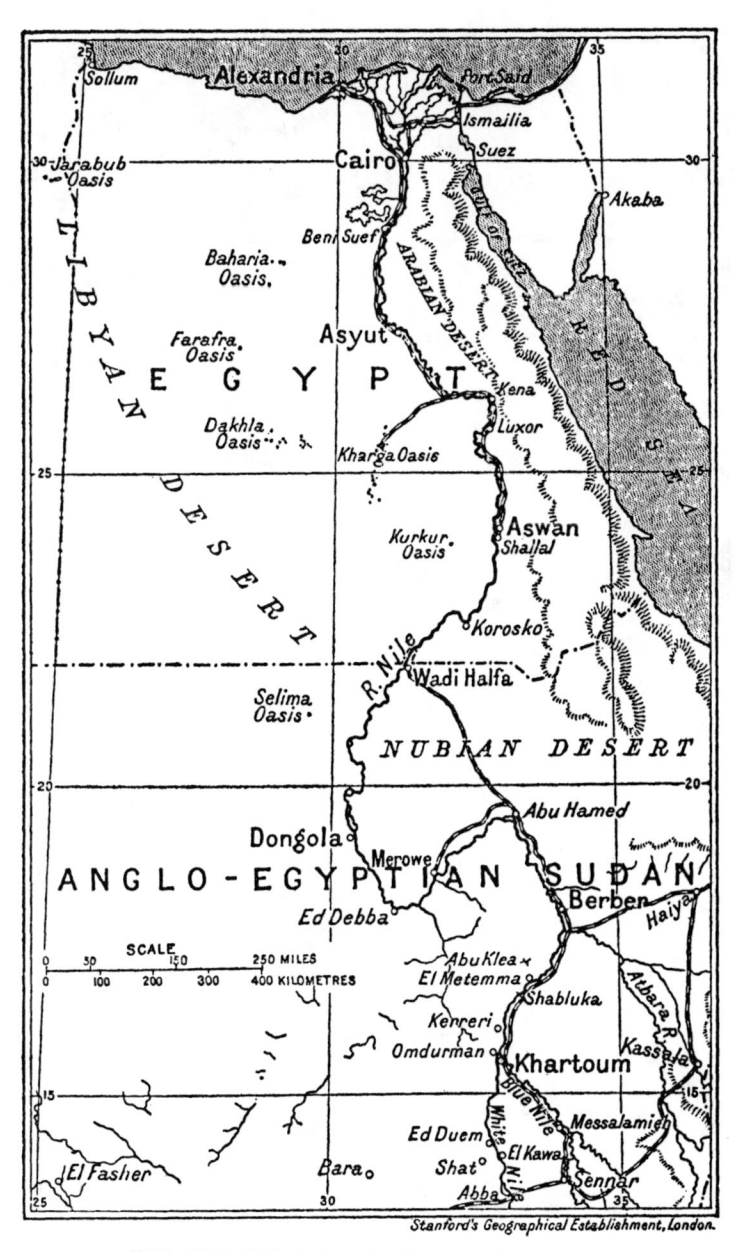

THE NILE FROM CAIRO TO KHARTOUM

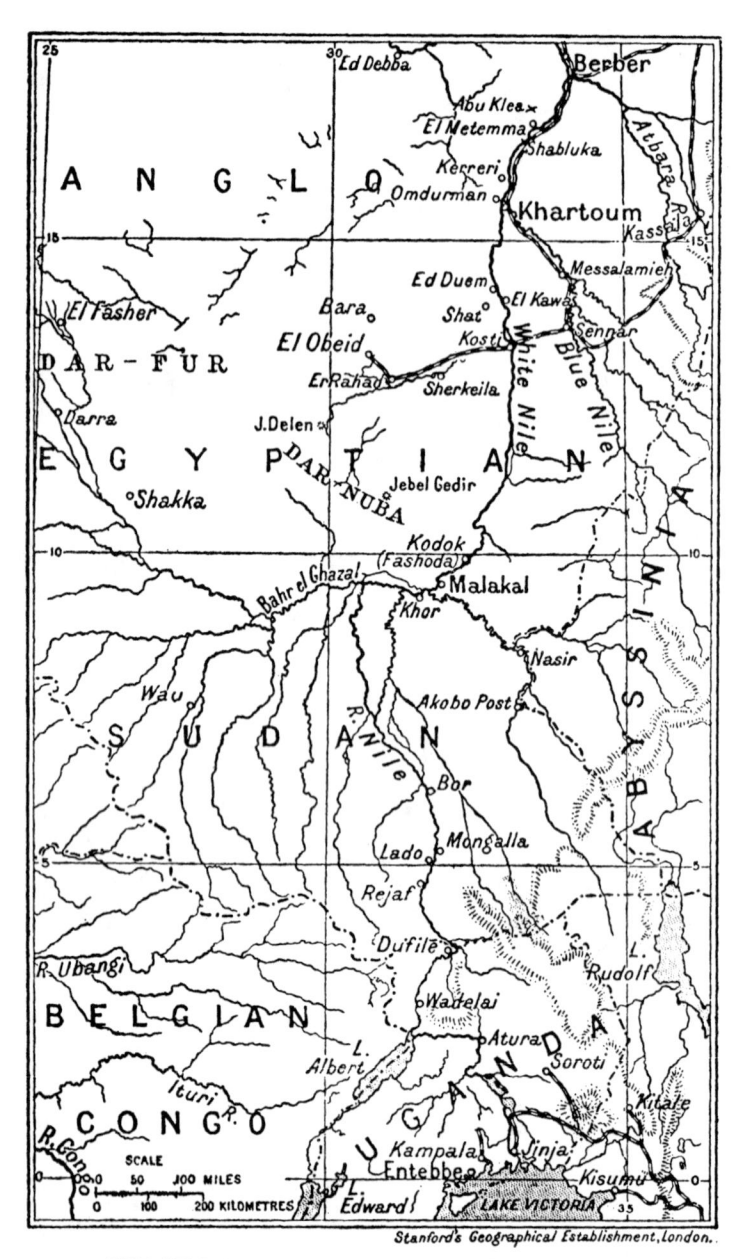

THE NILE FROM KHARTOUM TO LAKE VICTORIA

## NOTE

The description of the life of the Mahdi Mohammed Ahmed contained in this book is not founded on invention, but in all its details on historical evidence. Even such fantastic episodes as Gordon's experience with the laughing stork or the ride of the Senussi messenger to the Mahdi, the fate of Klootz the Prussian and that of the Frenchman Pain are mentioned in contemporary records.

Similarly, the speeches, proclamations, and letters of the Mahdi employed in the text are by no means freely invented, but are taken verbatim, unless they be somewhat abbreviated, from the collection of documents which Sir Reginald Wingate, then of the Anglo-Egyptian Intelligence Department, published after the archives of the Mahdi had been captured at the battle of Toski.

. . . .

The story of the Mahdi has so far only been related by the victims, or at least by the opponents, of his rule: by Slatin Pasha, by Father Joseph Ohrwalder, and by Karl Neufeld, who were imprisoned for long years in the Mahdists' camp; and by the Arab Nahum Bey Shuquair, who, as an employee of the Anglo-Egyptian Intelligence Service, took part in the Sudan campaigns. His book on the history of the Sudan (partly translated into German by Ernst Ludwig Dietrich and Martin Thilo) is, because the work of an Arab Moslem, perhaps the most interesting contemporary source of reference.

. . . . .

The present writer, during his journey through the Sudan, made the acquaintance of the Sayid Sir Abderrahman el Mahdi, and obtained from him exhaustive and in part entirely new information about the Mahdi's life history.

Also, the former prisoner of the Mahdi, Sir Rudolf Slatin, most kindly told the author many interesting details not contained in any book published hitherto.

.   .   .   .   .

Of the books used, only the most important need be mentioned here.

### Works dealing with the Mahdi Period

Rudolf Slatin: *Fire and Sword in the Sudan.*
J. Ohrwalder: *Aufstand und Reich des Mahdi im Sudan.*
Major F. R. Wingate: *Mahdism and the Egyptian Sudan.*
Richard Buchta: *The Sudan under Egyptian Rule.*
Gaston Dujarric: *L'État Mahdiste au Soudan.*
Ernst Ludwig Dietrich: "Der Mahdi Mohammed Achmed vom Sudan nach arabischen Quellen" (in the periodical *Der Islam*, vol. xiv).
Dr. Martin Thilo: *Zibehr Rahamet Pashas Autobiographie.*
Earl of Cromer: *Modern Egypt.*
Hasenclever: *Geschichte Aegyptens im 19. Jahrhundert.*

### Works dealing with Charles Gordon's Life and Death

General Gordon's letters and journals in various collections; several English biographies; above all, the fine essay by Lytton Strachey in his volume *Eminent Victorians.*
Sir Charles Wilson: *From Korti to Khartoum.*

### Dealing with the Reconquest of the Sudan

Steevens: *With Kitchener to Khartoum*; and the reports of several other war correspondents.

NOTE

BOOKS ON THE COUNTRY, PEOPLE, AND CUSTOMS

E. W. LANE: *The Manners and Customs of the Modern Egyptians.*
E. DOUTTE: *Magie et Religion dans l'Afrique du Nord.*
SHEIKH MOHAMMED BEN OSTMANE EL HACHAICHI: *Voyage au pays des Senoussia.*
PAUL KAHLE: "Zur Organisation der Derwischorden in Aegypten" (*Der Islam*, vol. vi).

. . . . .

The name of the Mahdi's first khalifa and successor is written in many historical books "Abdullah" or "Abdallah." The author has preferred the spelling "Abdullahi" because Slatin used it, and because one of the khalifa's sons, whom the author met, pronounced his father's name in that way.

# CHRONOLOGICAL TABLE

Year.
- 622. The Flight (Hegira) of the Prophet Mohammed.
- 1819. The Egyptian Viceroy, Mehemet Ali, occupies the Sudan.
- Jan. 28, 1833. Charles Gordon born.
- c. 1844. The Mahdi born near Dongola.
- 1861. Mohammed Ahmed becomes a disciple of Sheikh Mohammed Sherif.
- 1863. Ismail II becomes Khedive.
- 1871. The family of Mohammed Ahmed settles on Abba Island.
- 1873. Zubeir Rahamet conquers Dar-Fur for Egypt.
- 1874. Gordon becomes Governor-General of the Equatorial Province.
- 1877. Gordon becomes Governor-General of the Sudan.
- 1878. Gessi Pasha has Zubeir's son executed.
- 1879. Rudolf Slatin comes to the Sudan.
- 1879. The Khedive Ismail II abdicates in favour of his son Tewfik.
- 1879. Gordon leaves the Sudan.
- 1880. Mohammed Ahmed becomes the successor of Sheikh El Koreishi. Abdullahi joins him.
- Sept., 1881. Arabi Pasha's military revolt in Cairo.
- 1881. Mohammed Ahmed declares himself to be the Mahdi. The fight on Abba Island. Flight to Gadir.
- Sept., 1882. Wolseley's British army defeats Arabi at Tel-el-Kebir and occupies Egypt.
- Jan., 1883. The Mahdi captures El Obeid.
- Nov., 1883. Hicks Pasha's army destroyed.
- Jan., 1884. Slatin surrenders himself to the Dervishes.

## THE MAHDI OF ALLAH

| | Year. | |
|---|---|---|
| Feb., | 1884. | Gordon returns to Khartoum. |
| Jan. 17, | 1885. | The British relieving army gains a victory at Abu Klea. |
| Jan. 25, | 1885. | Khartoum falls. Death of Gordon. |
| Jan. 27, | 1885. | The two British steamers appear outside Khartoum. |
| June 22, | 1885. | Death of the Mahdi. |
| | 1895. | Slatin's escape. |
| Sept. 2, | 1898. | Kitchener captures Khartoum. |
| Dec., | 1898. | The Fashoda incident. |
| Nov. 24, | 1899. | The Khalifa falls in the action at Umm Debrekat. |

Printed in the United States
119381LV00008B/111/A